PRACTICAL REUSABLE UNIX SOFTWARE

PRACTICAL REUSABLE UNIX SOFTWARE

Edited by

Balachander Krishnamurthy

WILEY

John Wiley & Sons, Inc.

New York • Chichester • Brisbane • Toronto • Singapore

Publisher: Katherine Schowalter
Senior Editor: Diane D. Cerra
Managing Editor: Maureen B. Drexel
Text Design & Composition: Balachander Krishnamurthy

This text is printed on acid-free paper.

Published simultaneously in Canada.

Library of Congress Cataloging-in-Publication Data:

Practical reusable UNIX software / edited by Balachander
   Krishnamurthy.
      p. cm.
   Includes bibliographical references and index.
   ISBN 0-471-05807-6 (acid-free paper)
    1. Operating systems (Computers) 2. UNIX (Computer file)
 3. Computer software–Reusability. 4. Computer software–
  -Development. I. Krishnamurthy, Balachander, 1961- .
 QA76.76.063R48 1995
 005.1–dc20   94-37119
                                                 CIP

Printed in the United States of America
10 9 8 7 6 5 4 3 2 1

To my family in the United States and in India

Trademarks

X Windows System is a trademark of Massachusetts Institute of Technology.

UNIX is a registered trademark of X/Open Inc.

watchd, libft, REPL are registered trademarks of AT&T Corporation.

SoftBench is a trademark of the Hewlett-Packard Company.

Encapsulator is a trademark of the Hewlett-Packard Company.

DOMAIN is a registered trademark of HP-Apollo.

Foreword

This book describes a collection of software of a sort that people have known was needed for years, but has been neglected. Most of the computer-using population sees machines that run applications created by others. It's hardly surprising that most of the ink on paper and pixels on the screen, that talk about computers are devoted to the result–the quality, usefulness, and attractiveness of the applications. Most people don't program.

But someone has to create these applications, and the software industry has known for a long time that handcrafted software is expensive. AT&T, the company for which I work, has undergone a lot of change since I first joined it; one of the most profound, albeit not the most obvious from the outside, is its transformation to an essentially software-based organization. The communications services and the telephone switches AT&T sells are, in a real sense, enabled by an enormous number of lines of code in various languages, running on a vast assortment of hardware; writing and maintaining software dominates our development budget.

The tools and libraries described in this book show a variety of approaches to help reduce these costs. It doesn't claim to be a cure-all; it doesn't say, "Buy our object-oriented distributed gizmo and your problems are over." Instead it offers, for example, a library portable to many environments that improves software resilience in the presence of failure. It offers tools for understanding programs, for visualizing them, for keeping track of software development, for application building. It's a wide-ranging congeries, and pretty far from the slick shrinkwrapped box in the local software shop. Nevertheless, the contents share a valuable theme–by emphasizing portability and reusability, by being used in real projects, the software described in this book makes the insights and hard work that might have remained entangled in one software system available for others to use.

Dennis M. Ritchie
Murray Hill, NJ

Preface

In the mid-1990s, with new software paradigms being introduced on a regular basis, it might be instructive to take a step back and look at a successful experiment in creating practical reusable software. This book is a description of one such experiment. I came in midway through the experiment and have had the benefit of learning several of the lessons described here.

As a discipline, software engineering is still maturing; we believe that managing a software engine requires some key precepts to be kept in mind. The life cycle of software begins with good design and architecture, a proper environment in which it can be constructed. That environment should include a good repository of tools and ongoing help for the rest of the life cycle.

There is a great variety of hardware and software platforms on which modern software has to run; the environments change rapidly. It is no longer enough to build stable software on a specific platform—the software has to run and be maintained on *multiple* platforms. UNIX was well ahead of its time by being portable and introducing the concept of linking programs in pipelines to achieve a sum greater than the parts. In the past twenty five years, UNIX tools have become a key reason for the success of UNIX. With the explosion in sites running UNIX both in academia, and, increasingly, in business, the need for high quality portable UNIX software is felt increasingly. Within AT&T the number of UNIX-dependent projects soared and with it the need for quick solutions. Our department was formed to aid software developers and, in the process, we brought about high quality tools.

The origin of the term *software reuse* has been attributed to Doug McIlroy, a UNIX pioneer at AT&T Bell Labs, who compared the role of software routines to the role of screws or resistors in mechanical designs. For software in the large, one needs to have the full range of artifacts from high-quality library routines to generic architectural services that can be fitted into a variety of applications to as modular and reusable components. The collection of software described in this book covers this range.

Chapter 1 sets up the environment in which the software described in the rest of the chapters was constructed. It describes the assumptions under which we worked as well as the ADVSOFT repository and distribution scheme. As one of the lessons learned, we discuss our view of architectural style and services—ideas we consider important for reuse. In conjunction with Chapter 12, practical suggestions on how to run a reuse program are presented.

Chapter 2 is in some sense the core of our reuse repository: the collection of most of the highly reused libraries. The descriptions of the libraries are both at the conceptual level—what niche they fill—as well as the nitty gritty level, replete with examples. The libraries range from the porting base (*libast*) to graph and file system services. Chapter 2 also introduces the concept of *discipline* and *method*; techniques dealing with safe resource management and library portability. This chapter constitutes the substrate level of the four levels of partitioning that we have done.

Chapters 3 and 4 deal with the base level tools: *nmake*–a build tool that represents the state of the art amongst the successors of *make*, the original UNIX configuration and build tool; *n-DFS*–a *n-Dimensional File System* which provides a variety of operating system services; *ksh*–the widely used Korn Shell command interpreter; EASEL–a system for writing end-user applications via interactive constructs. The tools in this layer are considered base tools since we use many of them on an everyday basis for building and maintaining our software.

We now move up to the standalone layer: Chapters 5 and 6 discuss two program understanding tools–APP, an assertion system helping programmers specify what a program is meant to do and CIA, a tool that abstracts relationships between entities in programs for reverse engineering. Chapters 7 and 8 discuss two dynamic aspects of programs: security and high availability. Chapter 8 discusses three reusable components (*watchd*, *libft*, and REPL) that makes software fault tolerant. Tools at the standalone layer all reuse libraries at the substrate level as well as tools at the base level.

Chapters 9 through 11 discuss connected tools covering the areas of event action systems, software process, visualization, testing, and animation. In Chapter 9, YEAST, an extensible event-action specification system, is discussed, along with its extensive reuse of a variety of entities described earlier in the book. Chapter 10 discusses PROVENCE, a process visualization and enactment environment, made by combining several tools at the component level. Chapter 11 discusses four vertically integrated tools: *dotty*, a customizable graph editor; TESTTUBE, a tool for selective regression testing; *Xray*, a function call animator, and VPM, a real-time, network-wide process execution visualizer. The connected tools are all formed by linking to lower layer tools.

The practical bent of our software operating system illustrated by the thousands of users of our tools (for example, *sfio*, *ksh*, and *nmake*) as well as the fact that companies other than AT&T sell them as products (for example, Tandem's HATS version of *watchd/libft*). The cycle time between identifying a reusable component and its deployment has been steadily shrinking. Fortunately, we have a large testbed within our company, making rapid experimentation feasible.

I believe that our ongoing experiment will bear out our belief in rapid construction of higher-level connected tools. Our strengths include the strong foundation (libraries) that we build on, our understanding of the software development process, and the remarkable environment in which we work. The environment is not just the software tools environment but the Bell Labs culture that has engendered such a diverse, yet closely knit, collection of useful tools. We do not simply advocate our tools and methodology: We have tried and tested it, and it works.

A large number of people have contributed, in many different ways, to the efforts described in the book. Some have contributed to the book, while many more are colleagues and partners, researchers, developers, and those involved in technology transfer. It is impossible to thank all of them by name, but they are due thanks for their contributions.

I thank my department head David Belanger for encouraging me to pursue this book. He is largely responsible for creating a stable atmosphere in the department that enabled the creation of virtually all the software described in the book.

My thanks to to Dennis Ritchie for graciously agreeing to write the foreword and Brian Kernighan for his insightful review and valuable comments.

I thank Valerie Torres and Randy Hackbarth for jointly evolving the ADVSOFT process, Geeti Granger at Production Technology of John Wiley & Sons, Inc. (Chichester) for her LaTeX style file to build on, Terry Anderson and Steven Bellovin for freely sharing their LaTeX wisdom, Lorinda Cherry for her index-generating program, Berkley Tague, Moses Ling, Steve Lally, and Fred Douglis for their comments. I thank Diane D. Cerra and Maureen Drexel of John Wiley & Sons, Inc. (New York), for their help in guiding me through the editing process.

Above all, without the contributors this book wouldn't have come about: my thanks to all of them.

Balachander Krishnamurthy
bala@research.att.com

Historical Overview

In the mid-1980s, it became clear in AT&T Bell Laboratories that our primary development activities revolved around producing software for products and services. Having recently gone through divestiture, it was also clear that for AT&T to be more competitive in the marketplace products would have to be produced with less cost, higher quality, and in less time. One of the responses to this realization was to bring together, in 1986, a Software Technology Center chartered with delivering to AT&T developers the best software tools, technologies, and processes available. One group brought into the Software Technology Center was a small software research department then known as the Advanced Software Department. That department had been established a few years earlier as an experiment to connect software researchers more closely to the product development community. This book presents some of the work of that department.

The timing of this book is driven by a number of factors, most important of which is the coming together of a capability. The capability is to put together very quickly small teams of experts to create new software tools and systems that embody research breakthrough concepts that can be made available to nonexpert users. Examples are sprinkled throughout the book, with several concentrated in Chapter 11 ("Intertool Connections"). This process of integration is continuing, and it is quite exciting to view the sophisticated new applications that are now built in periods of weeks by small teams of researchers. These systems display the desirable characteristics of good prototypes in that they mature rapidly as they generate feedback from users. On the other hand, they have the characteristics of good products in that they are fast, portable, robust, and are in several cases used in AT&T Products & Services, sometimes by hundreds of users.

How did this capability come about? Simply through the efforts of some very good people in a stable environment. There is, however, more to the story. It is the evolution through several stages of knowledge on our part. The goal of the department was to have as much impact on AT&T's software proficiency as possible. Therefore, our software had to be usable in a wide variety of production environments. This approach had a significant impact on the way the research effort itself worked. In the beginning, tools were typically built as individual entities. There was not enough infrastructure to provide common support for the diversity and scale of the early tools. Original versions of tools such as EASEL, *ksh*, and *nmake* cooperated with each other but shared little code. As these tools were revised, a set of libraries was created and shared by these tools and newer tools. This process continued as tools that started with little relationship to the original core of tools, like graph layout tools (*dot, dotty*) and reliability tools (*watchd, libft*), became cores of integrated applications. Finally, the set of experts, along with the systems that they have created, have evolved into a village of experts with the ability to reuse code effectively in building integrated systems. The total amount of code that we distribute is now on the order of 750,000 lines divided across close to 100 tools and libraries.

Our strategy has been to support people who are experts in a software subject, such as configuration management or fault tolerance and experts in building software, and to do this over a diverse range of expertise. This created the breadth and depth required to meet a number of the software technology needs of AT&T. Of course, effort is required to manage such a diverse range of expertise. The software systems/tools/libraries we created were tested and matured in real environments like products/services with hard requirements and deadlines. Each of the currently mature tools/libraries has had one or two projects that provided early, real trials and greatly accelerated the technical maturity of the tools and the knowledge base of the researcher. The tools start as a concrete expression of a research idea. They evolve to embody not only the software product developer's requirements, but often their innovative suggestions, and sometimes their code. Working in partnership with the development community has led to wide acceptance of many of the tools, and early discovery of where tools did not meet an essential development need. Surveys and user counts show that the mature libraries/tools either have hundreds of users, or in a few cases (such as *nmake* and *ksh*) are de facto standards of large AT&T business units.

The evolution in maturity of reuse and system integration described earlier and documented within this book illustrates a crucial aspect of reuse. It is that the evolution through different stages of reuse was also an evolution through stages of knowledge. This has been a learning process that leads to successful reuse. It can be replicated but one cannot skip to the endpoint without obtaining the prerequisite knowledge.

David Belanger
Head, Software Engineering Research Department
AT&T Bell Laboratories

Contents

8   A Software Fault Tolerance Platform   223

Yennun Huang and Chandra Kintala

9   Generalized Event-Action Handling   247

David Rosenblum and Balachander Krishnamurthy

10 Monitoring, Modeling, and Enacting Processes 275

Naser Barghouti and Balachander Krishnamurthy

11 Intertool Connections 299

Yih-Farn Chen, Glenn Fowler, David Korn, Eleftherios Koutsofios,
Stephen North, David Rosenblum, and Kiem-Phong Vo

Color plates follow page 310

1

Software Reuse: A Decade-Long Experiment

David Belanger and Balachander Krishnamurthy

1.1 Introduction

This book describes several case studies of software tools and libraries
that have been developed by a software research program at AT&T Bell
Laboratories. It is organized to reflect the impact of these programs on
the reuse of software, both within research and by the software development community. The term *software reuse* means that a software entity
is used in multiple software systems, by multiple people, and by multiple organizations. The research program that generated these results
is part of a more comprehensive program of creating and distributing
software technology and methods throughout AT&T, with the aim of
building higher-quality software faster and at lower costs. Reusing large
amounts of software is one of the most promising approaches to achieving
this goal. Although the overall effort within AT&T includes participation
from many organizations, this book describes lessons learned to date in
a specific research project.

The contributors to this book all belong to the same department in
AT&T Bell Laboratories. The software described is used throughout
AT&T and in several cases outside of AT&T. This research program is
intended to be pragmatic. Although what has been learned may seem well

1

structured in this presentation, its unveiling was not. Many of the things
we learned were discovered in bottom-up and contorted ways. Most often,
the learning cycle proceeded from a general hypothesis of a need in the
product development community; to the creation of an experimental tool
to address the need; to the widespread, general use (or lack of widespread
use) of a tool; to a better understanding of software development and of
reuse. The ability to articulate a general structure for supporting reuse
trailed widespread use of the technology, sometimes by months or years.
As our understanding evolved, it in turn helped change the way we build
software.

The three basic principles that tie together the work described in suc-
ceeding chapters are:

- *Free-Market Assumption*: We had to deliver value that users would
  choose over alternatives. They might also be required to purchase software. This assumption extended to use in our own group. The model
  is that of producer/consumer, with the consumer free to choose other
  suppliers.
- *Rapid-Evolution Assumption*: We expected the rate of change of reused
  software to be high. Compared to product software, it was expected to
  experience more internal change but retain more stable interfaces. This
  implied a need for release control. As research was applied, this assumption was strongly confirmed and configuration management became a
  central focus of the effort.
- *Systems-Architecture Assumption*: For reasonable leverage, reused software must constitute significant parts of the software systems that reuse
  it. This implies that reuse must be enabled by including reusable components in the high levels of software design. In our terminology, this
  is called *software architecture*. It is a central concept to leverage reuse.

The book describes work that has been ongoing for about nine years.
It was at first a small effort with about ten people, but it has grown gradually over time to 25 people. Most are researchers who create prototype
software. A small number work at technology transfer, and manage the
reuse process. The wide scope of the research work enabled us to create
new technology and also serve as a fertile site for testing and accelerating
the maturation of the software systems. This environment has provided

effective feedback for conceptual and implementation improvements. The resulting levels of quality was key in encouraging reuse. Here are the results of this work:

- A reusable software distribution process called ADVSOFT, which receives over 1,000 requests a year for software or information (almost all requests for information are followed by requests for software). This process manages about 80 tools/libraries, with a total of about 300,000 lines of code). It is currently managing about half of the code of the systems distributed by our department. As with all of our software, the use of ADVSOFT is voluntary. ADVSOFT is evolving and expanding rapidly and the process includes all the software described in this book.
- A self-supporting, second-order distribution and support system for some tools and libraries. This support system takes technology transferred by us and, in turn, manages several times the customer load of ADVSOFT.
- A set of software components and tools that are used in software production in nearly every AT&T Business Unit. Some tools or components have thousands of users; others, hundreds; and many are just starting significant distribution.
- A reuse infrastructure internal to the department that has allowed us to create new and innovative software systems in time intervals that are ten times shorter than our previous experience.

The remainder of this chapter examines the general thought processes that this work depends on, and provides a framework for reading the book. Later chapters examine the details of the technology. The primary results as they apply to reuse are: the impact that the software has had on AT&T and on our organization, and the lessons that were learned in breaking free of some of the folklore surrounding reuse as a tool for software development.

1.2 The Free-Market Assumption

This assumption is probably the simplest of those adopted, but may be the most powerful in its implication. There are many approaches to encouraging large scale reuse. A straightforward option is to dictate to an organization. Our experience has been that this works largely where the organization is cohesive enough in its product line to have a shared technology base at the start, or where the software to be reused is of exceptional quality and is well supported (for example, the C language and the UNIX system). In the climate of the late 1980s and early 1990s, it was and is rare for a diverse corporation to reach agreement on common software components or reuse strategies to be used corporation-wide. On the other hand, it is common to see *de facto* standards emerge. Our view of a free market is that it encourages the emergence of *de facto* standards based on the best options available, and that the role of management is to support the free-market conditions and encourage the rapid convergence to *de facto* standards.

This has important implications for researchers and technology transfer agents. They include:

- *Quality* of the reused software is crucial, both in the beginning and throughout the life cycle. Quality means *better than other options*, as judged by the projects using the software; note that this has to happen at the time a project is deciding between options, not after.
- *Market share* is a crucial metric. As a software component was built to meet a need, it is easy to argue that the additional cost of making it reusable can be paid for if it is reused a few times. However, to manage a long term reuse program, the goal should be market share and should include an understanding of the probable length of the life cycle of the software involved.
- *Marketing and deployment*, often called *technology transfer*, is a necessity for success. A small group was established in our department which was specifically aimed at transferring technology from research to support organizations or directly to users.

A key fact to keep in mind is that while a piece of software may be intrinsically reusable, several constraints on the reusing application may make reuse difficult. Typical constraints include performance, portability, and suitability for new architectures (for example, multiprocessor or distributed).

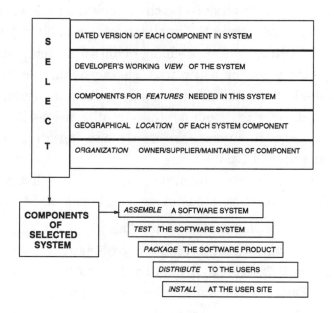

Figure 1.1   Software configuration management.

1.3   Rapid Evolution

Reused software evolves unusually quickly because it must meet the needs of a demanding and diverse community. Software Configuration Management [FHO92], with distribution capability, is the base technology necessary to address the problem. The various versions of the software must be easily stored, accurately recoverable, and automatically distributable. This requires a well-defined, controllable process. In our case, this process is known as ADVSOFT. This section contains an example of the use of the ADVSOFT process applied to a tool called YEAST.

Figure 1.1 is an illustration of the goals of a configuration management process. The general notion is that there is an existing *base* of software components from which the components of a specific system are chosen, assembled, tested, and distributed to a user.

This *Software Base* is partitioned in a variety of dimensions. For example, the actual software components may be stored in a variety of geographical locations, and components are used to create the desired *features* of the resultant application system. A specific application system is selected from available versions (such as revisions), views, and perhaps components from other systems. Finally, selection is often based on a set of Modification Requests from a change control system. Following this selection, a system is assembled, tested, packaged, shipped to a customer site, and installed. At that point, it is ready for customer use. This ability to create a system selected from a variety of dimensions is crucial to the multiple use of software objects. We have made considerable progress in this area for example [FKSV94].

As an example of the above concept, consider the delivery of a specific version of a tool, YEAST, to a customer. It might look like this:

```
For Customer - North Carolina Lab
Select the August 1993 Version of Yeast
    with Modification Requests for "NC" added,
    with Fault Tolerance & Security Features,
    using "libast" libraries.
```

The preceding syntax is fictitious (since these functions are currently not provided in a single tool), but the problem and capability are not. This delivery specification could result in selection and packaging of all changes to YEAST necessary to create the requested system from a computer in Murray Hill, New Jersey, and shipping only the changes to "North Carolina Lab" to update their YEAST configuration. Once the changes are delivered to North Carolina, the software is assembled, tested, and installed there. Note that though our customers use diverse software/hardware platforms, software requests as in the above example are free of platform specifications. This is because we view portability as fundamental to software reuse and strive to develop technologies and disciplines that ensure portable code. We also ship source code. Changes necessitated by a port to a new platform are considered equivalent to bug fixes. Chapter 2 discusses our approach to writing and maintaining portable software.

Our experience has been that software that is reused is subject to constant change. This is a corollary to the Second Law of Program Evolution [LB85]: "As an evolving program is continuously changed, its complexity, reflecting deteriorating structure, increases unless work is done to maintain or reduce it." Software that is reused widely will be subject to many requests for enhancement. If, as in our case, software creation is done in small aggressive teams (sometimes consisting of only one individual), the rate of change of reusable software can be substantial. This process is managed using the following principles:

- A single person owns responsibility for the process of distribution of software.
- A predictable process for freezing basic software components is in place (this has proven hard in practice).
- The responsibility of ensuring that software ready for distribution has been tested is a distributed process. The responsibility is currently that of the software's *creator*.
- Configuration, distribution, and process are replicated at user sites. The entire process can be reused.
- Configuration and distribution (and to a limited extent—testing) are part of a single process. The goal is to combine and automate the processes of: configure, assemble, test, package, ship, and install (see Figure 1.1).
- Few requirements can be enforced on the target (user) machine. The current assumption is that it is a UNIX-like system with at least a 7th Edition UNIX Shell and a C compilation system. Even these requirements are being relaxed.

Some of these principles have been easier to accomplish than others. There is a single responsible manager. Configuration and distribution are part of a single process, and few requirements are placed on either the target machine or on the capability of the distribution mechanism (for example, distribution is over wide areas and existing network facilities). Freezing the basic components in an environment in which changes are frequent has proven difficult. It could be done with a formal change management process, but we, as a research organization, have chosen to encourage change and work hard when freeze dates occur. Our choice is biased in the direction of frequent improvement, as opposed to control. Downstream distributors use formal change management. Their releases are less frequent but better controlled and tested. In Section 1.3.1, we trace the ADVSOFT process, as applied to a specific tool.

The technology in use for configuration and distribution is advanced and flexible. It uses a variety of new tools, including *n-DFS* and *ship/pax* (described in Chapters 2 and 3, respectively). On the other hand, the technology for testing is not as advanced and automated as that for configuration, assembling, packaging, shipping, and installation. Work is being carried out on automating and increasing the effectiveness of the testing process, but much is yet to be done. Today, those systems that are large, sophisticated, and/or critical to project operations are typically distributed to production users by downstream technology organizations (usually for a charge). In that case, our process supplies that downstream distribution channel.

1.3.1   ADVSOFT Process Example

In this section, we present an example of how we coordinate, configure, and track the development of a variety of software components that are distributed to organizations throughout AT&T. We use a tool called *ship*, which is a collection of KornShell command scripts (see Chapter 4) that packages components of a software distribution for a variety of hardware and operating system platforms in a portable way. *ship* requires that tools to be distributed be stored in a directory, together with an *item* file that lists the set of direct dependent entities of the tool (that is, libraries needed to build the tool). *ship* creates a portable archive (using *pax*) of the source and *nmake* (the build tool) files to be sent to the remote site. *ship*, *pax*, and *nmake* are described in Chapter 3.

The example in this section deals with how changes are automatically tracked in *libast*, a library on which YEAST and other tools depend. Taking advantage of the *ship* directory hierarchy and the item files, we are able to automate the generation of new versions of modified software via the ADVSOFT process. The automation itself, incidentally, is done via YEAST (see Chapter 9). The example is explained in more detail in Section 9.5.

Figure 1.2 depicts the process that ADVSOFT manages. In the figure, the circles represent subprocesses and the arrows represent data flow between subprocesses. Tool owners submit a copy of the newest version of their tools to ADVSOFT in cycles (about twice a year).

Figure 1.2 depicts in detail how the process is carried out for the tool

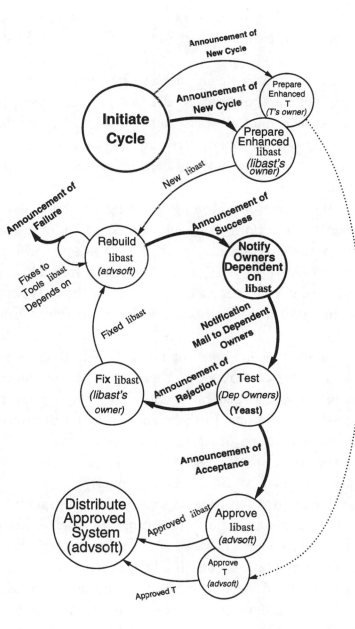

Figure 1.2 A software tool development and distribution process. Portions automated by YEAST are shown in boldface.

libast (solid lines), while showing that an identical process is carried out for all other tools T in parallel (dotted lines). The rest of the diagram is self-explanatory.

The configuration management tasks to be carried out by the AD-VSOFT process include coordinating changes (a new version of a tool requires notifying owners of all tools that depend on the modified tool), tracking the changes (some tool owners may reject the changes), and controlling the changes (waiting until all dependent tool owners accept the modified version).

The seemingly simple bookkeeping activities can be time-consuming and error-prone when performed by humans. Thus, automation of these responsibilities was undertaken. In particular, YEAST specifications automate those portions of Figure 1.2 that are shown in boldface.

The details of how YEAST is used to implement the ADVSOFT process are described in detail in Section 9.5. We simply present a brief outline here.

We first generate specifications for all tools and all owners that are under the management of ADVSOFT. YEAST watches for the creation of new versions of tools, and generates notifications about the successful building of these new versions. In the example, the notifications are sent to tool owners dependent on *libast*, causing them to test their tools with the modified version of *libast*. YEAST also generates appropriate error messages if the new versions did not build properly.

Tool owners run regression tests on their tools and generate a YEAST announcement (a user notification) indicating that they either accept or reject the modified version of *libast*. YEAST keeps track of all acceptance and rejection announcements. If all dependent tool owners indicate acceptance, the modified version of *libast* is considered to be ready for distribution. If *any* of the dependent owners indicate rejection, the owner of *libast* is notified and the process involving *libast* is recommenced.

As dependencies among existing tools change and as new tools and new versions of existing tools come into existence, obsolete YEAST specifications are automatically deleted and new ones added.

1.4 Systems Architecture

A key to reuse at every level of software components is stability of the interface. At the basic—component—level of reuse, such as the UNIX System Libraries, a standard must be established at the level of C function calls, parameters, return values, and names, most of which remain unchanged across versions. However, at higher levels of reuse, a framework must be in place to establish standards for a larger variety of things. For example, in many systems a language is necessary to express and execute *actions* for the system. This language is not, typically, part of the system itself—if each system has a unique *action* language, reuse will be severely impacted. In later chapters, there are examples of tools that have separated out the action language: YEAST, EASEL, and *nmake* are three such tools. Nearly all of our high-level systems currently use the *ksh93* version of the KornShell as the *action* language. Thus, it is important that the KornShell language evolves mostly in an upward compatible way.

Over time, a better understanding of the interaction between reuse and system architecture has evolved. These notions are the result of observation of the use of many application developers, as well as our own work. In general, they are built around the common notions of separation of roles in a way that encourages reuse. This discussion is framed in the context of application systems, often driven by data management and user interfaces, but it also applies to tool applications.

Three principles were observed in practice:

- A standard, high-level, comprehensive, action language is essential. To minimize learning curves, it is essential that this language be widely distributed, understood, and accepted. We have used an extended UNIX System Shell, KornShell, for this purpose. Because it is also the command interpreter for many of the computer systems used by our customers, it has led to widespread understanding without extensive training.
- Application systems should clearly identify their Architectural Styles and separate their implementation from that of the Application Domain Specific Components. Architectural styles show how components of an architecture can be arranged. It is easy to glean the proper-

ties of an architecture once the style is known. This was learned, over time, largely from the development and use of a system called EASEL (Chapter 4). EASEL is a tool that supports the efficient construction of application systems that can be built as a network of *tasks*. A task can be a variety of activities, with one of the most common being an interaction with a user of the application. Data is passed among tasks, control is from task to task, and a rich variety of user interface types are built into the tool.

- An emerging area of reuse is Architectural Services, which should be identified and leveraged for reuse. Architectural services are capabilities that are required independent of architectural style. They support the non-feature requirements of application systems. For example, most network management systems require high levels of availability and security, but these are not part of their application feature sets. A list of some such services is included in Figure 1.3. These capabilities are crucial to most software products, and make up a significant part of the software in application systems. They have also become areas of some depth in their own right. This creates ideal conditions for the reuse of software: valuable/necessary functionality that is technically difficult to get right. Recent work in this department in the area of software fault tolerance (Chapter 8) has reinforced the value of this notion. This work has achieved widespread use in products in a shorter time than any equivalent project. Within a year of development, these techniques were in use or committed to by more than ten projects across several AT&T Business Units.

Figure 1.3 illustrates a way of describing the structure of application systems that is aimed at increasing levels of reuse. Envision a system as defined by a basic structure (*style*), chosen from a small set. The architectural styles range in complexity from simple pipelines, to complex transaction processing and real time applications. In the ideal case an architectural style is supported by a tool. For example, systems using a *Transaction Processing* style [GR93] would likely use one of several transaction processing monitors. Independently of the architectural style, users should expect services, such as fault tolerance, security, portability, and

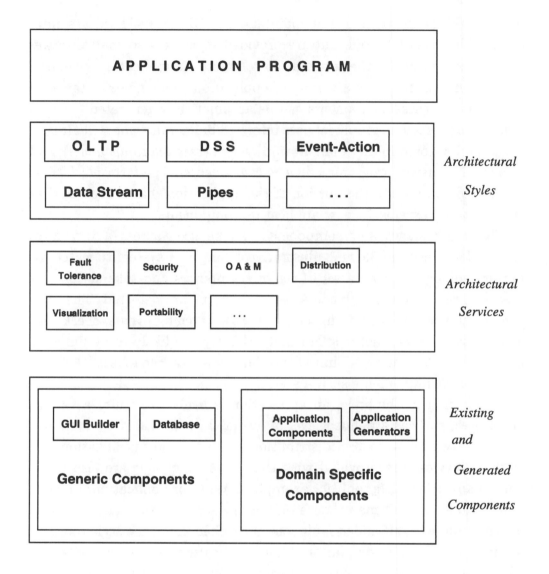

Figure 1.3 Structural components of reuse.

operations administration and maintenance (OA&M). These are integrated with the *style* tool, but are provided separately so that all *styles* can take advantage of the services. To complete an application system, a programmer must attach a variety of application *components* to the *style* tool. Some of these components can be automatically generated (*component builders* such as graphical user interface builders); some will already exist and be stored in the configuration system (*existing components*); and some will be newly programmed (*new components*). The term *platform* is often used to describe the portion of the application that is reused, that is, everything except the new application components.

Figure 1.3 shows how components can be used across a variety of styles. Consider the following illustrative example: A system to watch for patterns of signals from a set of remote computers and take action (for example, raise an alarm) when selected patterns are detected. The *style* can be called event/condition/action, that is, watch for events, check conditions, take defined actions. Formally, this style is likely to be modeled by a tool implementing a Finite State Machine or a Petri Net. YEAST is one tool that implements such a style.

In addition to the style, an application is likely to require a variety of services, such as a defined level of availability (provided by fault tolerance software), wide-area distribution, security, and visualization. All of these services are provided with the YEAST tool, but are also available to any other *style* tool (for example, EASEL) or application. In some applications, YEAST may choose only a few services, such as, wide-area distribution, without added fault tolerance. Combining the style tool and services provides a basic platform. The application can be completed by adding application-specific components. For example, user interfaces will be created using a graphical user interface (GUI) builder—an example of a component builder; specific actions will be collected if they exist or written if they are new. In the end, a complete application is created by gluing together pieces of an existing *platform*; writing scripts in the *style* tool's language (here YEAST) and in the language of the *action* tool (KornShell); and writing (hopefully, only a few) new components.

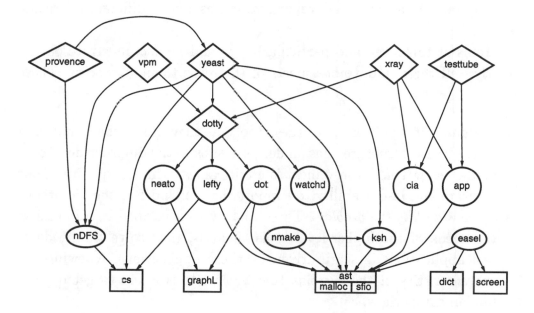

Figure 1.4   Four levels of the software described.

1.5   Four Levels

The software described in this book can be partitioned into four levels: substrate, base, standalone, and connected tools. Reuse is achieved at each of these levels: intralevel and interlevel. Figure 1.4 illustrates this four-level structure as it applies to the tools described in this book. Readers should note that the distinction between these layers is internal; application developers who build tools on top of our software will have a different notion of where the tools fit in their hierarchy.

Each of the nodes in Figure 1.4 corresponds to a tool/library; an edge between two nodes indicates a dependence by the higher-level node on the lower-level node. All of the tools/libraries are discussed in the rest of the chapters of this book.

1.5.1   Substrate

The lowest layer, the substrate (shown by rectangles in Figure 1.4), consists of a collection of libraries. These include *ast*, which is a library including three fundamental components: *sfio*, *malloc*, and a set of functions to help portability by standardizing variances among different operating systems.

Tools at this level, and particularly *sfio* and *malloc*, illustrate particularly well three important aspects of the reuse thought process. These are:

- *Dynamic life-cycle*: Each of these tools, as they are at the foundation of the reuse structure, has undergone substantial improvement over many years. This improvement is a critical factor in the quality of our software and in our ability to support the remainder of the hierarchy.
- *Understanding the problem*: These tools were developed in response to the needs of the higher-level tools. That is, they solve the needs of real applications and are driven by those applications. Knowing the characteristics of the systems that you write is a key to getting the fundamentals right.
- *Reuse induction*: The substrate tools have evolved to become general tools by solving problems for a sequence of real systems, and by concentrating on improving the abstract model of the solution at each step.

The libraries are all described in Chapter 2.

1.5.2   Base

The second layer consists of what we label *base* tools (shown by ovals in Figure 1.4). These tools are important for the environment in which other tools are built. The primary difference between tools at this level and the substrate layer is the complexity of their interfaces and how they are reused. The substrate is a collection of libraries with simple C function interfaces that can be reused as pluggable components, while the base tools provide languages and filters that encode knowledge reusable with some programming.

Tools that embody the *style* of an architecture important to a family of applications (for example, EASEL) typically become *base* tools, as do those that provide essential standards on which other tools depend (such as, *ksh93* and *nmake*). Tools that support architecture services also exist at this level. *n-DFS* supports services such as fault tolerance and synchronization of data. It will likely support many other services as it matures.

nmake and *n-DFS* are described in Chapter 3, *ksh* and EASEL are described in Chapter 4.

1.5.3   Standalone Tools

The standalone tools (shown by circles in Figure 1.4) layer comes next. Tools at this layer reuse libraries in the substrate layer and are built in the environment of the tools in the second layer. The standalone tools perform a focused task and are not as generic as the base tools. For example, *cia*, a reverse engineering tool, uses *libast* in the lowest layer. *cia* is generic within a reasonably bounded application class. However, *cia* is not as generic as *ksh*, which provides a language in which arbitrary scripts can be written.

Both *cia* and APP are tools that aid program understanding. *cia* provides static analysis while APP aids in analysis at runtime. *cia* extracts C program entity relationships, while APP processes assertions (specified as pre- and post-conditions) to generate self-checking C programs. Both *cia* and APP use *libast* and *libpp*.

The *watchd* tool (together with the *libft* library) provides a mechanism to add fault tolerance to existing programs. *watchd* reuses *libast*.

Several tools have been written on top of *cia* forming the CIA system. APP and CIA are described in Chapters 5 and 6, respectively. While we do not have a tool that provides security as an architectural service, we discuss security aspects of software engineering in Chapter 7; *watchd* and *libft* are described in Chapter 8.

1.5.4   Connected Tools

The connected tools (shown by rhombuses in Figure 1.4) are application systems. They are constructed from lower levels of library and tool, and they, in turn, are used to build other application systems. Thus, for example, YEAST from the viewpoint of its developers is a *connected tool* in that it is built using *ksh*, *watchd*, *lefty*, and *dot*, as well as *libast* and *libcs*. On the other hand, to an application developer using YEAST to provide the architectural style for his/her system, YEAST is a *base* tool, and the application (or part of it) is a *connected* tool.

PROVENCE, an open process-centered software development environment, is another connected tool. PROVENCE's components are: MARVEL (a tool developed outside AT&T), *Enactor*, YEAST, *dotty* and *n-DFS*. *dotty*, a graphical editor/layout tool, consists of *dot* and *lefty*. TEST-TUBE, formed by connecting *cia* and APP, identifies subsets of test suites that need to be run when a new version of a system is created (thus helping in minimizing the number of tests). *Xray* animates programs and visualizes the dynamic aspects of program execution either *live* or by playing back a recorded session. *Xray* is formed by connecting *cia* (to get relational information between entities in the program), APP (for instrumenting the code to output useful information during the run), and *dotty* (for visualizing). VPM, a visual process monitor, permits dynamic monitoring of running processes across multiple machines. VPM is formed by linking *n-DFS* and *dotty*.

YEAST and PROVENCE are described in Chapters 9 and 10, respectively. *dotty*, *Xray*, TESTTUBE, and VPM are all described in Chapter 11.

1.5.5   Reuse Experiences

Reuse from existing component libraries, internal to this department, is shown in Table 1.1. The first column shows a partial list of tools we distribute (the tools are described in detail in the book). The second column shows the actual lines of source code in the tool (referred to as NCSL, or noncommented source lines), while the third column shows the total lines of code shipped (including all the libraries needed by the tool). On average, it is greater than five lines reused per line of code written.

But there are two important factors that we have to consider: Even though an entire library is linked, only a subset of the functions in the library is actually referenced by the reusing entity. Thus, if we consider the code in the library actually used by the tool, we get the numbers in the fourth column. These numbers were computed by using *cref* and *subsys* (tools that are part of the CIA system), described in Sections 6.3.2 and 6.5.1, respectively. We should stress that the analysis is based on static information.

The second factor is that there is also a hierarchy of reuse at the system level among the tools in Table 1.1. For example, *ksh93* provides the action language for YEAST, EASEL, *nmake*, and *coshell*; these tools support a variety of architectural styles. Also, tools, such as *watchd*, support several other tools by providing architectural services, such as YEAST. These reuse values are not in the table because they are in separate executables, but they represent large integer factors in terms of effort reduction, both for tool builders and in learning time for tool users.

Table 1.1 Software Reuse

Tool	NCSL	S-NCSL	R-NCSL
3DFS	11099	83069	18466
APP	5881	57097	11462
cia	5327	52914	13166
coshell	3884	49166	14026
cs	1723	45724	14092
dot	12952	16585	14245
dotty	1413	75918	27674
easel	25782	48024	38901
incl	1085	43868	5245
ksh	31310	69407	39288
lefty	12730	59333	18601
nmake	17319	64687	28663
pax	6479	42225	15344
probe	345	34943	7278
proto	208	47389	2124
ss	504	42272	5867
subsys	360	41194	7301
VPM	1100	115621	40043
watchd	3133	10694	3552
YEAST	7288	56397	14913

NCSL: Non-commented source lines
S-NCSL: Shipped NCSL
R-NCSL: Reused NCSL

1.6   An Example of Architectural Style and Service

In this section, we present an illustration of architectural styles and services as a way of building new applications out of reusable components. First, we briefly discuss YEAST, an event-action specification tool, as an example of a tool that enables an architectural style. YEAST is described in detail in Chapter 9. Next, we show how two architectural services, namely fault tolerance and visualization, have been added to YEAST. Fault tolerance is described in more detail in Chapter 8 and visualization in Section 11.2.

1.6.1   Architectural Style

YEAST runs as a daemon on a single machine on a network and accepts client specifications from users. When these specifications are matched, user-specified actions are triggered by YEAST. Client commands—such as, add, remove, and suspend specifications—can be issued from any of several machines in the network. YEAST permits arbitrary actions to be triggered when event patterns of interest are matched. It can match temporal events and nontemporal events, such as changes of attributes in objects belonging to a variety of object classes. The list of predefined attributes for these object classes can be extended, as can the classes themselves. With the use of external event notifications (called *announcements*), YEAST can model a wide range of applications that follow the event-action paradigm.

YEAST supports an event/condition/action architectural style, making such platforms easier to build. The application first decides on the set of events of interest and the manner (both temporal ordering as well as combination of patterns) in which the events should be detected. Then, a collection of YEAST specifications is registered with a YEAST daemon. Several applications have been built on top of YEAST, ranging from automatic coordination of database files from a network of machines to a schedule maintenance system.

1.6.2   Architectural Services

We next look at two architectural services that dramatically improved the power and capability of YEAST. The first is the fault tolerance service provided by a combination of a library and a watcher process. The second example is visualization support provided via a language mechanism.

1.6.2.1   Fault Tolerance

Software fault tolerance is a way to make software withstand faults that arise during execution. It is significantly more than checking boundary conditions and several techniques have been identified. It is not enough to rollback, recover, and restart; nor is it enough to test *adequately*. Some faults in programs fall in the category of *transient* failures resulting from a particular input sequence or a set of environment conditions. The approach taken in *libft/watchd* is to provide a platform that, with some modifications to the software, provides an acceptable level of recovery from catastrophic conditions, as well as an opportunity to modify software faults when an exception happens.

The first half of the fault tolerance technique is a library that, when linked with application programs, provides a checkpointing facility for recovering from failures. The second half is a *watch daemon* that aids in locating the fault. The library and the watch daemon free individual application programs from having to do their own separate fault tolerance. A significant amount of useful code is thus reused.

Consider the example of YEAST, of which some customers require fault tolerance. YEAST clients do not know where the YEAST daemon process is running on the network. If the machine on which the YEAST daemon is running crashes, two problems arise: The existing set of specifications is no longer being matched, and new client commands cannot communicate with a YEAST daemon. Ad hoc solutions, while reasonable, require a significant amount of code to be added to YEAST, none of which deals with event-action matching—the stated purpose of the application.

The *libft/watchd* technique is suited for a distributed environment. The list of data structures significant to YEAST is isolated in a section of

YEAST code and the YEAST daemon process is registered with *watchd*. *
This requires minimal modifications to YEAST. Upon a machine crash,
the shadow process restarts a YEAST daemon on another machine on the
network with the most recent value of the significant data structures. This
enables continued matching of the existing specifications with no loss of
state. Additionally, new client connections are automatically routed to
the new daemon process, thus making the machine crash transparent to
the users on the network.

1.6.2.2   Visualization

Visualization is often a key component of interfaces and application front
ends. Visualization can be static or dynamic, depending on the application needs. For example, graph layouts are often a useful way to present
visual information, especially when dealing with software entities. A flexible way to provide this is to use a graph description language consisting
of nodes and edges at a simple level, and attributes (such as color) and
abstractions (such as clusters, groupings) at a higher level. The choice for
a visual representation language is driven by simplicity that minimizes
the time spent in learning an additional language.

Unlike *libft/watchd*, where a library is used, a language is used here
to describe the service. A graph drawing program should be able to
parse a graph description language and construct a picture quickly.
dot [GKNV93] is a tool that reads and writes graphs in an attributed
graph description language. By combining *dot* with *lefty* [KD91] (a programmable graphics editor), *dotty* was created. *dotty* can be used as a
standalone tool or as a front end for applications that use graphs. In
dotty, the *lefty* program implements the insertion and deletion of nodes
and edges, the drawing of the picture, and functions that map user actions
to operations on the picture. *dotty* can thus read *dot* input and create a
dynamic front end that can be controlled through simple commands. *dot*,
lefty, and *dotty* are all described in Section 11.2. Section 9.6.2.2 describes
the visualization of YEAST specifications in more detail.

The graphical front end for YEAST took a couple of hours to build and

---

*In the most recent version of *libft* with global checkpointing, the need for even this modest step
has been obviated.

needed an addition of about 50 lines of code to YEAST. This technique has since been replicated for other tools in the department—a recent example is for a software process visualization environment, PROVENCE (see Chapter 10).

We have examined how one tool (YEAST) has taken advantage of the architectural services that are available separately from the basic tools that they serve. Other examples can be found in this book.

1.7   Summary

Our experience shows that there is considerable value in a reasonably comprehensive set of reusable items of mixed levels (component, service, style, platform) when supported by strong marketing and distribution capabilities. The set can be put together in a variety of ways. A reuse factor greater than five has been achieved locally using libraries (with a *real* reuse factor of 2 to 2.5 when the actual percentage usage of library functions is considered). The real impact is much greater than that if the use of architectural roles and levels is considered, but we do not yet have accurate measures of that effect.

The book follows the four-level structure described in Section 1.5. The software entities in the substrate and base levels concentrate on the principles on which they were built and the reusability they offer to the higher-level tools. The standalone tools chapters begin with a description of the tool, describe their architecture, and highlight the lower-level components reused by them. They also point toward how they were used as components to the tools in the later chapters. The chapters dealing with connected tools discuss the reuse of the standalone tools at the component level and show how they were assembled efficiently.

1.8   Reading This Book

There are a number of ways to read this book.

One is as a presentation of a collection of tools and libraries that perform a variety of interesting and valuable tasks. These tasks include:

basic library support for software development (Chapter 2), configuration management (Chapter 3), static and dynamic code analysis (Chapters 5 and 6), secure/reliable application systems (Chapters 7 and 8), high level languages for system development (Chapters 4 and 9), and integrated applications (Chapters 10 and 11). They describe software that is in widespread use and reflect what we have learned in several application areas.

A second is as a collection of tools and ideas that, when taken together, provide a platform for effective software development. The software described in this book supports the technique of obtaining high-leverage reuse by division of software into several architectural roles. From this point of view: Chapter 2 describes basic components; Chapters 4 and 9 describe tools to support certain architectural styles using high-level languages; Chapters 5 and 6 describe development environment support; Chapters 7 and 8 describe architectural services; Chapters 3, 10, and 11 describe integrated applications. Development activity is supported both within the development environment and for reuse within developed systems. Particular attention is paid to such issues as portability and configuration for the development of large-scale software.

A third way to read the book is for ideas and processes that can lead to an effective software development strategy based on multiple use of software entities. This strategy has been successful in our research environment. It is implicit in the way the software in each chapter relate to each other, rather than the contents of a specific chapter. It is best understood by following the relationships in Figure 1.4 as you read the book. Keep in mind that this strategy it is not limited to research, to the production of software tools, or to the specific technologies described in this book. We encourage you to consider, as you read the remainder of this book, concepts and techniques that you can take from our experience and use in your software development and specifically your reuse strategy.

2

Libraries and File System Architecture

Glenn Fowler, David Korn, Stephen North, Herman Rao, and Kiem-Phong Vo

2.1 Libraries

Libraries are the most widely understood and used form of code reuse. A collection of generic routines that can be simply plugged into diverse applications is often a strong motivating factor for reuse. However, there are several principles that have to be kept in mind to create a successfully reusable library. This chapter deals with a broad cross section of software ranging from memory allocation to operating system services. The software is organized into a collection of libraries called the *ast* libraries that form the backbone for the rest of the tools described in the book.

The main sections of the chapter are:

- Section 2.2 gives an introduction to the *ast* libraries along with a detailed discussion of the design principles used in writing them. This section also overviews some of the main components of *ast* including the porting base *libast*.
- Section 2.3 deals with a resource acquisition and management parameterization technique—*disciplines* and *methods*—that enhances library

---

The left running heads in chapters 2, 3, 4, and 11 indicate the author(s) of each section.

flexibility and portability, which are *key* requirements for widespread reuse. This section describes four libraries written using this technique.

- Section 2.4 describes a general purpose graph library based on a standard graph data language, that is used by a variety of tools described in this book.
- Section 2.5 discusses a file system service substrate called *n-DFS*. Of the wide variety of services offered by this logical file system that has been implemented as a library, several, such as viewpathing, versioning, and event notification, are used by tools described later in this book.

2.2   The *ast* Libraries

In the early years of C and UNIX programming, many general purpose libraries were produced and widely distributed. These libraries provide a wide variety of functions for mathematics, buffered I/O, dynamic memory allocation, and so on. Their availability led to a tremendous growth in programmer productivity. By virtue of their widespread use, the libraries became *de facto* standards and were commonly called the standard C libraries. These libraries stand as some of the best examples of successful reusable software.

Unfortunately, in the early 1980s, the creation of widely available reusable C libraries came to a virtual standstill. One can debate the factors that contributed to this. Certainly, within AT&T and probably in the industry at large, the main focus of most UNIX development organizations was more on hardware and kernel development than on general reusable libraries. This direction of work was driven by the belief that except for application-specific products, the main value of software was to help sell hardware. This assumption was always dubious and is certainly no longer valid at current prices for high-performance stock hardware.

From a language point of view, an important factor was the lack of direct support for modularization in C. Though conventions could be formed to alleviate the problem, such conventions were either ill-defined or, more often, ignored when available. This situation was worsened by the explosive growth of the UNIX system as a platform for building software applications. During this gold rush, more effort was dedicated to building application-specific products than reusable software. The latter was sometimes viewed as an unnecessary luxury. As applications have expanded and branched into families and demands have increased for quick turnaround of new features, the need for standard reusable software components has become critical.

The introduction of the C++ programming language in the mid 1980s put an additional damper on the development of new C libraries. C++ had better support for interface encapsulation than C. This simplified the creation of new libraries. Moreover, since C++ was in its infancy, there was no backward compatibility to contend with. The result was that much of the recent best library work in the C family of languages occurred in the C++ arena (including many reimplementations of C libraries as C++).

Despite the lack of support for modularization in the C language, it is possible to write high-level reusable libraries in C. With some effort, such libraries can even be written to be compatible with any variant of the C language, including C++. Over a period of several years, we have been writing and distributing a collection of high-level reusable C libraries under the *ast* (advanced software technology) umbrella. The *ast* libraries were developed as a part of a research program to build highly portable advanced software development tools. The algorithms and data structures underlying these tools are encapsulated in library components to increase general reuse, avoid code duplication, and maximize portability. Over the years, the libraries have found wide use both within our own work and other applications, including commercial products.

The *ast* libraries cover a broad spectrum, including functions traditionally provided in *libc* (but more portable), general network connection functions, C expression evaluation, data compression, and others. *ast* has been ported to virtually every combination of UNIX software/hardware platform, including various versions of System V, BSD and AT&T Bell Laboratories Research UNIX systems, and Windows and Windows NT. The remainder of this section describes in detail the design conventions used, and overviews a few components of *ast*. A few *ast* components are based on the idea of disciplines and methods that parameterize resource acquisition and management. These are overviewed in Section 2.3, which discusses disciplines and methods in detail.

2.2.1   Design Considerations

The primary goals in building the *ast* components are applicability, efficiency, ease of use, and ease of maintenance. However, there is no simple set of rules that would guarantee the simultaneous achievement of these goals. Often enough, the goals conflict and decisions have to be made to balance the trade-offs. Below are an eclectic set of design considerations used as guidelines in building the *ast* software.

2.2.1.1   Necessity

A component is not reusable unless it is used. This means that a reusable component should be built out of real needs. A way to meet this condition is to first plan some applications, then build the functions that make up the applications as one or more libraries. Because libraries are often used in different ways, this approach has the additional advantage of forcing the programmer to think in advance about different usages resulting in better code quality.

An example of writing a library before writing a command is the *libpp* library (Section 2.2.9). *libpp* defines the token parsing and symbol processing engine in our K&R [KR88], ANSI [ANS90], and C++ [Str91] compatible C preprocessor. Besides this original use, *libpp* has found use in other important language related tools, such as CIA (Chapter 6), a system for storing and finding information about C programs, and *app* (Chapter 5), a preprocessor to annotate C code with assertions.

2.2.1.2   Generality

Except for efficiency concerns, reusable components should be designed for their most general applications. Often, this means putting together separate but related concepts into a single unifying interface. This is important because applications often use similar mechanisms (for example, various search structures) in different ways (such as for storing objects of different types). Unifying the different mechanisms in a standard set of functions both simplifies application construction and increases their ease of maintenance. A further important effect of generality is that it often opens up new uses.

The dictionary library *libdict* (see Section 2.3.3) shows an example of how related concepts are unified under a single general interface. Ordered and unordered objects are treated uniformly. Efficiency is guaranteed by switching storage methods between hash tables for unordered objects and self-adjusting binary trees for ordered ones.

An aspect of generality related to portability is to provide common abstractions that hide the differences in the underlying platforms. Though our software is UNIX-based, it is no secret that no two versions of UNIX are the same. In the short term, the existence of standard bodies, such as POSIX [POS90], actually worsens the situation, as the standards tend to be some amalgam of existing systems but unlike any of them. Sometimes, when the differences in extant implementations of a desired feature are wide enough, the standards may even shy away from defining one. In Section 2.2.2, we describe a set of functions and header files that combine features from various UNIX flavors. Our tools are written based on this interface to increase portability.

2.2.1.3   Extensibility

In building a library, certain low-level but critical functions from the underlying platform are frequently required. Sometimes it is profitable to abstract such dependencies and let applications provide appropriate processing functions. This is similar to the idea of virtual functions in C++, which parameterize the operations of an abstract class. Section 2.3 discusses disciplines that are interfaces designed to capture external resource dependencies. This allows applications to redefine such resource requirements for a library without tampering with its internals.

2.2.1.4   Efficiency

Efficiency is a primary consideration in the construction of a reusable component, because the performance of such a component is amplified by its repeated use. When a reusable component does not perform adequately, programmers will be tempted to hand-code and create applications that are hard to maintain. There are two aspects of efficiency: internal and external.

Internal efficiency This means, first, that library components are implemented using the current best-known data structures and algorithms. Then, even if general algorithms may have good performance over a large class of operations, it is sometimes beneficial to optimize code based on its most popular use or local hardware and platform features. An example of this type of optimization is the numerical conversion algorithm from an internal representation to an ASCII format in the `sfprintf()` family of functions in the *sfio* library (Section 2.3.1). Here, because base 10 is most commonly used, it is handled using a fast customized algorithm. Other bases are handled by a general but slower method.

External efficiency: This means that the library interface is designed so that critical resources managed by the library can be efficiently accessed by applications. An example of this is the `sfreserve()` function of the *sfio* library that allows an application to directly and safely access the internal buffer of an I/O stream. For applications accessing large chunks of data, this can dramatically reduce the number of memory copying operations between stream and application buffers while still minimizing system calls. We have rewritten many system commands, such as *pack* and *wc*, based on `sfreserve()` with up to a factor of four in performance improvement over the BSD4.3 versions of the same commands.

2.2.1.5   Robustness

A successful reusable component should be robust with respect to stresses on critical resources. There are two aspects of robustness: internal and external.

Internal robustness This means that the library components should be well tested in a variety of environments, that their implementation does not impose any artificial constraints on resources, and that they can respond well to unexpected events. The *ast* components are continually tested and used on nearly every UNIX platform. Artificial constraints, such as fixed size arrays, number of bits in an `int`, etc., are duly avoided. As an additional measure of internal robustness, the *ast*

code is written in a style compilable under the K&R C, ANSI C and
C++ dialects. This allows the code to be tested with the type checking mechanisms of many C compilers, each with its own strengths and
weaknesses. In addition, the code can be used transparently by applications based on different C dialects.

External robustness: This means that the library design should prevent
applications from making inherently unsafe usage and provide them
with ways to deal with exceptions. An example of inherently unsafe
usage is the *stdio* gets() function, which takes as input a buffer with
unspecified size and returns data of unspecified length in the buffer.
Since neither buffer size nor data size are known in advance, there is
no precaution that either the library or the application can make to
prevent buffer overflow. By contrast, the *sfio* library provides a function sfgetr(), which returns a pointer to a record delineated by some
application-defined record separator. The space for the record is internally managed by the library, as only it can know how much space is
required.

An aspect of external robustness related to extensions is to design
global data structures so that applications see only what they require.
For example, an application based on the *sfio* library does I/O via
stream handles of the type Sfio_t. However, from the application's
viewpoint, such a handle contains only the elements necessary to implement fast operations, such as sfputc() or sfgetc(). Other members
of the structure are hidden from view. By doing this and by being careful to use memory allocation instead of static arrays, we can guarantee
that, even at the binary level, application code will not be affected
should the Sfio_t structure need extensions.

2.2.1.6 Modularity

Modularity means that components and functions are sufficiently insu-
lated from one another so that the implementation of one will not severely
affect the implementation of another. It also means that the components
and functions can be used independently. Modularity is important because it reduces the complexity in interrelations among components. By
and large, the *ast* libraries can be used in arbitrary order. Of course, using

some of them may mean that others will be implicitly required, but such requirements are transparent at the application level.

For example, the *ast* error-handling component uses *sfio* to format error messages, so using an error-handling routine would implicitly mean using *sfio*. But this does not mean that any understanding of *sfio* is required to use the error-handling functions. Within a library, to the extent possible, the functions are designed to be orthogonal. For example, similar to *stdio*, the *sfio* package allows an application to set its own buffer for a stream. Unlike *stdio*, which requires that the buffer be set before any I/O operation is performed, *sfio* allows arbitrary buffer change. This may seem to be a trivial improvement but for the fact that *sfio* lets applications create string streams to access memory buffers, and being able to switch such buffers at any time is important.

2.2.1.7   Minimality

Next to having an awkward or inconsistent interface, having too much in the interface is another factor that steepens the learning curve for users. As a general rule, an interface should not be provided unless it does something that cannot be done otherwise without significant loss of efficiency or convenience. For example, unlike *stdio*, which provides a multitude of convenience functions, such as `getchar()` and `putchar()` in addition to general stream manipulation functions, such as `getc()` and `putc()`, *sfio* simply insists that the standard functions `sfgetc()` and `sfputc()` be used.

The downside of minimizing the interface is awkward and redundant code at the application level when certain aggregate operations are commonly performed. In such a case, a compromise should be reached. An example is the `sfprints()` function of *sfio* that creates a formatted string in some system provided area and returns a pointer to that string. This function avoids the buffer overflow problem that often arises with the `sprintf()` function of *stdio*. Here, strictly speaking, an application can create the effect of `sfprints()` using a combination of a string stream, `sfprintf()`, `sfseek()`, and `sfreserve()`, but this is too awkward to repeat in every application.

2.2.1.8 Portability

Given the multitude of hardware and software platforms available today, portability is an absolute requirement for successful software. There are two dimensions to portability: code and data. At the code level, the *ast* libraries are portable to nearly all known UNIX and UNIX-like platforms (including Windows and Windows NT). This is aided by the *iffe* probing mechanism and an accompanying coding discipline (see Section 3.2) that allows recording knowledge learned during porting and enables code configuration without user intervention.

At the data level, it is desirable that persistent data (for example, disk files) or data communicated among processes also be portable. That is, such data should be independent of the local hardware representations. This is a hard problem and a complete solution for aggregate data types would require much more cooperation from the languages and compilers than currently available in any flavor of C. However, for primitive types, the problem is more amenable to treatment. Assuming that the order of bits in bytes is the same across hardware platforms, the *sfio* library provides function to transparently read and write integers and floating point values.

2.2.1.9 Evolvability

A successful reusable library will undergo revisions as its design and implementation are stressed by usage or technology advances. When the interface is sufficiently general, certain types of revision can be kept hidden within the package, and the interface can be maintained as is. However, weakness in the design is often not revealed until challenged by new needs; then, the interface must change. Sometimes, this amounts to adding new functions to alter the states of the library.

An example along this way is the method idea discussed in Section 2.3, which allows customization of the abstract interface by selecting a new method. In other cases where new, clean, and well-designed interfaces provide much more benefit than previous ones, compatibility must be broken. Then, it is important to help users ease the transition. An example is the *stdio* source and binary compatibility packages provided with *sfio*. These packages allow applications based on *stdio* to either recompile or simply link with *sfio* transparently. This means that a software project can take advantage of new technologies immediately without too much upheaval in their programming practice.

2.2.1.10   Naming Conventions

Good interface conventions help to ease the learning curve of a software package and reduce name clashing when different packages are used together in a single application. As libraries are developed by different people at different times, it is hard to achieve a uniform set of conventions.

Sometimes the interface is already defined by earlier packages (for example, the *screen* library in Section 2.2.4), so new conventions cannot apply. By and large, the naming conventions followed in *ast* are:

- *Standard prefixes:* Constants, functions, and variables used in a package are always named using a small and unique set of prefixes that clearly identify the package, including the name of the package. For example, the prefixes SF, Sf, and sf are used for the *sfio* package.
- *Standard argument ordering:* Functions typically manipulate some structures that carry states across calls. Such state-carrying structures always come first in a argument list. For example, in all *sfio* calls, the stream argument is always the first. Sometimes arguments come in pairs (for example, a buffer and its size). Then, the one containing data or used to store data comes first (for example, the buffer comes before its size). Finally, flag arguments are always last in the list.
- *Object identification:* A library typically defines and uses many different objects. It is helpful to use naming conventions that distinguish different object types. Preprocessor symbols or macros (for example, SF_READ) are defined using uppercase letters. Nonfunctional global symbols (for example, Sfio_t) often start with an uppercase letter. Sfio_t also shows that a library-defined type often has an affixed _t. Function names (for example, sfopen()) are always in lowercase.
- *Reducing private global symbols:* Global data private to a single library is often placed in a single struct so that only one identifier in the data name space is taken. For example, all private global data of the *sfio*

library are kept in a structure _Sfextern. The leading underscore in
_Sfextern further emphasizes that it is a private symbol.

2.2.1.11   Architecture Conventions

Architecture conventions help to fit a library into other families of libraries, simplify the library design, and ease the learning process for new
users. Below are some of the conventions used in the *ast* libraries.

Reusing well-known architecture conventions: Inventing a new library
   does not necessarily mean inventing new software architecture and
   conventions. It is often advantageous to follow already familiar conventions. For example, in many libraries, the *modus operandi* is to create
   some data structure, manipulate it, and finally destroy it. A good existing convention is practiced by the UNIX file-manipulation system
   calls: open(), read(), write(), lseek(), and close(). Here, open()
   creates a file descriptor, a data structure that carries states across system calls–and close() destroys this data structure. The file descriptor,
   that is, the object being manipulated, is always the first argument to
   other calls, such as read() or write(), that require it. This is one of
   the architecture conventions employed in *ast*.

Saving and restoring states: C and its sibling languages are stack-like in
   their function-call convention. Certain data structures in the libraries
   are shared across function calls, so it is good to architect the library
   functions so that state information can be saved and restored seam-
   lessly. A good convention for functions that alter states is to always
   return the previous state. This allows an arbitrary function to call a
   library function to perform some work, then restore the data structures to their previous state before returning. For example, the function sfset() of *sfio*, used to set the flags controlling a stream, always
   returns the previous set of flags.

Information hiding: A structure publicly advertised by a library needs
   to reveal only as much of its internals as required by the interface implementation. Revealing too much of the private structure members
   makes it difficult to improve or extend the library without violating
   object-code compatibility. So, for example, the Sfio_t structure of *sfio*

reveals only as much of its members as required for implementing fast macro functions, such as `sfputc()`. Other members are visible only to the *sfio* functions. This prevents application developers from improper use of information. Further, as the structure is incomplete, certain information, such as its size, is meaningless in computation. On numerous occasions, this has helped to prevent applications from having to recompile when `Sfio_t` was extended.

Meaningful use of exceptional values: Separate operations can often be merged into one using certain exceptional values. An example is the *sfio* call `sfstack(base,top)` that specifies a `base` stream and a `top` stream to be pushed on top of `base`. I/O operations on the stream stack identified by `base` are performed on the `top` stream. Thus, `sfstack()` is useful for applications that process nested streams, such as the C preprocessor and `#include` files. Now, an operation required for a stack is the ability to *pop* the top element. Instead of providing a separate pop function, *sfio* does this with `sfstack(base,NULL)`. As `NULL` is often an error value (for example, for `malloc()`), using it in a meaningful way like this also induces programmers to be more aware and check for it.

2.2.2   *libast*: The *ast* Base

libast is the base library for the *ast* tools. It provides a common header and function interface for many UNIX systems and C compilers. Implementation specific details are confined to *libast*, with the effect that most *ast* tools are programmed without architecture-specific `#ifdefs`. While encouraging clean tool design, *libast* also provides a convenient framework for portability. Many interface issues are addressed and these are categorized below.

2.2.2.1   Header Interface

Determining the set of `#include` headers to use for a given system is one of the hardest portability challenges. Missing headers can be handled with simple feature testing (see Section 3.2). More difficult are system headers that omit information or define constructs that conflict with other headers. This is especially true with the introduction of function prototypes in ANSI C and C++ compiler headers. Traveling along the migration path between K&R and ANSI C adds more complications.

The header `ast_std.h` provides a union of the following ANSI and POSIX headers:

```
stdarg.h, stddef.h, stdlib.h, string.h, locale.h,
limits.h, sys/types.h, unistd.h, fcntl.h
```

`ast_std.h` is self-consistent across UNIX system and compiler variants. Consistency is attained by supplying omitted headers, providing defaults for omitted definitions, and fixing up botched constructs in existing local headers. For example, the type `size_t` is typically defined in `stddef.h` for ANSI C and `sys/types.h` for UNIX systems. In the latter case, it is sometimes not defined. As `size_t` is a symbol defined by the ANSI C standard, the header `ast_std.h` guarantees that this type is always defined.

`ast_std.h` includes local headers whenever possible (thus, it may define nonstandard symbols). Others are generated as necessary for the compiler that installs *libast* using iffe probes (Section 3.2). The `ast_std.h` header can be safely used with the C compiler used to generate it. It can also be used with other C compilers if the *libpp* C preprocessor (the default preprocessor for *nmake* users) is used.

2.2.2.2 Missing Functions

libast provides implementations for common system calls not supported by the local system. Some calls, like `rename()`, are emulated using `link()` and `unlink()`. Others, like `symlink()`, cannot be emulated, so the library provides a stub that always fails with `errno` set to `ENOSYS`. Nonfunctional stubs allow applications to be written against a single system call model.

2.2.2.3 Replacement Functions

Many of the functions in *libc* have changed little since their introduction in the late 1970s. Since then, better algorithms and optimizations may have been discovered. *libast* provides interface-compatible replacements for the best of these. `getcwd()` takes advantage of the `PWD` environment variable maintained by *ksh* and other modern shells. By comparing the value of PWD with ".", the more complex search algorithm can be almost always avoided. Another example illustrating the dark side of standard headers and function prototypes is getgroups(). The POSIX function prototype is int getgroups(int size, gid_t* groups), but the library implementation on most current systems follows the traditional BSD int getgroups(int size, int* groups). This is untenable on systems where sizeof(gid_t)!=sizeof(int) (most implementations define gid_t as short). *libast* solves this by providing a macro getgroups that calls _ast_getgroups() with the proper gid_t* prototype. _ast_getgroups() then handles the gid_t*/int* inconsistency.

2.2.2.4   New Functions

libast is also a common repository for new functions that are shared among the *ast* tools. Application specific functions, like the *coshell* interface described below, generally warrant their own library. There are over 200 public functions in *libast*. All are used by at least two of the *ast* tools. Some, like *sfio*, are used by all of the *ast* tools. There are too many functions to list, but one particular class should give a flavor of library. The str* routines convert char* strings to other C types. struid() converts a string to a uid_t, and strperm() converts a *chmod* file mode expression to a mode_t. For each of these there is an inverse conversion routine. fmtuid() converts a uid_t into a char*, and fmtperm() converts a mode_t to a *chmod* expression string.

2.2.3   *libcmd*: Enhanced UNIX Commands

To enhance efficiency and to test the libraries, we have rewritten many common commands in the IEEE POSIX 1003.2 Standard for shell and utilities. Each command is implemented as a self-contained library function whose name is b_*name*, where *name* is the name of the command. For example, b_cat() is the function corresponding to the command *cat*. Then, an actual command is just a simple main() that passes on its arguments to the respective function. For convenience, these functions are grouped together in the *libcmd* library. An advantage of *libcmd* is that such functions can be directly built into applications to avoid the *fork/exec* overhead of running commands. Recent versions of *ksh* support dynamic linking of built-ins. By building *libcmd* as a shared library, any or all of these commands can be made built-ins to the shell as desired. Since the built-in version uses the same code as the command version, they are always compatible.

libcmd contains many of the simple commands that take more time to invoke than to run, such as `basename`, `dirname`, `logname`, `mkdir`, `pathchk`, and `tty`. It also contains commands that descend the file hierarchy, such as `chmod`, `chgrp`, and `chown`. Finally, to enhance I/O efficiency, *libcmd* contains commands, such as `cut`, `join`, `paste`, `wc`, and other utilities.

2.2.4 *screen*: Character Screen Management

The *screen* library is a collection of functions to manipulate character terminals. It can be used as a replacement for the *curses* library [Arn84, Hor82] (because of this, *screen* does not follow the standard *ast* naming conventions.) The original *curses* library was distributed with the BSD4.1 UNIX system. This version suffered from many serious bugs (such as memory violations), rendering it virtually unusable.

The library was based on the *termcap* terminal description language and database used in the *vi* editor [Joy80], but it did not make full use of terminal capabilities, such as hardware scrolling and line/character insert/delete. A later version released with the System V Release 2 UNIX system fixed many of these problems. This version of *curses* was based on the *terminfo* language and database for terminal description. In terms of functionality, this version was relatively complete, but it suffered from performance both in terms of space requirement and time. There were a few idiosyncrasies in the interface, such as the distinction between windows that fit a screen and windows that extended beyond screen boundaries (these were called *pads*).

When the EASEL system (Chapter 4) was developed in 1982, neither of the existing *curses* versions was adequate. This was not just a matter of performance or portability but also because many key features were lacking. The *screen* library was built to deal with such problems. An early version of the library was used as a base for more modern versions of *curses* starting from UNIX System V Release 3.2. Beyond *curses* functionality, below are the key contributions of *screen*.

2.2.4.1 Logical Window Hierarchy Model

The library handles windows and derived windows consistently so that any change in the image of a window in the hierarchy is accurately reflected in the others. New functions, such as `wsyncup()` and `wsyncdown()`, allow applications flexible and efficient manipulations of window images and screen updates.

2.2.4.2 Efficient Screen Update Algorithm

The library implements an efficient screen update algorithm that uses all defined terminal capabilities, including scrolling and character/line insert/delete. The algorithm also correctly deals with variations in video attribute handling, including various types of *magic cookies* [Hor82]. The line update part of the algorithm is based on the Minimum Distance Longest Common Subsequence algorithm [JV92], which minimizes visual disturbance due to line jumpings.

2.2.4.3 Internationalization

The library can deal with a wide range of character code sets, including ASCII, 8-bit European code sets, and other multibyte character sets commonly used in the Orient. There are many different code sets for multibyte characters defined by different vendors. The *screen* library is still the only implementation of *curses* that can deal with most existing code sets.

2.2.4.4 Terminal Handling

In contrast to other *curses* implementations that can use only one of the *termcap* and *terminfo* databases, the *screen* library can use either database or even both in the same process if necessary. On modern workstations with pointer devices, such as the mouse, the library supports their use for interactive screen manipulations.

2.2.4.5   New Functions

The library adds many new functions to perform higher-level data manipulations. Examples are wmenu() to interact with matrices of menu options, wview() and wunview() to create textual descriptions of window images, and wedit(), which defines a virtual screen editor.

Below is an example of editing a string in a small window. The example is prototypical of how a form package would create form fields using *screen*. Lines 2 to 17 define the keyboard interface for editing. Here, arrow keys are used for cursor motion, the control-D character ends editing, and any other alphabetic keyboard input is inserted in front the cursor. The full set of editor commands supplied by wedit() is rich enough to simulate all screen interactions of editors, such as *vi* or *emacs*. Lines 18 to 20 create a window with 1 line and 10 columns, turn it to inverse video, and enable function key interactions. Line 18 invokes the editor with the string "abcd" as the initial text. wedit() returns the edited string.

```
 1: #include <curses.h>
 2: static kbf(WINDOW* win, EDIT_ARG* arg)
 3: {   int  ch;
 4:     while(1)
 5:     { switch((ch = wgetch(win)) )
 6:       { default        : if(isalpha(ch))
 7:                             return ch;
 8:                          else continue;
 9:         case KEY_LEFT : return EDIT_LEFT;
10:         case KEY_RIGHT: return EDIT_RIGHT;
11:         case KEY_DOWN : return EDIT_DOWN;
12:         case KEY_UP    : return EDIT_UP;
13:         case ERR       :
14:         case CTRL(D)  : return EDIT_DONE;
15:       }
16:     }
17: }
    ...
18: win = newwin(1,10,10,10);
19: wbkgd(win,A_REVERSE);
20: keypad(win,TRUE);
21: str = wedit(win,0,kbf,"abcd",0,0,0,0,0,0,0);
```

2.2.5   *stak*: Stacklike Memory Allocation

Interpreters (such as *ksh*) frequently build parse trees and text strings by substitution of text patterns (for example, values of shell variables). The typical construction of these objects involves several allocations but no frees, and, when the object is deleted, all allocated space is freed at once. Though *malloc* could be used for this purpose, the overhead can be high. Interfaces, such as alloca() [UNI86] and the Vmlast method described in Section 2.3.4, are more suitable, but the function call overheads are still high when many characters or small strings are being glued together. alloca(), which, if available, allocates from the stack, is also unsuitable if the constructed object must live beyond the life of the function that builds it. The *stak* library provides a set of macros and functions to conveniently and efficiently build stack-like objects.

A stack abstraction consists of an ordered list of contiguous memory regions, called stack frames, that can hold objects of arbitrary size. A stack is represented by the type Stk_t defined in header stk.h. A Stk_t structure is derived from a Sfio_t structure, so *sfio* calls for output can also be used on Stk_t. Stacks are opened and closed with stkopen() and stkclose(). Variable size objects can be added to a stack. All objects, once frozen, can be referred to by pointer. The last object (called the current object) can be built incrementally. During such a construction process, the object location may be moved, so it is necessary to reference this object with relative offsets. Allocation of a frozen object is done with stkalloc(). The current object can be frozen with stkfreeze() so that pointers can be used to refer to locations within it. Applications that require only one stack can use the standardly provided stkstd.

```
1: int myopen(const char *dir, const char *name)
2: {   long offset = stktell(stkstd);
3:     sfputr(stkstd,dir,-1);
4:     sfputc(stkstd,'/');
5:     sfputr(stkstd,name,-1);
6:     sfputc(stkstd,'\0');
7:     stkseek(stkstd,offset);
8:     return(open(stkptr(stkstd,offset),0));
9: }
```

The example above shows the function myopen() that constructs a pathname on the standard stack stdstk from a directory name, and a filename, then opens the corresponding file and returns the resulting file descriptor. Line 2 obtains the current location on the standard stack, which is reset on line 7 so that the memory can be reused in future calls.

The `stkptr()` call on line 8 converts the current `offset` into a memory address that should point to the constructed pathname.

2.2.6   *libcoshell*: Shell Coprocess

libcoshell provides a flexible alternative to the traditional *system* or *fork, exec, wait* paradigms for command execution. Instead of executing a separate shell for each job (related sequence of shell commands), *libcoshell* supports the shell as a coprocess. This coprocess spans the lifetime of the calling process. The coprocess may be either *ksh* or *sh* executing on the local host, or it may be the *coshell* daemon with access to shells on hosts throughout a local network. Local, concurrent and remote job execution are all handled through one interface.

Although full *fork/exec* semantics are not supported (for example, open file descriptors are not passed to the jobs), the library passes most of the caller's environment and relays signals from the caller's process to each job. The interface is defined in the `coshell.h` header and is implemented in the *coshell* library. Each coprocess is created and closed by `coopen()` and `coclose()`. `coopen()` returns a handle of the type `Coshell_t*`. Then, each job is executed by `coexec()`, which returns a handle of type `Cojob_t*`. This handle can be used to wait on a job and to get its accounting information.

The following example shows a simple command interpreter. Line 7 opens a coshell using default parameters (all zeros). Thus, by default, *ksh* is used as the coshell, but that can be overridden by setting, for example, `COSHELL=coshell` to run commands on other lightly loaded hosts on the local network. Line 9 reads commands from standard input. Line 10 executes the commands. Line 12 waits for the running command to complete before getting the next one. Lines 14 to 17 prints the termination status of the command and its user and system times. Line 19 terminates the coshell after all commands have been read and executed.

```
1: #include <ast.h>
2: #include <coshell.h>
3: main()
4: {   char*      cmd;
5:      Coshell_t* csh;
6:      Cojob_t*   job;
```

```
 7:     if(!(csh = coopen(0, 0, 0)) )
 8:         exit(1);
 9:     while((cmd = sfgetr(sfstdin,'\n',1)) )
10:     {   if(!(job = coexec(csh,cmd,0,0,0,"label=cosh")))
11:             exit(1);
12:         if(!(job = cowait(csh, job)))
13:             exit(1);
14:         sfprintf(sfstdout,"status=%d usr=%s sys=%s\n",
15:             job->status,
16:             fmtelapsed(job->user, CO_QUANT),
17:             fmtelapsed(job->sys, CO_QUANT));
18:     }
19:     coclose(csh);
20:     exit(0);
21: }
```

2.2.7 *libcs*: **Connect Streams**

The internet service addressing scheme for remote service names and interprocess communication is complicated to program. Service naming in the flat IP address and port number name space is like naming files and commands by device and inode numbers instead of hierarchical pathnames. This is not a pleasant process. An additional complication is the interface difference between BSD sockets and System V TLI. As a result, most applications either resort to a *super-server*, like *inetd*, for establishing communications or copy boilerplate initialization code from other programs.

libcs solves the problem by placing service names in the file system namespace and providing a common interface based on either BSD sockets or System V TLI. A *connect stream* is a pathname that names a service. Connect stream files allow unrelated processes to rendezvous. A server first creates a connect stream; then, each client open of the connect stream received by the server presents a unique bidirectional pipe connection between the client and server.

Connect streams may be *local* or *remote*. Local connections support file descriptor exchange via **cssend()** and **csrecv()** that allows one process to open a file and an unrelated process to operate on it. Remote streams support pipe or datagram semantics.

Connect stream names match **/dev/***proto*/*host*/*service*[/*options*], where *proto* is **fdp** for local streams and **tcp** or **udp** for remote streams.

host is either a host name (**local** names the local host) or an IP *n.n.n.n* address. The special host name **share** names one service that serves all hosts on the local network; otherwise, the service may run one per host. *service* is either a service name (for new services), **inet**.*service* (for standard services in **/etc/services**), or an integer port number (for old internet services). The *options* are slash-separated and further qualify the connect stream: **user** [=*uid*] restricts the service to the current user [or *uid*]; **group** [=*gid*] restricts the service to the current group [or *gid*]; **other** (default) specifies no user or group service restrictions. Other options are service-dependent and are used to name different instantiations of the same service; different connect streams name different services. For example, two different process instances of the **coshell** daemon program are named by **/dev/fdp/local/coshell/user** and **/dev/fdp/local/coshell/group=ship**.

Most servers reside in the directory **libcs**/*proto/server. server* is the name of the server executable in this directory. For remote connect streams, the file **hosts** lists the hosts on which the service can be automatically started. If not specified, then the file **lib/cs/share** is used. If **hosts** is empty, then the service must be manually started. Otherwise the service is started by the first user open of the service. Service maintenance is trivial, as no modifications to the kernel *init* sequence or *rc* files are necessary.

A server announces its connect stream with **csserve()**, which also handles the bookkeeping for new connects, read and write requests, and timeouts. Clients connect to the server by **fd=csopen(** *"connect-stream"*,**0)**. Normal **read()** and **write()** calls are then used on **fd** to communicate with the server.

libcs provides routines for host status monitoring (such as, load average, user idle time), host attributes (such as, mips rating, cpu type), and service monitoring. For example, the *cs* command lists the active connect streams visible from the local host:

```
$ cs -lp
# connect stream                process
/dev/fdp/local/coshell/user     /proc/17692
/dev/fdp/local/dev/user         /proc/20112
/dev/tcp/share/dbm/group=ship   /n/toucan/proc/6486
/dev/tcp/share/yeast/local      /proc/20463
```

libcs also supports `msgsend()` and `msgrecv()`, which are used to pack and unpack system call messages that may be sent over stream (socket) pipes. System call messages are used to monitor processes, as well as to provide alternate system services. The message format is byte-order and word-size independent.

A glaring omission in the UNIX IP address-port IPC interface is client authentication. In a modern computing environment, services must be able to identify clients or service integrity may be compromised. Traditionally, authentication requires some form of encrypted key exchange between client and server, but such an intrusive mechanism would break the file-based illusion of *libcs* connect streams.

A *libcs* server can choose to enable client authentication when it creates the connect stream with `cscreate()`. Each client `csopen()` then initiates the authentication protocol and handshakes with `csserve()`.

Rather than inventing a new authentication scheme, and in the interest of doing as much work in user space as possible, *libcs* relies on standard UNIX file access mechanisms for client authentication. Authentication is based on challenge-response. A client `csopen()` requests a challenge sequence from the server. The challenge is a file pathname and two 32-bit numbers in ASCII format. The client must create the file with the access and modify times set to the two given numbers (using the `utime()` system call). In addition, the set-uid, set-gid, user-read, and user-write permission bits are set and all other permission bits are cleared. On UNIX systems, only the file owner could create such a file. The client sends a null message back to the server and the server authenticates the client by calling `lstat()` on the file, verifying the challenge numbers, and then using the file owner and group as the client user identity. If the file does not verify, then the connection is dropped. Otherwise, the server sends back a positive acknowledgement and accepts the connection. The client then deletes the authentication file and continues.

Client authentication between server and client hosts that do not share a file system is slightly more complicated. In this case, the client uses the remote shell *rsh* to run an authentication agent command on the server host. The client and server handshake just as above, but the agent does the file create and delete. In this case, remote client authentication is as strong as, or as weak as, *rsh* authentication.

The main advantage of *libcs* authentication is that no new privileged service is required; it is based on mechanisms already present on UNIX systems.

2.2.8   *libexpr*: C Expression

Runtime program control is a common feature of many UNIX tools. Much of this control is provided by so-called *little languages*, such as in *expr*, *find*, and *test*. Although they get the job done, the downside is that commands like these provide different and incompatible expression syntax for the same basic constructs or, worse, the same syntax with inconsistent usage. For example, *expr* numeric equality syntax is *num1=num2*, while the same syntax is used for string matching in *test*. This leads to confusing expressions, such as 0 = 00, which is true in *expr* but false in *test*. Unfortunately, old commands are sometimes beyond repair because of the weight of existing practice and standardization.

libexpr is an alternative for new commands that require runtime expression evaluation. It provides routines that parse and evaluate simple C-style expressions. The C syntax was chosen because it is almost second nature to most UNIX system users, and C functions are a natural for command-specific extensions. Also, the control constructs `while`, `if`, `for`, and `switch` are included.

One diversion from C is that string operands are accepted for == and !=, and the right operand is interpreted as a *ksh* file match pattern. *ksh* patterns were chosen over *ed* regular expressions because, like *ksh*, *libexpr* is biased toward command level evaluation. *ksh* also offers pattern negation, which is beyond the scope of basic regular expressions. Since *libexpr* expressions are often entered as command line arguments from the shell, string literals may use either "..." or '...' quoting styles.

Interface definitions are contained in the header `expr.h`. Before interpreting expressions, a parser context must be allocated with `exopen()`, which returns a handle of type `Expr_t`. Arguments to `exopen()` define application-specific symbols and access functions for referencing, getting, setting, and converting values. An expression context is deleted via `exclose()`. Expressions must be first compiled with `excomp()`, then evaluated with `exeval()`.

Each expression context maintains a set of expression procedures. The default or main expression has no name–all others are named:

```
name == "*.c"  /* default expression */
void action()  /* action expression */
{   printf("found %s\n", name);
}
```

Because `goto` is not supported, `goto` style labels provide a convenient shorthand:

```
name=="*.c"; action: printf("found %s\n", name);
```

libexpr was originally designed for the *tw* [FKV89] file tree walk command, a replacement for *find* based on the *libast* `ftwalk()` tree traversal function (upon which the POSIX `fts_*()` was based). The following *tw* expression selects files matching the shell pattern `*.[ch]` that have been modified since yesterday:

```
'name == "*.[ch]" && mtime > "yesterday"'
```

In some respects, *tw* (and *find*) are database query programs, where the database is the file system. This observation led to *cql* [Fow94], a flat file database query program based on *libexpr* expressions. A flat file database is a sequence of `newline` terminated records with `delimiter` separated fields. Given a database schema description, *cql* expressions can be written on the schema field names. The following example shows a *cql* schema for `/etc/passwd` (tokenized but not parsed by *libexpr*).

```
passwd {
    register char*  name;
    char*           passwd;
    register int    uid, gid;
    info            info;
    char*           home, shell;
}
info {
    char*           name, address, office, home;
}
delimiter = ':';
input = "/etc/passwd";
```

register identifies fields that are good candidates for hash indexing. *cql* can use this to optimize the query and database scan to eliminate records that cannot match the query.

The following query lists the names of all users with **uid** less than 10 and no encrypted password:

```
uid < 10 && passwd == ""
action: printf("%s\t%s\n", name, info.name);
```

2.2.9   *libpp*: C Preprocessor Library

libpp is a C preprocessor library that is runtime compatible (only one preprocessor executable) with all C dialects: K&R, ANSI, and C++. For use with *cc*, a standalone *cpp* was generated from a 30-line *cpp* **main()** linked with *libpp*. Except for option and pragma settings, the library interface is fairly simple and consists of two main functions, **ppop()** and **pplex()**.

The call **pplex()** returns the token identifier for each fully expanded token in the input files. The token identifiers are suitable for *yacc* grammars, and the library provides the *yacc* **%include** file **pp.yacc** for this purpose. **pplex()** places the token name in the global **char* pp.token**.

The call **ppop(int op,...)** sets preprocessor options and states. For example, for C++, the call **ppop(PP_PLUSPLUS,1)** enables recognition of **//** comments and the **.***, **->*** and **::** tokens.

ANSI C requires a tokenizing preprocessor, so *libpp* must follow C syntax rules for the multicharacter operators, as well as identifiers and numeric and literal constants. This is different from the usual K&R preprocessor that passes off most of the token-splitting rules to the compiler front end. **ppop()** allows over 100 option settings. This may seem out of hand but it merely reflects the state of C compilation systems. Compiler vendors cannot resist the temptation to extend C. Some PC compilers have more than doubled the number of compiler-reserved words (**near** and **far** are just the tip of the iceberg). GNU C and C++ are not far behind. Others add new directives: **#import** in Objective C, **#ident** in System V, and **#eject** (to control program listings!) in Apollo C. If the *libpp* user were responsible for detecting all of these incompatibilities, application programming would never get beyond the **ppop()** stage. *libpp* handles this by probing each native compiler (at the first run) and posting the probe information for all users. The probe information includes predefined macros, dialect-specific pragmas, nonstandard directive and pragma maps, and other non-K&R preprocessor-reserved words. The probe information is a header file that is included to initialize the preprocessor. The following is an example of predefined macros probed by *libpp*:

```
#pragma pp:predefined
#define __unix          1
#pragma pp:nopredefined
```

Probing at runtime to generate pragmas helps maintain a surprisingly stable user and programmer interface. The interface has weathered three lexical analyzer implementations, the last one, based on a lexical finite state machine from Dennis Ritchie, brought *libpp* speed within 10 percent of the K&R "Reiser" *cpp* which is still the most efficient preprocessor for K&R C.

From a programming perspective, *libpp* operates in either *standalone* or *compile* mode. *standalone* output is a text file that is passed on to the compiler front end pass. All macros and include files are expanded and the output also contains special line synchronization directives that identify the source file and line number for all preprocessed input. Since not all output tokens need to be delineated, standalone mode can skip some ANSI details; these will be picked up by the next compiler pass. `void ppcpp(void)` encodes the standalone optimizations in a single routine. On the other hand, *compile* mode does full tokenization and hashes all identifiers into the symbol table `Hash_table_t* pp.symtab`. In this mode, `pplex()` sets `struct ppsymbol* pp.symbol` to point to the symbol table entry for each identifier token. `void* pp.symbol->value` is a pointer, initialized to `NULL` and free for use by the *libpp* user.

Compilers can use `pp.symbol->value` to hold symbol type and scope information. The `PP_COMPILE ppop()` that sets compile mode accepts an optional reserved-word table argument, allowing `pplex()` to do all C-related lexical analysis.

The following code fragment lists each C source identifier once (after macro expansion):

```
ppop(PP_DEFAULT, PPDEFAULT);
optjoin(argv, ppargs, NULL);
ppop(PP_COMPILE, ppkey);
ppop(PP_INIT);
while(n = pplex())
    if (n == T_ID && !pp.symbol->value)
    {   pp.symbol->value = (void*)"";
        sfputr(sfstdout, pp.token, '\n');
    }
ppop(PP_DONE);
```

2.2.10   Discussion

The *ast* libraries have been in use for about ten years and currently stand at about 50K lines of noncommented C code. The libraries have proved to be a good base for building new efficient and portable tools and continue to evolve along with the construction of such tools. Aside from well-known tools, such as *ksh*, *nmake*, and EASEL, we have also written many POSIX and UNIX commands, such as *ls*, *pack*, and *pax* which are much faster than other standard implementations. All the tools are more or less freed from architecture-specific `#ifdef`, yet they have been ported to all known UNIX platforms with little effort.

In the continuing effort of building and maintaining *ast*, we have learned many lessons and developed support technologies to build and use reusable code. There is no easy path toward building such code. They arise out of necessity but must be chiseled and formed until their essence is revealed and their applicability fully realized. The design and implementation considerations described in Section 2.2.1 guide us both in building the software and in the continuing examination of it. None of these considerations are individually deep and hard, but the success of *ast* does testify to the value of debating and applying them as appropriate.

2.3   Disciplines and Methods

As with any product, software or otherwise, desirable characteristics of a good library are simplicity, applicability, and performance. Achieving these characteristics is a balancing act difficult even for experienced software designers. On the one hand, too much concern about performance over simplicity may lead to multiple packages with essentially the same interface but different implementation methods. An extreme example is the multitude of libraries for dictionary look-up, such as the *map* [Koe88] package for C++ and the *lsearch*, *tsearch*, and *hsearch* packages in UNIX System V [SVR90]. All these packages perform more or less the same abstract operations of search, insert, delete, and iterate but their interfaces are all distinct. On the other hand, extreme concern with simplicity can make software designers fail to anticipate variations in the underlying computing substrate. This leads to software not as generally applicable as it could be. For example, the various implementations of the *malloc* package for memory allocation in C programs deal very well with heap memory but are not usable with other types of memory, such as shared memory. This is a pity, because a great deal of time and effort was put into developing sophisticated algorithms for such purposes [KV85]. Design failures of the types discussed can often be traced to the lack of consideration of two factors: *resource acquisition* and *resource management*.

Insufficient consideration for resource acquisition means that methods to obtain resources are assumed without analyzing their availability or variations in their usage. For example, I/O libraries on UNIX systems often assume that data can be read or written via the system calls `read()` and `write()`. Thus, these system calls are simply used by the libraries but their usage is completely hidden from applications. Now, in a sense, this is a purpose of the library: to hide certain low level implementation details. However, by doing so, the library design limits the library's applicability, as it does not permit applications to specify alternative implementations for resource acquisition. Further, implicit assumptions of this type introduce hidden external dependencies that may be hard to trace, for example, during porting such an I/O library to a non-UNIX system. Thus, to increase the usability of a library, we assert that its external resource requirements should be analyzed up front. Then, if applicable, the interface to such data structures and functions should be defined explicitly as a part of the library's public interface. This interface is called a *discipline*.

Insufficient consideration of resource management means the avoidance of analyzing and dealing with distinct usage scenarios where different efficiency levels and features may not mix well. At worst, the available code is not usable in a particular application. More often, we end up with fragmented and inconsistent interfaces as in the case of multiple online dictionary packages. Such interface differences make it difficult to mix and match usage of the libraries in a single application. At a more subtle level, the variance among packages prevents application writers from experimenting to find the right trade-off in efficiency and features. Clearly, it is desirable to have a uniform abstract interface to common operations even if the underlying data structures and algorithms may vary due to performance or other requirements. Such variations should be analyzed and captured as different scenarios of using the abstract interface. An interface packaging of a usage scenario to vary some common abstract interface is called a *method*.

The ideas of discipline and method are useful to keep in mind when designing a library interface. A discipline defines a *disciplined* way for applications to extend the library functionality by altering the behavior of its external dependencies. Further, during any porting effort, a large amount of work is done to identify external dependencies and establish their validity in different environments. By considering such external dependencies up front and defining the interface to them in disciplines, the library code is also more readily portable. Methods provide an architecture that allows applications to select and tune for certain predefined usage scenarios. A library based on this architecture is also easier to extend without losing upward compatibility as new manipulation methods are implemented.

In the rest of this section, we support the above hypothesis by overviewing four example libraries built based on the idea of disciplines and methods: *sfio* [KV91] for buffered I/O, *vdelta* [KV] for data differencing and compression, *libdict* [NV93] for online dictionary management, and *vmalloc* [Vo] for general purpose memory allocation.

2.3.1   *sfio*: Safe/Fast I/O

One of the main contributions of the UNIX system is the notion of byte streams for I/O. The byte streams, be they disk files, terminals, tape devices, or communication channels (such as pipes), are uniformly accessed via the system calls: `read()`, `write()`, and `lseek()`. As system calls can incur significant costs, it is advantageous to implement some scheme of buffering to reduce the number of such calls. The *sfio* library does this and more. It starts by defining the type `Sfio_t` as an abstraction of byte streams, then provides high-level functions, such as `sfread()` or `sfwrite()`, to read/write data to such streams. Internally, a stream may use a buffer or a memory mapped area via `mmap()` [SVR90] for efficient I/O manipulations. In its common use, the *sfio* library is similar to the *stdio* or standard I/O functions in the *libc* library found in any UNIX or ANSI-C distribution. In fact, *sfio* was originally written to replace *stdio* and correct a number of deficiencies in its design and implementation. To ease transition of existing code, *sfio* provides packages to emulate *stdio* both at the source and object levels. Beyond *stdio*, *sfio* provides a number of new features:

String streams: In many applications, it is frequently desirable to manage memory as if it were a file. String streams allow applications to read and write to memory, using the same stream operations. Buffers of write string streams are dynamically reallocated as necessary to accommodate data.

Portable numerical data: The library provides standard functions to perform I/O of integral and floating point values in portable formats. The coding of these values is optimized so that small values may use less space than required in their internal representations. This allows applications to transport data across heterogeneous hardwares without resorting to ASCII, which implies some space wastage in the case of integers and loss of accuracy in the case of floating point values.

Safe and efficient buffer access: The function `sfgetr()` is used to read variable length records. For example, the call `sfgetr(sfstdin,'\n',1)` reads a line delineated by the newline character. The third argument, 1, means that the newline character should be replaced by the null byte to make the line into a C string. `sfgetr()` keeps the string in the buffer if possible; otherwise, it builds the string in some other stream-managed area. Thus, this example shows a feature similar to *stdio* `gets()` but without any possibility of buffer overflow.

For more general buffer access, the function sfreserve() can be used. For example, sfreserve(sfstdin,1024,1) reserves a data segment of size 1024 from the standard input stream. The third argument, 1, indicates that the stream should be locked from further access until the data segment is released. sfreserve() gives applications the same I/O power as sfread() and sfwrite(), but applications do not have to worry about buffer size and avoid multiple intermediate buffer-to-buffer copies. This is particularly efficient for streams that use mmap() for disk access.

Stream stacks: Streams can be nested using sfstack(base,top), which pushes the stream top onto the stream stack identified by the stream base. Any I/O operation on base will be performed on top. This is useful for processing nested files, such as #include files. Position synchronization information can be detected by installing disciplines with appropriate exception handlers to watch when a stream is finished.

The last item brings us back to the issue of how methods and disciplines parameterize an I/O package. In this case, the standard method implemented by *sfio* is deemed sufficient, so there is no need for alternative methods. However, external resources managed by the library are streams of bytes, that, by default, are obtained by the system calls read(), write(), and lseek(). Thus, these functions can be packaged abstractly using disciplines. Taking in the additional consideration for exception handling, an *sfio* discipline structure of type Sfdisc_t contains at least the following members:

```
int (*readf)();
int (*writef)();
long (*seekf)();
int (*exceptf)();
```

The first three functions are self-explanatory. The (*exceptf)() function is called on various exceptional events. For example, the call (*except)(f,SF_READ,disc) is raised when an error (or end of file) condition is detected while reading raw data into the stream f. Other exceptions announce events, such as stream being closed, or the manipulation of the discipline stack itself.

The following is an example of filter code that translates input data from lowercase to uppercase, then outputs the transformed data. Lines 1 to 8 define the function `lower()`, which will be used as the `(*readf)()` discipline function on line 9. Note that raw data is read via the function `sfrd()` on line 4. `sfrd()` may invoke lower disciplines on the discipline stack, if any, or simply call `read()`. In this way, several disciplines can cooperate to process data into the final form that the application requires. Line 10 shows how the discipline is inserted into the standard input stream. Then, on line 11, the `sfmove()` function is invoked to move data from this stream to the standard output stream.

```
1: lower(Sfio_t* f, void* argbuf, int n, Sfdisc_t* disc)
2: {   int    c;
3:     unsigned char* buf = (unsigned char*)argbuf;
4:     n = sfrd(f,argbuf,n,disc);
5:     for(c = 0; c < n; ++c)
6:         buf[c] = tolower(buf[c]);
7:     return n;
8: }
9: Sfdisc_t Disc = { lower, 0, 0, 0 };
   ...
10: sfdisc(sfstdin,&Disc);
11: sfmove(sfstdin,sfstdout,SF_UNBOUND,-1);
```

Though simplistic, this example shows how disciplines can be used to greatly extend the range of data processing. Here is another example to show how the data output to a stream can be transparently duplicated to a second file (perhaps on a different networked machine) to increase software fault tolerance (see Chapter 8). Because the discipline must know the identity of the second file, we extend it to contain the file descriptor of this file:

```
typedef struct _dupdisc_s
{ Sfdisc_t disc;  /* actual sfio discipline       */
  int      fd;    /* descriptor of duplicated file */
} Dupdisc_t;
```

Before a stream can be instrumented, a discipline structure of type `Dupdisc_t` must be created. The discipline function `(*writef)` is defined below. For simplicity, we did not check error status of the `write()` calls on lines 2 and 4. Note that the cast `(Dupdisc_t*)` on line 4 is valid because the *sfio* discipline is included as the first member of `Dupdisc_t`.

```
1: dupwrite(Sfio_t* f, void* buf, int n, Sfdisc_t* disc)
2: { int w = write(sffileno(f),buf,n);
3:   if(w > 0)
4:     (void)write(((Dupdisc_t*)disc)->fd,buf,n);
5:   return w;
6: }
```

So, suppose that a discipline structure of type Dupdisc_t, say dupdisc, has been created; we can use it to instrument an output stream f like this:

```
sfdisc(f,(Sfdisc_t*)dupdisc);
```

The *sfio* library is in use worldwide on many different platforms including UNIX, DOS systems, and others. Disciplines have proved to be a good ground for extending the library functionality and a good source of reusable code. A more complete version of the above duplicated file discipline and a discipline to read files compressed by the UNIX *compress* program are among the disciplines regularly distributed with *sfio*.

2.3.2   *vdelta*: Differencing and Compression

Data differencing and data compression are techniques to reduce data storage by exploiting redundancy in data sources. A data compression tool exploits redundancies in a single data source and computes a compact representation of that source. Popular data-compression tools are the *pack*, *compress*, and *gzip* programs. A data-differencing tool takes two related data sources and produces a transformation to transform the first to the second. The idea is that if the second data source is similar to the first, then storing the transformation would require substantially less storage than storing the second source explicitly. In fact, if the two sources are very similar (for example, different versions of a source code), the size of the differencing transformation should be much smaller than that of the compressed data for any compression technique on the second data source. A well-known data-differencing tool is the *diff* program that, given two text files, produces a set of line insert/delete operations that transform the first file to the second. The *diff* transformation underlies the storage schemes of popular source-code control systems, such as *SCCS* [Roc75] and *RCS* [Tic85].

The *vdelta* library both compresses and computes data differences. It uses a variation of the Lempel-Ziv data-compression method [ZL77, Tic84] with a time and space efficient string-matching algorithm and an encoding technique suitable for byte streams. The encoding method is portable across hardware platforms. Thus, it is possible to compute the transformation on one machine type (perhaps a large machine) while applying it on another machine (perhaps a small PC).

For compression, *vdelta* generally produces smaller compressed files than *compress* (especially text files) but larger than *gzip*. In terms of speed, *vdelta* compression is comparable to *compress*, which is about two to three times faster than *gzip*, while *vdelta* decompression is two to three times faster than either *compress* or *gzip*. This makes the method suitable for applications, such as remote software updates, where compression is typically done once but decompression is done many times. When used for differencing, applications that update software versions based on the *vdelta* transformation have reduced the amount of data transmitted by an order of magnitude.

The call **vddelta(src, n_src, tar, n_tar, disc)** does both compression and differencing. Source and target data are of size **n_src** and **n_tar**. Compression corresponds to the case where **n_src** is zero. The source/target data can be given in array form if **src/tar** is not NULL. Otherwise, the data will be obtained via the discipline **disc**. The corresponding function **vdupdate()** recomputes the target data.

A *vdelta* discipline is a structure of type **Vddisc_t**, which contains at least the following members:

```
int (*readf)();
int (*writef)();
long window;
```

The **(*readf)()/(*writef)()** function is used to read/write data from/to a *vdelta* transformation or the source or target data. The **window** member of **Vddisc_t** defines a segment size to partition large data sets. This is useful to speed up **vddelta()** as it constructs a large data structure to process data (about 5 bytes per input byte). If **window** is nonpositive, an internal value (2^{16}) is used.

The *vdelta* function interface and discipline are designed to permit applications a range of usage from compressing/differencing pure memory arrays to compressing/differencing pure data streams via the discipline I/O functions. As working with memory arrays is most efficient while working with data streams is most general, this allows applications to select what best fits their needs. Finally, it is worth noting that an early version of the *vdelta* library directly relies on the *sfio* library for I/O. Even though the selection between memory arrays and streams is unified under the *sfio* string streams, the dependency on *sfio* means that it is hard to use *vdelta* as an independent library and in applications where only memory manipulations are required. Defining I/O dependency in terms of a discipline solves this problem.

2.3.3   *libdict*: Online Dictionaries

The dictionary library, *libdict*, provides a set of functions to manage objects in runtime dictionaries. Aside from certain engineering features, the main abstract operations on a dictionary are search, insert, delete and iterate. There are two distinctive classes of objects: those that are totally ordered and those that are unordered. Ordered objects are compared as less than, greater than, or equal, while unordered objects are compared as equal or not equal. To avoid search degeneracy in managing ordered objects, either balanced trees or some form of self-adjusting data structure [Knu73, Sed78, ST85] should be used. With a properly defined object comparator, unordered objects can be taken as a special case of ordered objects. However, for good performance, hashing techniques should be used so that each primitive operation can be performed in constant time on the average.

The availability of multiple algorithms for essentially the same purpose but with different performance levels induces a great temptation to create separate packages tailored to different types of applications. Indeed, this is the case on various C and C+- platforms. On System V UNIX systems [SVR90], ordered dictionaries are handled by `tsearch()`, a tree-based package, while unordered dictionaries are handled by `hsearch()`, which maintains a hash table. These packages employ distinct interfaces so that it is not easy to take advantage of their services in applications that require simultaneous manipulation of both ordered and unordered objects. `hsearch()` also imposes a severe limitation of only one hash table per application. In the C++ environment, the `map` class library is a popular package for online dictionaries. `map` requires that the objects be ordered, thus sacrificing efficiency when objects are unordered.

By contrast, *libdict* provides a single abstract interface. To handle the distinction between ordered and unordered objects and the implied performance trade-off, *libdict* provides two methods for object maintenance: `Dttree` and `Dthash`. When `Dttree` is in use, objects are stored in a splay tree [ST85]. This data structure guarantees that, with amortization, the cost of each operation is O(log*n*) time, where *n* is the number of objects. Further, the data structure adapts well to applications where search patterns may be biased. When `Dthash` is in use, objects are kept in an extensible hash table with chaining.

Interface definitions are given in the header file `dict.h`. A dictionary is opened with some initial discipline and method using `dtopen(disc,meth)`, which, upon success, returns a handle of type `Dict_t`. The discipline and method of a dictionary can be changed at any time using `dtdisc()` and `dtmethod()`, respectively. A dictionary, `dict`, can be closed using `dtclose(dict)`.

Searching for an object is done via `dtsearch(dict,proto)`, where `proto` defines a prototype of the object being searched. Similar functions, `dtinsert()` and `dtdelete()`, insert and delete objects.

The simplest way to iterate on a dictionary is `dtwalk(dict,func)`, which causes the call `(*func)(obj)` to be issued on each object in order. Note that the object order is well-defined only for an ordered dictionary. For an unordered dictionary (such as under `Dthash`), some arbitrary order will be used. This order is maintained as long as there are no inserts or deletes. There are other ways to iterate on a dictionary. The code below shows how to iterate either forward or backward in explicit loops:

```
for(obj = dtfirst(dict); obj; obj = dtnext(dict,obj))
for(obj = dtlast(dict); obj; obj = dtprev(dict,obj))
```

For applications that build dictionaries in nested scopes (for example, symbol tables in nested braces in a C-like language), dictionaries can be linked together using `dtview(dict,view)`. This makes all objects in `view` visible in `dict`. Thus, a search or a walk starting from `dict` will continue as necessary to **view** (and any other dictionaries continuously viewable from it).

In *libdict* case, discipline is not just a mechanism to increase usability; it is required so that applications can supply information about objects to be managed. The discipline structure **Dtdisc_t** contains at least the following members:

```
int    key, size;
void*  (*makef)();
void   (*freef)();
int    (*comparf)();
unsigned long (*hashf)();
```

Objects are compared by their keys. The **key** and **size** fields define how to get the key of an object from the object address. For example, if **key** is negative, then the object's address itself is the key. Otherwise, it defines an offset into the object structure where the key resides. The function members are optional. If given, (**makef**)() and (**freef**)() are used to make or free objects. (**comparf**)() compares keys and returns a negative, zero, or positive value to indicate whether or not the first key is considered smaller, equal, or larger than the second. However, when the dictionary is unordered, the return value of (**comparf**)() is only significant in whether it is zero or non-zero. Likewise, (**hashf**)(), if given, is used to hash keys.

The following is an example of reading a collection of words with many duplications possible and writing out the unique words in a lexicographic order (as defined by the ASCII character set). Line 2 defines a discipline using the **strdup**() function for creating words and the **strcmp**() function to compare them. Note that the **key** field is set to −1 to indicate that the object itself (such as the word) is the key. Line 3 creates a new dictionary using this discipline and the hashing method. Lines 4 and 5 read words from the standard input and insert them into the dictionary. Here, we are assuming that words are given one per line. Because dictionary objects must be unique with respect to the comparison function, duplicated words are automatically rejected. Note also that by using hashing in this phase, duplications are found quickly. Line 6 changes the method to **Dttree**, which causes words to be sorted lexicographically. Finally, lines 7 and 8 output the words in this order.

```
1: char*    word;
2: Dtdisc_t disc = { -1, 0, strdup, 0, strcmp, 0 };
3: dict = dtopen(&disc,Dthash);
4: while((word = sfgetr(sfstdin,'\n',1)) != 0)
5:     dtinsert(dict,word);
6: dtmethod(dict,Dttree,0);
7: for(word = dtfirst(dict); word; word = dtnext(dict,word) )
8:     sfprintf(sfstdout,"%s\n",word);
```

As the preceding example shows, an interesting aspect of *libdict*'s method architecture is that a dictionary may dynamically change its method. As we see next in *vmalloc*, method switching is not always possible, because the objects created and managed by the library may contain states associated with the method in use. Still, it is useful that such a possibility exists.

2.3.4   *vmalloc*: Virtual Memory Allocation

The virtual memory allocation library, *vmalloc*, provides a set of functions to manage any type of runtime memory: that is, memory that can be accessed via pointers, such as the usual heap memory (obtained via sbrk(2) on UNIX systems), shared memory, or even stack space.

Memory is allocated from regions. The call vmopen(disc,meth,mode) creates a region with discipline disc and method meth. The library provides two standard disciplines, Vmdcsbrk and Vmdcheap. The former obtains memory using sbrk(2), while the latter uses *vmalloc* calls on the standardly provided Vmheap region. Vmheap is an example of how regions can be built out of memory from other regions. A region, vm, can be closed with vmclose(vm), which releases all memory associated with vm via the associated discipline.

The call vmalloc(vm,size) allocates a segment of memory, which, in turn, can be freed with vmfree(vm,addr). Note that the memory to be freed must have been allocated from vm. vmresize(vm,addr,size,type) and used to resize a previously allocated memory segment to fit the given size. It is similar to *malloc* realloc() but more general. Here, if type is zero, vmresize() will fail if the segment cannot be resized in place. If type is not zero and it is not possible to resize the block in place, a new area will be created to fit size. Then, data is copied to the new area only if type is positive.

Different types of memory can be managed by *vmalloc* via the use of disciplines. A *vmalloc* discipline of type **Vmdisc_t** contains at least the following fields:

```
void* (*memoryf)();
int (*exceptf)();
```

The function **(*memoryf)()** obtains or reduces memory of a region. Exceptional events are announced by **(*exceptf)()**. For example, a failed attempt to get **size** bytes of memory is announced by the call **(*exceptf)(vm,VM_NOMEM,size,disc)**. Other events announce region opening and closing, or that some allocation operations were given bad data.

vmalloc provides a number of allocation methods for different important cases of dynamic memory allocation:

Vmbest: A general purpose allocation strategy. It uses a best-fit allocation strategy which is good for space compaction. Free memory areas are kept in a splay tree for fast search. For heap allocation, private simulation studies using real programs showed that this method performs as well as or better than most other *malloc* implementations.

Vmlast: A strategy good for building complex structures that are only deleted in whole (for example, via **vmclose()**). Thus, only the block allocated last can be freed or resized. Unlike **Vmbest**, there is no space overhead for every allocated block.

Vmpool: A strategy for allocating blocks of one size. This size is set on the first **vmalloc()** call after **vmopen()**. Like **Vmlast**, there is no space overhead for every allocated block.

Vmdebug: A strategy with stringent checking. It is useful for finding misuses of dynamically allocated memory, such as writing beyond block boundary or freeing a block twice.

Vmprofile: A strategy that records and prints summaries of memory usage. It is useful to find memory leaks and to analyze memory usage patterns.

As an example of using *vmalloc*, consider a language interpreter that may construct several parse trees for different language fragments. Since all nodes, edges, and associated attributes in a parse tree are allocated together and freed together, it is advantageous to allocate from a region using the **Vmlast** method as follows:

```
1: Vmalloc_t* vm = vmopen(Vmdcheap,Vmlast,0);
2:... Build tree with vmalloc()...
3:... Processing...
4: vmclose(vm);
```

The **Vmlast** method ensures that there is no space overhead associated with allocated areas and the search for free memory is trivial and fast. This example also uses the discipline **Vmdcheap** to obtain space from the library-provided **Vmheap** region. One can imagine situations where different instances of an interpreter may want to share a parse tree. If a discipline is available to obtain shared memory, say **Vmdcshare**, allocating shared data structures can be done by simply changing line 1 to:

```
Vmalloc_t* vm = vmopen(Vmdcshare,Vmlast,0);
```

A major part of *vmalloc* is a package that emulates the familiar ANSI-C *malloc* interface. Using this package, a particular allocation method can be selected by setting some appropriate environment variable. For example, **export VMETHOD=vmdebug** turns on debugging, while **export VMPROFILE=/dev/tty** turns on profiling and directs profiling output to the terminal. This allows applications based on the current *malloc* interface to select appropriate allocation methods at runtime. The following is an example C program with various memory bugs.

```
 1: #include <stddef.h>
 2: #include <vmalloc.h>
 3: char* copy(char* s)
 4: { char* news = malloc(strlen(s));
 5:    strcpy(news,s);
 6:    free(s);
 7:    return news;
 8: }
 9: main()
10: { char* s = copy("1234");
11:    free(s);
12: }
```

Lines 3 to 8 define a function `copy()` that makes a copy of an input string, frees the old string, and returns the new copy. Line 10 calls this function to copy a string. The first indication of bugs was seen after compiling and running the program for the first time:

```
$ cc -DVMFL t.c -lvmalloc -o t
$ t
Bus error(core dump)
```

Now, if an error like this was found during development, the developer can try to debug. But if this error happened at a customer's site, it would be hard to figure out. However, because the program was based on *vmalloc*, we can try turning on memory debugging:

```
$ VMETHOD=vmdebug t
corrupted data:region=0xc638:block=0xe6a0:bad byte=4:
    allocated at=t2.c,4:
free error:region=0xc638:block=0xc17a:unknown address:
    detected at=t2.c,6:
```

The first error message says that the block allocated on line 4 (that is, the space for the new string) was overwritten. Further examination of the code shows that the programmer forgot the null byte at the end of a C string, so the allocation on line 4 was one byte short. The second error message says that the **free()** call on line 6 attempted to free a block that was not previously allocated. Indeed, this was the case, as **copy()** was called with a literal string. This was the cause of the bus error. Note also that the program ran *successfully* this time (that is, without causing a core dump). This is because the **Vmdebug** method checks for invalid calls, such as the erroneous **free()** call in the example, and prevents them from going too far.

The point in the above examples is that by anticipating and isolating different usage scenarios into separate methods, applications can be built that are both powerful and efficient. Applications based on the *malloc* part of *vmalloc* can run at high efficiency in normal mode, yet they still can detect certain classes of memory errors by turning on the debugging method as necessary. This is to be contrasted with memory debugging packages, such as Purify [HJ92a] that requires building separate executables if debugging is desired. Though Purify is more comprehensive than **Vmdebug**, executables built with it cannot be shipped to customers.

2.3.5   Discussion

We have described the idea of analyzing resource usage for a library as a part of defining the library interface. Resource usage is further categorized as acquisition and management. The interface to the former is called discipline, while the interface for the latter is called method. Library designers routinely assume these resource aspects and avoid analyzing their requirements. This leads to libraries that are not easily extensible and, in some cases, unusable due to nonportability or poor performance. We proposed and showed via examples that the functionality of a library package can be greatly extended by explicitly defining disciplines and methods as parts of the library interface.

Methods allow flexibility in customization of resource management in certain predefined scenarios to add functionality or to tune for performance. The *libdict* library allows applications to tune for performance at the right time by switching the managing method of a dictionary to use hash tables or binary trees. The *vmalloc* library provides an extensive set of methods ranging from efficient allocation to memory debugging or profiling. Architecting different usages of the abstract interface of a library with methods also makes it easy to extend the library as new methods are discovered. Since a method must be specifically named to use, this architecture also helps to reduce application code size if the library implementation is structured so that different methods are either isolated or share only minimal code. This is due to the way that most C link editors work. If symbols in a module (C source file) of a library are not referred to directly or indirectly, the module is not linked to the final executable code. For example, if Dthash is never mentioned in an application based on *libdict*, the code for the hash method is not linked to the application executable code. This increases the usability of a library in environments where memory may be limited.

Disciplines allow applications to extend library functionality or customize it to specific resource requirements. *libdict* disciplines provide an example of customizing object descriptions in dictionaries. This use of disciplines is somewhat similar to class inheritance in object-oriented languages, where member functions of a discipline structure are virtual methods that operate on the specific object type. However, the dynamic specification of the key location in an object representation allowed by *libdict* disciplines is not as easily done in a language, because class members can only be accessed by names. The *sfio* library shows how the underlying I/O system can be extended for data processing, using disciplines. Isolating resource acquisition functions in disciplines (as in *sfio*) also means that much of the external dependencies in a library package have been analyzed and anticipated. This helps to simplify any porting effort.

The described discipline examples parameterize only the resource acquisition parts of the respective libraries as applied to certain library objects. There are other resource acquisition functions that may benefit from such parameterization. For example, dynamic memory allocation is traditionally done via a single interface *malloc*. With the introduction of a library such as *vmalloc*, it may be desirable to parameterize dynamic memory allocation so that structures can be allocated from different types of memory. A difficulty with doing this in general is that such a parameterization must be done for a library as a whole, not just for a library object. For example, the creation of a stream in *sfio* involves dynamic memory allocation and file opening (typically via the **open()** system call) so, if parameterized, alternatives to these functions must be specified before the stream is created. Perhaps, some notion of discipline that applies to a library as a whole would be useful.

Finally, as discipline interfaces are well-defined, disciplines are a good source of reusable code. This is amply demonstrated with the *sfio* and *vmalloc* libraries, which have the most generally defined discipline interfaces. There are currently about half a dozen standardly distributed *sfio* disciplines ranging from making an unseekable stream seekable (by shadowing data in temporary files as necessary) to making transparent I/O on compressed data. Users of *vmalloc* have written disciplines to manage shared memory via both **shmget()** and **mmap()**. This ability to write reusable code to create variations of a library without having to tamper with its internals is a key toward general library reusability.

2.4   *libgraph*

Graphs are fundamental data structures with many applications. In software engineering, graphs can model the dependencies between the types, variables, functions, modules, and files that make up programs, as well as data structures containing pointers or finite state machines and Petri nets, to name a few examples.

Many CASE systems use graph layouts to display software structure, and, for some purposes, users appreciate these diagrams as an alternative to text output. Our experience with graph layout programs began with creating the *dag* layout utility [GNV88]. It iteratively reads a graph, computes a layout, and emits graphics code for a picture. Its algorithm combines heuristics and mathematical optimization to make hierarchical layouts of directed graphs. *dag* is more general-purpose than most integrated CASE tools. It is not tied to any particular application or type of graph, such as call graphs or class hierarchies. *dag* is language-based. Though it can work with a compatible interactive front end, it doesn't have to be operated manually with a point-and-click interface. This permitted us to concentrate on layout style and algorithms, not GUI design. Because *dag* was conceived as part of the *troff* suite, its input language resembles PIC [Ker84]. Its syntax is reasonably easy to learn, predictable, and forgiving. Thus, programmers find it straightforward to write generators to convert other data into *dag* files. While *dag*'s successor, *dot* (*dag of tomorrow*), and some applications will be discussed further in Chapter 11, we have introduced these tools here to provide background and motivation for the design of an underlying graph library.

A serious problem with *dag* is that its data language was not designed to be reusable. The need for reuse arose when users requested an interactive graph browser, filters to cut large graphs down to size, and other graph tools. *dag* does not have any foundation library to help in writing such utilities. Though it does have a *little language* for graph specification, this language has hard-wired keywords and layout control statements (for example, to set shapes or constrain rank assignments). It is not general enough for other tools. Also, *dag*'s parser is entangled with its internal layout data structures.

When creating *dot*, we addressed this need by writing *libgraph*, which defines a *standard* graph data language and a small collection of C data types and primitives. Consequently, *libgraph* programs can trivially share graphs and possibly share code as well. (After gaining further experience with *dot*, *libgraph-2* was designed to address other problems. Most of the following discussion pertains to both versions, except as noted.)

libgraph deals only with representing graphs in memory and in files. It does not include depth-first search, planarity testing, layout functions, or a GUI. Including such routines in a base library is a mistake; it is much better to keep them separate in higher-level libraries. Dependencies on a specific window system or widget set are particularly undesirable because of the resultant loss of portability.

2.4.1   Previous Work

Some examples of recent work in graph toolkits are Edge [PT90], GraphEd [Him89], the Tom Sawyer commercial graph layout toolkit [Tom], and XmGraph [You]; with new systems appearing regularly now. These systems vary considerably in scope and complexity, but most of them focus on a graphical user interface and layout algorithms. Generally, these systems were designed from the viewpoint that graphs will be manipulated interactively, so the core system contains a user interface. New graph operations are programmed by compiling and linking them to the main system. These systems were not designed with the idea of making it easy for individual tools to be composed as shell command pipelines, which we consider one of the most effective forms of tool construction and reuse in UNIX.

All these systems define basic data structures for graphs, nodes, and edges that are typically maintained in hash tables or linked lists. This is a common approach, but, for writing our tools, we felt that we needed a richer graph model incorporating efficient random access, programmer-defined and external file attributes, and general subgraphs. Also, to enable the design of reusable libraries, these data structures need to support layering application-specific data. It's not difficult, but the only other system that supports this is GraphEd, using essentially the same solution as ours.

Most of these systems do not address reusable graph file representation adequately. The problem is how to support application-dependent attributes. Edge was first in providing a data language for graphs; unfortunately, its parser was implemented only as a prototype, with hard-wired keywords and data structures much like *dag*'s design. GraphEd, a later design, has flexible attributes (which can even be nested); however, GraphEd's attributes are hard-wired, and non-GraphEd attributes are silently deleted by the scanner when a graph is read. GraphEd also has a facility to handle graph grammars; this has applications in graph theory (for example, these files can succinctly encode circles, trees, complete graphs, outerplanar graphs, and, by also supplying a graph parse derivation, data flow graphs). In comparison with the other systems, including *libgraph*, GraphEd has many advanced features. The price may be paid in complexity: The entire system, including contributed layout code, is 230,000 lines of C.

In contrast to the examples just mentioned, the USL C++ graph class library [Wei92] and the Stanford GraphBase [Knu93] are non-GUI programming libraries, so they are closer in spirit to *libgraph*. The USL toolkit adopts C++ conventions, such as inheritance and iterators, so it appeals to a slightly different audience of programmers. It lacks a file language, and its representation of node and edge sets as digital tries raises some questions about time and space efficiency. GraphBase was written to support experiments in implementing efficient graph algorithms; it employs *ad hoc* file formats instead of a common language. Also, for our purposes, because of the choice of data structures, it is missing functions we want, such as node and edge deletion. In summary, while most of these systems reflect similar design criteria, none has all the features needed for writing straightforward, reusable graph processors.

Other previous work deals with persistent data structures. Examples include IDL [NNGS90] and P-Graphite [WWFT88]. They are similar in calling records *nodes*, and pointers *edges*. But these systems were created not for programming graph algorithms, but to address issues of storing arbitrary data structures on disk in relocatable, machine-independent format. The *libgraph* model is more specific, and higher-level. For example, subgraphs are built-in and do not have to be simulated by arrays or some similar technique. Also, an edge is not simply an address pointer, but may carry attributes, such as cost, color, or node port identifier.

2.4.2   File Language

To support writing effective tools, the graph data language should have certain properties.

- *Readable.* Although, in practice, most graph files are automatically generated and never seen by a human, there are still occasions when people must read and even edit graph files. This happens when debugging graph generators or fine-tuning important diagrams. If the graph specification syntax is *reasonable*, such tasks can be a little easier.
- *General.* Although compatibility precludes application-specific syntactic constructs in the graph language, it must nevertheless be general enough to encode important concepts, such as constraints on sets of nodes and edges, and layout controls. *libgraph* relies on a built-in notation for nested, attributed subgraphs. A constraint can then be expressed by creating a subgraph and labeling it with some distinguishing attribute for relevant tools to recognize.
- *High-level.* Our intended applications operate on abstract graphs. Thus our data language aims higher than just giving an exhaustive list of nodes and edges and their attributes. For example, the *edge creation operator* applies not only to node pairs, but also subgraphs (interpreted as node sets).

Examples of the graph data language and the corresponding layouts are shown in Figures 2.1 to 2.6. Main graphs and their subgraphs are enclosed in brackets. These define contexts for creating and initializing new subgraphs, nodes, and edges. These are also implicitly inserted into containing graphs; thus, the main graph has global node and edge sets. A node is created explicitly by giving its name and an optional list of attribute settings, or implicitly if it does not already exist when named in an edge. Edges are created by connecting endpoints (nodes or subgraphs) with an edge operator. Edges also may have attribute settings.

A graph file may contain additional statements to set graph attributes, change default values for initializing nodes and edges, or change values of previously created graph elements. Some attributes are special. The key of an edge distinguishes multiple edges between the same node pair.

```
 1:    digraph finite_state_machine {
 2:        rankdir = LR;  size = "5,4";
 3:        node [shape = doublecircle]; LR_0 LR_3 LR_4 LR_8;
 4:        node [shape = circle];
 5:        LR_0 -> LR_2 [ label = "SS(B)" ];
 6:        LR_0 -> LR_1 [ label = "SS(S)" ];
 7:        LR_1 -> LR_3 [ label = "S($end)" ];
 8:        LR_2 -> LR_6 [ label = "SS(b)" ];
 9:        LR_2 -> LR_5 [ label = "SS(a)" ];
10:        LR_2 -> LR_4 [ label = "S(A)" ];
11:        LR_5 -> LR_7 [ label = "S(b)" ];
12:        LR_5 -> LR_5 [ label = "S(a)" ];
13:        LR_6 -> LR_6 [ label = "S(b)" ];
14:        LR_6 -> LR_5 [ label = "S(a)" ];
15:        LR_7 -> LR_8 [ label = "S(b)" ];
16:        LR_7 -> LR_5 [ label = "S(a)" ];
17:        LR_8 -> LR_6 [ label = "S(b)" ];
18:        LR_8 -> LR_5 [ label = "S(a)" ];
19:    }
```

Figure 2.1 *dot* source for finite state machine.

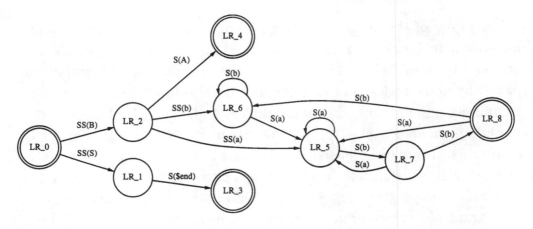

Figure 2.2 Finite state machine.

```
1:   digraph G {
2:       node [shape=record];
3:       struct1 [label="<f0> left|<f1> middle|<f2> right"];
4:       struct2 [label="<f0> one|<f1> two"];
5:       struct3 [label="hello\nworld
                    |{ b |{c|<here> d|e}| f}| g | h"];
6:       struct1:f1 -> struct2:f0;
7:       struct1:f2 -> struct3:here;
8:   }
```

Figure 2.3 *dot* source for compound node structure.

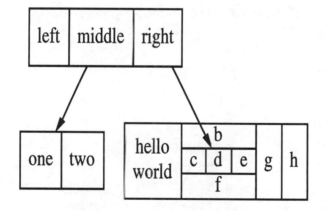

Figure 2.4 Compound node structure.

```
 1:    graph G {
 2:            run -- intr;
 3:            intr -- runbl;
 4:            runbl -- run;
 5:            run -- kernel;
 6:            kernel -- zombie;
 7:            kernel -- sleep;
 8:            kernel -- runmem;
 9:            sleep -- swap;
10:            swap -- runswap;
11:            runswap -- new;
12:            runswap -- runmem;
13:            new -- runmem;
14:            sleep -- runmem;
15:    }
```

Figure 2.5   *dot* source for process status.

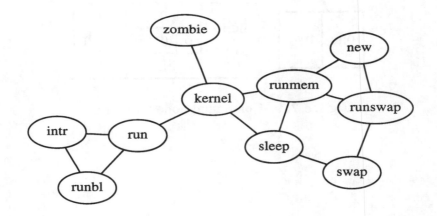

Figure 2.6   Process status.

If no value is given, an internal key is generated. Also, for convenience, edge `tailport` and `headport` values are supported with special syntax in *libgraph*'s parser and printer, using the colon notation, as can be seen in lines 6 and 7 of Figure 2.3.

2.4.3   Primitives and Implementation

We now consider the interface that *libgraph* presents to C programmers. Most programmers can write basic graph data structures and functions in a few dozen lines of code. A typical approach is to store nodes in a hash table and give each node an out-edge list. Attributes are hardwired as fields in the node and edge structs. This approach is simple and usually efficient. The problem is that it does not permit much sharing of code or of graph data files. Usually, if files are considered at all, they are programmed to have fixed field, line-oriented formats that are not compatible between applications that employ different attribute sets. As argued previously, we need a richer, more flexible model. To support this model, *libgraph* has about 30 entry point functions. They can be classified into the following groups:

- Create, search for, or delete graphs, subgraphs, nodes, and edges.
- Attach, get, or set attributes.
- Traverse node or edge lists, or subgraph trees.
- Read or write files.

The basic data structures defined by *libgraph* are graphs, nodes, and edges. As a client program runs, it can decorate these with attributes. *libgraph* also supplies a few auxiliary data structures to manage attributes. There are two kinds of attributes. String attributes are name-value pairs with default values, and are intended principally for I/O. For example, when *libgraph* reads an external file, the string attributes are automatically attached to graphs, nodes, and edges.

The other kind of attributes are runtime records defined in C by application programmers. These attributes allow programs to operate on values, such as weights, counts, and marks, using efficient native representations. In *libgraph-1*, programmers define one record type shared throughout the entire client program. This proved to be a serious limitation because it impedes the design of layered graph libraries; all functions generally must share the same compile-time definition of attributes.

libgraph-2 allows multiple runtime records. Each record has a header containing a unique name (a string, such as `layout_data` or `union_find_fields`), a pointer to the next record in the list, and application-specific fields. These records are kept in a circularly linked list attached to a node, edge, or graph. Thus, a function can find its runtime data by searching for the record with a given name. It is up to application programmers to manage this name space sensibly. Because it is clearly undesirable to search this list on every data reference, *libgraph-2* has an optional *move-to-front* search on this list, with hard and soft lock requests, making frequently referenced data available in one pointer reference within a set of compatible functions.

Any desired conversion between runtime and string values must be written explicitly by application programmers. Usually, conversion functions are called immediately after reading or before writing graphs. For example, a program may convert a numeric weight in a runtime record to a string attribute for printing in a graph file.

libgraph's node and edge sets are stored in *libdict* splay tree dictionaries. An advantage of splay trees over hash tables is the support for ordered sets. If nodes and edges are labeled and stored in their input sequence order, filters may process graphs without scrambling their contents, as would be the case if only hashing were employed. Further, some algorithms seem more predictable to users if they process nodes or edges in a known sequence, not some seemingly unpredictable order. *libdict* also allows changing dictionary ordering functions, and we take advantage of this to order nodes and edges by external keys sometimes, and by internal number at other times. User-defined ordering functions are also permitted. Though we have not exploited this much, it may be useful in coding geometric algorithms.

While *libdict* provides many convenient features, naive use for node and edge sets as we just described would incur significant overhead. For example, calling `Dtnext` to move from one item to the next in a splay tree dictionary set involves a function call and possibly several comparisons and pointer operations for tree rotation. Ideally, to compete with the hash table/linked list representation of graphs, we would like the cost of moving from one element to the next in a set to be just a few machine instructions or perhaps even just one. This cost is critical when coding an algorithm whose inner loop involves scanning edge lists.

Our solution is to give *libgraph-2* a function to temporarily linearize or *flatten* node and edge sets. This makes the splay tree look like a linked list: the root node or list head is set to the smallest element, and the *left* and *right* tree pointers are *prev* and *next* in the list. *libgraph* also defines macros or inline functions to traverse these lists very quickly. This means that a graph is either in *edit* mode (having efficient random access), or *traversal* mode (having efficient sequential access). A boolean flag in each graph records its mode; this flag is tested by random-access operations to trap related errors as early as possible.

Naive use of *libdict* also costs memory in the form of container objects for dictionary members. Each container object has left and right tree pointers and a user object pointer. *libgraph* eliminates these containers by using the *libdict* option of embedding the headers in user objects (in this case, the graphs, nodes, and edges). A slight complication is that an edge needs to belong to two dictionaries (both in- and out-edge sets). Accordingly, *libgraph* creates two structs for every edge; each has a pointer to one endpoint node and to its partner edge. Each node and edge struct consumes 7 words (plus additional storage for node names and any attributes that are attached).

2.4.4   Experience

libgraph supports a collection of tools, including *dot*, *neato* (*Network Embedding Automatic Tool* for undirected graph layout by spring models), *tred* (a transitive reduction filter), *sccmap* (a strongly connected component decomposition utility), *gpr* (a generic filter to apply a predicate to nodes and edges and perform path contraction on unselected nodes), and *colorize* (a filter to algorithmically color nodes from seed values). *libgraph* was essential in the development of these tools. Of particular importance is that the data language is general enough to support new features without breaking existing tools or data sets. While *libgraph-1* was a success for creating graph tools, it was too inflexible for writing layered graph libraries. Initial experience with *libgraph-2* has been satisfactory in this area; for example, the network-simplex solver has been rewritten as a separate library.

2.5 *n-DFS*: The Multiple Dimensional File System

The Multiple Dimensional File System (*n-DFS*) is a logical file system layered on top of UNIX-like file systems. Inspired by its predecessors, the Three Dimensional File System (*3DFS*) [KK90], AT&T Bell Laboratories' Plan 9 [PPTT90], and the Jade File System [RP93], the goal of *n-DFS* is to tailor traditional UNIX-like file systems to meet the needs of configuration management in software development environments. *n-DFS* allows new services to be added to the underlying file system. Examples of services include naming services (for example, viewpathing [KK90], semantic naming [GJSO91], and attribute-based naming [Pet88]); monitoring file systems operations and communication [KK92]; replicating critical files in underlying file systems to remote backup file systems [FHKR93]; accessing Internet-wide file systems [RP93, Sum94]; and providing versioning of files [LCM85, KK90]. *3DFS* was named the Three Dimensional File System because it introduced a third *physical* dimension (viewpathing) to the UNIX file system. Conceptually, we view each new service in *n-DFS* as a new *virtual* dimension to the file system, and thus we call *n-DFS* the Multiple Dimensional File System. The versioning service, for example, is analogous to a *time* dimension to file systems.

The design philosophy of *n-DFS* is that overloading file system semantics can improve software reusability and customer acceptability when compared with the alternative of creating a new interface that is incompatible with existing applications. For example, UNIX tools, such as *nmake* [Fow90] and *build* [EP84], have demonstrated the usefulness and power of viewpathing in configuration management. This notion has been implemented by adding extra code to each of these tools. *n-DFS*, however, embeds viewpathing into the file system so that not only do all tools (for example, UNIX commands ls, vi, and so forth) take advantage

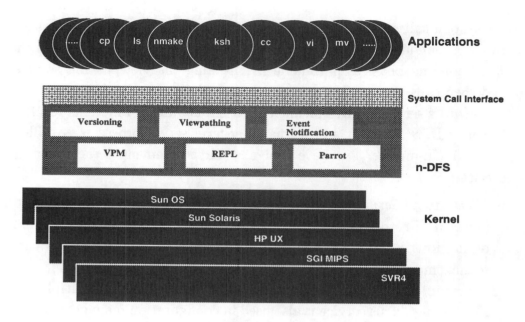

Figure 2.7   The Multiple Dimensional File System.

of viewpathing without any modification, but they also share the same view of the underlying file system. As another example, by implementing a versioning service as the front end of a source code control system (for example, SCCS [All86] and RCS [Tic85]), *n-DFS* introduces to UNIX-like file systems a new repository that supports versioning of files. Hence, users are able to reuse the **ls** command to browse different versions of a file.

Rather than considering individual functionality separately, our focus is to provide a generic and extensible architecture that allows new functionality to be added. Conceptually, *n-DFS* introduces a *logical layer* between the operating system and user applications, as illustrated in Figure 2.7. This layer presents applications with the same interface that the underlying system provides. However, it also allows users to *mount* services on nodes (such as directories or files) in the name space by maintaining a per-process name space. *n-DFS* intercepts system calls from applications and then passes them to the mounted services. For example, consider the viewpathing service that allows a virtual directory to refer to a sequence of physical directories. Users define a directory as a virtual directory by attaching the viewpathing services to the directory. When the system call *open* is invoked by an application (for example, vi) to access a file under this directory, *n-DFS* translates the pathname into the corresponding physical pathname by invoking the viewpathing service, and then calls the real system call *open* on the physical pathname.

n-DFS's services are implemented either as built-in functions resident in the *n-DFS* layer, or as external user-level server processes. As illustrated in Figure 2.7, we have designed and implemented the following services:

- *Viewpathing Service:* Allows a logical directory to refer to a sequence of physical directories/trees, the virtual content being an ordered union of files in the physical directories. This service is used in configuration management (see Section 3.3.1).

- *Versioning Service:* Supports a repository that provides multiple versions of files. This service is also used in configuration management (see Section 3.3.1).

- *Event Notification Service:* Collects file access events and notifies remote event-action servers, such as, YEAST (see Chapter 9).

- *Visual Process Manager (*VPM*):* Monitors interaction among a group of processes by collecting system calls invoked by them, and displays the result graphically in real time (see Section 11.5).

- *Tree Replication Service (*REPL*):* Replicates files under *replicated trees* in underlying file systems to a backup file system whenever their context/attributes are changed [FHKR93]. Software fault tolerance uses this service to backup critical data (see Section 8.2.3).

- *Parrot Service:* Presents users with a coherent, single-copy view of two loosely connected replicated physical file systems.

These services demonstrate the extensibility and generality of *n-DFS*. Indeed, *n-DFS* has been used as a research vehicle, enabling us to explore a variety of new services for different application domains.

n-DFS is unique in that the logical layer is realized as a library that is linked by applications and run in the application's address space. For systems, such as Sun OS 4.1 [Sun88], that provide the concept of dynamic linking of shared libraries, we are able to replace the standard C shared library with *n-DFS*'s library so that such applications may access *n-DFS* without any change. For systems without dynamic linking of shared libraries or applications with static linking, we need to relink applications with *n-DFS*'s library. In either case, *n-DFS* is transparent to the kernel and applications; no modification of the kernel or applications is required, and the syntax and semantics of system calls are preserved. Built-in services are accessed by local function calls without requiring any context-switch overhead.

With the library approach, *n-DFS* is more portable than the approach of modifying the kernel (for example, semantic file system [GJSO91] and watchdogs [BP88]) and adding new drivers (for example, Pseudo Devices [WO89]). Furthermore, *n-DFS* runs in the client side. It uses standard UNIX system calls to access the underlying file system, regardless of what access protocols are provided by file servers. Hence, heterogeneity is another advantage. The drawback to the library approach, however, is that it requires that all commands be linked with the library in order for everything to work correctly. Fortunately, most systems use dynamic linking, and nearly all the standard utilities are dynamically linked to the system call library. In most cases, we have been able to get third-party software vendors to provide dynamically linked versions of their software.

As shown in Figure 2.7, we have an implementation of *n-DFS* running on Sun OS 4.1, Sun Solaris, HP-UX, SGI MIPS, and SVR4, all of which support dynamic linking of shared libraries. The implementation includes the services described above. Most UNIX tools and commands, such as *vi*, *nmake*, and ls, are able to run on *n-DFS* without any modification, and without relinking for systems supporting dynamic shared libraries. *n-DFS* and its predecessor, *3DFS*, have been used as a software development environment in our department and other AT&T organizations for several years by hundreds of active users.

In the rest of this section, we describe the design and implementation of *n-DFS*, while detailed descriptions of services are in other chapters. Section 2.5.1 presents *n-DFS*'s architecture, focusing on its per-process name space and a mechanism of attaching services on the name space. Section 2.5.2 describes implementation of the current system. Section 2.5.3 evaluates the system by measuring overhead of the logical layer and the cost of the viewpathing service. Section 2.5.4 offers further discussion of

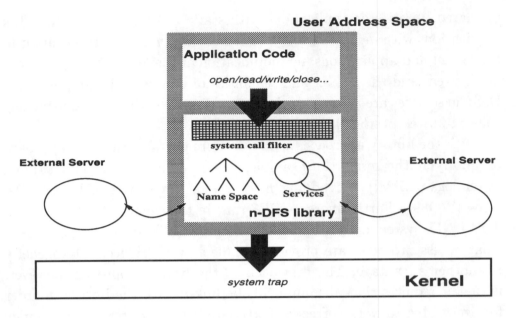

Figure 2.8   System architecture.

n-DFS in comparison to related projects, and Section 2.5.5 provides a summary.

2.5.1   Architecture

Layered between an application and the operating system, *n-DFS* extends the functionality of the underlying file system by providing additional services. *n-DFS* maintains a per-process name space that allows a service to be *mounted* on a subtree in the name space. Whenever a system call is made by an application for a file that lies in the subtree where the service is mounted (we say that the service is *mounted* on the file), *n-DFS* invokes the service to handle the request.

   As a replacement of the system call library (such as *libc*), *n-DFS* is linked to the application code and run at the same address space as the application code. Figure 2.8 illustrates its architecture, including a system call filter, a name space, built-in services, and an interface for interacting with external servers. The system call filter catches system calls from the application code, such as, *open, read, write, close*, and *fcntl*. It then locates and calls the mounted service. If no services are mounted on files referred by the system call, *n-DFS* simply passes the call to the kernel.

n-DFS provides a set of built-in services, which are implemented as regular function calls and reside in the application's address space. No context switch is required to access these services. The viewpathing service, for example, is implemented as a built-in service. In addition to these built-in services, *n-DFS* also provides an infrastructure to implement external services supported by external servers, which run in different address spaces or even on different machines. The infrastructure includes a naming mechanism to name servers, a library to implement servers (called *libcs*), and a message protocol for communicating between *n-DFS* and each server.

Each running *n-DFS* server has a unique global name in a distributed environment, as follows:

/**dev**/*proto*/*host*/*service*[/*options*]

The details of the syntax are described in Section 2.2.7. For example, /**dev**/**fdp**/**local**/**coshell**/**user**, /**dev**/**fdp**/**local**/**coshell**/**group**=**ship** both name different processes running the coshell daemon program. It is also possible to interact with the running server at the shell level. For example,

```
$ echo  "I did it" > /dev/tcp/share/logger
```

sends the message "I did it" to the shared server `logger`.

A service is defined by *mounting* a server on the service's pathname, as follows:

```
$ mount    /dev/proto/host/server_name    /#fs/service_name
```

/**dev**/*proto*/*host*/*server_name* refers to the name of the running server that provides the service and the second argument /**#fs**/*service_name* is the service pathname. Users may choose different pathnames for the same service. The binding of a service and its server may change dynamically. It is also possible to turn on/off services temporarily.

The mapping between a pathname and its mounted service is maintained by a name space. Like Plan 9, *n-DFS* maintains a per-process name space. Unlike Plan 9, the per-process name space resides inside the user address space rather than in the kernel. The name space is modifiable on a per-process level. It is, however, inherited across the *fork* system call, in that the child process has the same name space as its parent after *fork*. Users construct their own private name spaces using two system-wide, global name spaces: a name space supported by the underlying operating system and a name space of naming servers provided by *n-DFS*. At the beginning, the per-process name space contains only these two global name spaces. Users then are able to *attach* services onto their per-process name spaces.

Services supported by *n-DFS* can be classified into three categories: naming services, file services, and monitoring services. *n-DFS* intercepts system calls and then invokes the corresponding services. A service defines which calls it wants to intercept. Usually, naming services are invoked only to resolve pathnames in system calls, while file services may be called from all system calls that are related to file operations. Users can specify the system calls that are to be monitored by the monitoring services.

2.5.2   Implementation

The original version of *3DFS* was implemented by modifying the function that maps names to *i-node*s in the kernel. It proved too hard to maintain this version, since it relied on specific UNIX kernel implementations. To avoid this, *n-DFS* is now implemented as a user-level library that contains versions of many of the UNIX system calls. This library can either be merged with *libc*, or kept separately. Systems that do not have dynamic shared libraries require that programs be relinked to get the *n-DFS* extensions.

With the *n-DFS* library installed, each system call that *n-DFS* needs to know is intercepted and interpreted. As necessary, zero or more system calls are made by *n-DFS* to carry out a given action.

Because *n-DFS* runs in the user address space, it is not possible to guarantee that it will not affect an application that uses it. If the application writes into a random location that happens to lie in its address space, it could overwrite data that is critical to one or more *n-DFS* services. However, *n-DFS* was designed to be as unobtrusive as possible so that it could be used with existing programs. For example, since the vi editor uses the *sbrk* call to obtain heap memory and expects consecutive calls to *sbrk* to return contiguous memory, we could not use `malloc` to get heap memory needed for *n-DFS*. Instead, *n-DFS* maintains a static data area along with a 4K buffer to handle dynamic information. This space is more than adequate to handle the compact per-process information.

The *mount* system call is used to communicate with *n-DFS* itself. We chose to extend the *mount* call rather than adding another call so that any program that needs to use *n-DFS* services directly will not have an unsatisfied external reference when run *without* the *n-DFS* library. The arguments to *mount* are chosen so that the real *mount* returns an error code if *n-DFS* is not involved.

Each process using *n-DFS* requires tables of information relating to each of its dimensions, and this table needs to be inherited by each child process. With *3DFS*, the *execve* system call inserts an environment variable named "_" to the front of the environment list to pass down these tables. The first system call intercepted by *3DFS* reads the environment, extracts this information, and then deletes this environment entry. This creates two problems. First, it is possible for a user program to modify the environment before making any system calls, so the correct information may not be present. Second, programs that are close to the **ARG_MAX** limit of the size of the argument list plus environment are pushed over this limit with the additional *3DFS* data. To circumvent this problem, *n-DFS* passes down this information in an open file. Since *n-DFS* intercepts the *close* system call, there is no way that the user program can delete or modify this information before it is read by *n-DFS*. To save the time of creating and unlinking a file, *n-DFS* uses a UNIX pipe whenever the amount of information that is necessary is less then the

PIPE_MAX, the number of bytes that can safely be written on a pipe without blocking. A second optimization is done when a process that has not made any *mount* calls executes an *exec* call; the *n-DFS* table that was passed to this process can be reused to pass to the child process.

n-DFS uses *libcs* to implement external servers as explained earlier in Section 2.2.7.

2.5.2.1   Shell Interface

At the shell level, the **vpath** command controls the *n-DFS* namespace. Like other commands that control per-process system information (for example, **cd** and **umask**), **vpath** is a shell built-in. **vpath** uses the *mount*(2) system call, intercepted by *n-DFS*, to specify relationships between pairs of pathnames:

```
$ vpath    path1    path2
```

If *path1* and *path2* are directories, any reference to the directory hierarchy under *path1* will be mapped to the ordered union of the *path1* and *path2* hierarchies, where files under *path1* take precedence over files under *path2*. *path2* of the form /#* controls the *n-DFS* internal state. For this case, a *path1* of "−" can serve as a placeholder to preserve the **vpath** argument pairs. For example,

```
$ vpath    −    /#option/debug=5
```

sets the *n-DFS* debug trace output level to 5.

```
$ vpath    −    /#option/trace
```

prints the intercepted *n-DFS* systems calls on standard error for all child processes.

Replication is specified by first defining the replication service

```
$ vpath    /dev/tcp/share/rpl/user
/#fs/rpl/monitor/regular/write/call=open,close,write/ack=write
```

where **/dev/tcp/share/rpl/user** is the pathname of a per-user replication server that is shared among all hosts in the local network. **/dev/tcp/***host***/rpl** names a specific server running on *host*. /#fs defines a new file system service. The replication service is a file service that has the name *rpl* (usage described below), with the following attributes:

- *monitor:* Intercepted calls are run locally but also passed on to the service.
- *regular:* Monitors regular files (no directories, special devices, and so forth).
- *write:* Monitors only files open for write.
- *call=... :* Monitors only these intercepted calls.
- *ack=... :* Blocks for server acknowledgment for these calls.

Replication hierarchies are then specified by mounting directories on the replication service:

```
$ vpath   dir1   /#rpl   dir2   /#rpl
```

where *rpl* is the name from the /#fs mount above. The service can be switched off by

```
$ vpath   –   /#fs/rpl/off
```

and on by

```
$ vpath   –   /#fs/rpl/on
```

without breaking the service connection.

Finally, the command **vpath** with one argument prints out the physical path associated with the input logical path. **vpath** without arguments lists a complete configuration mapping. This can be saved into a file and used to restore an *n-DFS* configuration sometime in the future.

2.5.3   Evaluation

We measured the overhead of the logical layer and the performance of the viewpathing service using the Andrew Benchmark [HKM+88]. The input to the benchmark is a read-only source subtree consisting of about 70 files. These files are the source codes of an application program and total about 200 kilobytes in size. The benchmark includes five distinct phases, as listed in Table 2.1.

Table 2.1   Five Phases in Andrew Benchmark

MakeDir	Constructs a target subtree that is identical in structure to the source subtree.
Copy	Copies every file from the source subtree to the target subtree.
ScanDir	Recursively traverses the target subtree and examines the status of every file in it but does not read the contents of any file.
ReadAll	Scans every byte of every file in the target subtree once.
Make	Compiles and links all the files in the target subtree.

The hardware for testing is a Solbourne 5/800, running Sun OS 4.1 with a local disk. We compared three cases. In the first case, applications directly access files located on the local disk; we call this a UNIX file system case. In both the second and third cases, applications run on *n-DFS*, which, in turn, is layered on top of a UNIX file system. There is no viewpathing service defined by users in the second case, while in the third case, applications run on an empty directory that is on top of the source directory. Table 2.2 shows the performance results. The numbers presented in this section were derived from ten runs, with the average of those runs reported. The standard deviations of the experiments were small.

Table 2.2   Performance Results

	UNIX File System	*n-DFS*	
		No Layer	One Layer
MakeDir	5 sec	5 sec	-
Copy	15 sec	17 sec	-
ScanDir	18 sec	24 sec	25 sec
ReadAll	26 sec	36 sec	39 sec
Make	41 sec	48 sec	49 sec
Total	105 sec	130 sec	-

The second case (that is, *n-DFS*/No-Layer) shows the overhead of the logical layer introduced by *n-DFS*. Most of this overhead comes from pathname resolution done in *n-DFS* in order to locate mounted services. *n-DFS* needs to translate a relative pathname to an absolute pathname and then to look up the mapping table for mounted services. In the phases **ScanDir** and **ReadAll**, which access individual files using their relative pathnames, this process costs 33 to 38 percent compared with the UNIX case. However, this cost becomes less important when applications do more computation, as in the phase **Make**. The third case, *n-DFS*/One-Layer, shows the overhead of the viewpathing service. As shown in Table 2.2, the overhead is less than 10 percent.

2.5.4   Discussion

There are many research efforts that share our philosophy of overloading file system semantics to improve system uniformity and utility, software reusability, and customer acceptability. Examples of the research include Watchdogs, Killian's process file system [Kil84], Pseudo Device Drivers, Semantic File System, and Automount daemon [CL89]. All these projects introduce new functionality by modifying the kernel or implementing new drivers. *n-DFS*'s predecessor, *3DFS* , was originally implemented by modifying the kernel. Because it relies on a specific UNIX kernel implementation, *3DFS* proved too hard to maintain.

n-DFS, on the other hand, implements a logical layer using the library, which is running on the application's address space. As mentioned above, for systems providing dynamic linking of shared libraries, we are able to replace the standard C shared library with *n-DFS*'s library, and applications with dynamic linking may access *n-DFS* without any change. For systems without dynamic linking of shared libraries or applications with static linking, we need to relink applications with *n-DFS*'s library. By porting the library to a variety of platforms, we have shown that the library approach is more portable than modifying kernels or implementing new drivers.

Most modern UNIX-like operating systems [GLDW87, NH93] support dynamic linking of shared libraries to reduce sizes of program images and to improve page sharing between different programs running the same libraries. We take advantage of the dynamic linking feature to avoid relinking applications with *n-DFS*'s library.

Plan 9 and Spring [KN93] provide an architecture for extensible file systems. Plan 9 supports a per-process name space and a message-oriented file system protocol. All services implement a file system-like interface. Users are able to attach new services to the per-process name spaces dynamically. Spring provides a general, global naming structure to name objects with interfaces not restricted to that of the file system. It also provides an architecture that enables the extending of file system functionality by *stacking* new services on top of existing file systems. Like Plan 9 and Spring, *n-DFS* supports an infrastructure that allows new functionality to be added into existing file systems. Unlike Plan 9 and Spring, however, this infrastructure runs in the user address space rather than in the kernel address space. Spring and Ficus [GHM+90] also support a *stackable layers* architecture to permit coexistence of multiple functionality. For programs with static linking and no source code available for rebuilding, we have a shell script **vex**, that replaces each virtual filename with a physical name and executes the original program. Child processes of statically linked programs that spawn dynamically linked processes will inherit the *n-DFS* environment correctly. This approach doesn't handle the case in which the program opens a file whose name is not given as an argument to the program. In addition, monitoring services are not severely curtailed for these processes.

2.5.5   Conclusion

n-DFS provides a generic framework that allows new functionality to be added without any modifications of the kernel or applications. By porting *n-DFS* to a variety of UNIX-like operating systems, we have shown that *n-DFS* is more portable than other systems. By implementing a set of novel services, we have also demonstrated the extensibility and generality of *n-DFS*. *3DFS*, the predecessor of *n-DFS*, has been in production use for several years in many software development organizations at AT&T primarily because of its viewpathing capability. *n-DFS* has replaced *3DFS* in day-to-day work. REPL is currently being used by two projects in AT&T.

2.6   Summary

This chapter described a wide ranging collection of libraries in daily use throughout our company and, in some cases, worldwide. The libraries were constructed with specific design goals in mind, with portability as a key design goal. Methods and disciplines help in exposing external dependencies at an early stage and enabling later extensions. *libgraph* has shown how a language-based approach permits sharing at multiple levels. The *n-DFS* service infrastructure above the file system has resulted in many novel applications (Chapters 8, 9, and 10).

3

Configuration Management

Glenn Fowler, David Korn, Herman Rao, John Snyder, and Kiem-Phong Vo

3.1 The Common Bond

We manage software using our own tools: *nmake*, *n-DFS*, *pax*, and *ksh*. *nmake* builds executables and libraries from source; *n-DFS* partitions host-specific generated files from the source and allows transparent source sharing; *pax* efficiently records source changes for distribution to other hosts; and *ksh* scripts provide a concise user interface that ties the tools together.

Our *ast* software management is an evolutionary process made possible by the flexibility of its underlying tools. Portability, reuse, and minimal user intervention are the driving forces behind this evolution. In retrospect, the process has benefited from the evolution: We could not have anticipated the current process, because the tools it is based on have evolved and improved along with the process itself.

We describe each of the following six activities that characterize the *ast* software management process:

- *Build*—generate executables, libraries, documentation, and so on from source files.
- *Test*—test, debug, and improve the source.
- *Install*—place generated files in public directories.
- *Package*—collect source or generated files for use on other systems.

- *Bootstrap*—build and install on other systems, possibly in the absence of *ast* tools.
- *Version management*—manage multiple versions of software.

3.1.1   Build: *nmake*

nmake is the build tool. It is a modern variant of the traditional *make* [Fel79] with an important difference: *nmake* maintains state that records information for future runs. The state includes:

- File modification times
- Explicit prerequisites (from makefile assertions)
- Implicit prerequisites (from #include scanning)
- Action text (used to build targets)
- Variable values
- Target attributes:

    .BUILT—a generated file

    .MAKE—sends action to *nmake* rather than the *shell*

    .TERMINAL—a source file (not generated)

    .VIRTUAL—a target that is not a file

State *and* a language to manipulate it finally make concise makefiles a reality–concise because rules traditionally placed in each makefile can now be implemented in a general way in a single *base rules* file. The base rules are such a fundamental part of *nmake* that most of its visible features are controlled by them.

For example, a clean rule is traditionally supplied (by the user) with each makefile. This rule deletes generated files in the current directory. The **nmake clean** rule is in the standard base rules. The base rules version generates a list using a loop that selects all makefile targets that satisfy the following conditions:

- Has the .BUILT attribute.
- Exists as a file.
- Path is rooted in the current directory.

The traditional **clobber** rule is just **clean** with the path test omitted.

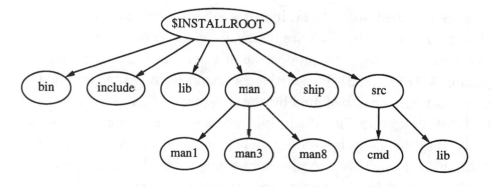

Figure 3.1   File hierarchy.

Similarly, the *pax* base rule creates a *pax* archive of all source files by generating a list of all .TERMINAL files rooted in the current directory.

Since the base rules are written in the same language as user-level makefiles, customization is simply a matter of providing global rules files that replace or augment the base rules assertions. There are several ways to access global rules: direct makefile include, the -g command line option, and assertion operator definition files (described below).

Makefiles play an important role in the layout of the source hierarchy. They conveniently partition the software into manageable components, where each component represents a single library or group of commands. *ast* components form a directory hierarchy, rooted at $INSTALLROOT that contains:

- bin: installed command executables
- lib: installed libraries and command-related data
- include: installed library interface headers
- src: component source files, src/lib for the libraries, and src/cmd for the commands
- ship: staging area for shipment to/from other systems
- man: manual pages for commands

Much of the power and simplicity in *ast* comes from file naming conventions. Figure 3.1 illustrates the prototype file hierarchy.

Intermediate files are built directly in the src subtree by *nmake*. nmake install places the installed files in the bin, lib, man, and include directories. By convention, commands are installed in bin, library interface headers are installed in `include`, libraries are installed in `lib`, and command related information files are installed in `lib/`*command*.

The naming conventions support application-position independence. By placing `$INSTALLROOT/bin` in the command `path` search, command-specific information can be found by searching for `../lib/command/info` in the `PATH` directories. Installed files that have been moved to another directory may be used by simply changing `PATH` to include the new `$INSTALLROOT/bin`. This also allows user overrides for information traditionally reserved by the system. For example, a user can reference a private `magic` file `$HOME/lib/file/magic` for the *file* command by inserting `$HOME/bin` before `$INSTALLROOT/bin` in `PATH`.

The *nmake* `:PACKAGE:` operator provides a convenient way to select portions of the `$(INSTALLROOT)` hierarchy. Many *ast* makefiles contain the line

```
:PACKAGE: ast
```

that asserts that the directory `$(INSTALLROOT)/include/ast` is searched for C header files and that all commands are linked with the library `-last` if it exists. The `:PACKAGE:` assertion also specifies that installed headers are to be placed in `$(INSTALLROOT)/include/ast`. Additional packages can be asserted. The first is the *main* package and specifies where include files will be installed, whereas the remaining packages provide include and library access. As with most *nmake* assertion operators, `:PACKAGE:` isolates makefiles from third-party software installation changes. For example, *ast X11* application makefiles assert

```
:PACKAGE: ast X11
```

The best makefiles specify only source dependencies; metarules in the *nmake* base rules file determine the underlying object and executable transformation commands. Command makefiles contain another assertion that specifies the command name, the source files, and any additional library dependencies:

```
calc :: README calc.1 calc.h main.c misc.c calc.y calc.l -lm
```

By using only source dependencies, the effects of implementation details and local naming conventions are eliminated. For example, on most UNIX systems, `main.c` generates the object file `main.o` that, when linked with the other object files and the library `/lib/libm.a`, generates the executable `calc`. On PCs, `main.c` generates `main.obj`, links with `libm.lib`, and generates the executable `calc.exe`. To further complicate matters, different compilers on the same system may have their own naming conventions. For example, if the compiler supports DLLs (dynamically linked libraries), then `-lm` might map to `libm.so`, `libm.so.n.m`, or `libm.sl`. DLL library timestamps are ignored because applications need not be relinked when a DLL changes. *nmake* automatically probes the `$(CC)` compiler at runtime to determine local conventions for the standard include directory, the library directory, file suffix conventions, and common options. It needs this information for accurate include, library, and option dependency evaluation. For example, `<stdio.h>` might bind to `/usr/include/stdio.h` for *cc*, but may bind to `/usr/local/CC/include/stdio.h` for *CC*.

In a similar fashion, the `:LIBRARY:` operator eliminates local library naming conventions from the abstract description:

```
ast 4.0 :LIBRARY: ast.h sfio.h sfio.c hash.h hash.c misc.c
```

On traditional UNIX systems, this produces `libast.a`. If the local system supports DLLs and the variable `CCFLAGS` contains `$(CC.PIC)` (the options to generate object files specifically for shared libraries), then `:LIBRARY:` also produces `libast$(CC.SUFFIX.SHARED).4.0` (where the value of `CC.SUFFIX.SHARED`, usually `.so` or `.sl`, is set according to local convention).

The *probe* generated compiler conventions are placed in `CC.*` variables (like `CC.PIC` and `CC.SUFFIX.SHARED` above), providing an abstraction to an otherwise out-of-control interface. Using the probe information *nmake* accurately determines include and library timestamps.

A library may also reference other libraries. For example, on some systems the socket and network routines are placed in `-lsocket` and `-lnsl` rather than in `-lc` (as was the tradition in BSD UNIX). The `-lcs` library (see Section 2.2.7) provides a consistent IPC abstraction on top of either sockets or streams, but, incredibly, the socket and stream library support may be found in one or more of eight different libraries, depending on the local implementation. To avoid specifying and testing these libraries for each command that uses -lcs (and to avoid editing all command makefiles to update the library list should it ever change), the optional libraries are simply asserted on the right-hand side of the :LIBRARY: operator in the makefile for -lcs:

```
cs 1.2 :LIBRARY: cs.3 csopen.c cssend.c ... \
    -lin -lipc -lnetcompat -lnetinet \
    -lsocket -linet -lnsl -ldl -lintl
```

If any of the *rhs* libraries exist, then a reference to -lcs also pulls in those libraries. As long as the cs library makefile is correct, makefiles like the one below are portable to all systems on which *cs* builds.

```
netcommand :: netcommand.c -lcs
```

The :MAKE: operator controls the makefile hierarchy itself. $INSTALLROOT/src/Makefile is:

```
:MAKE: lib - cmd
```

The *rhs* are directories in which separate *nmake* commands will be executed. The command line arguments are passed down using the built-in variable $(=) and the options are passed using $(-) (both quoted for the shell). Prerequisites may be built concurrently (the -jn option directs *nmake* to build up to n targets concurrently) but they are still queued for building from left to right. A '-' prerequisite is a synchronization point; *nmake* blocks until all prerequisites to the left complete. In the example above, all the libraries will be built before the applications.

Not all operators are defined in the standard base rules. Users and administrators may define their own operators by placing the definition for :OPERATOR: in the file $INSTALLROOT/lib/make/OPERATOR.mk. The first time :OPERATOR: appears, the file will be included to get its definition. The *cs* library uses this technique for servers using the :SERVICE: operator defined in $INSTALLROOT/lib/make/SERVICE.mk:

```
:PACKAGE: ast

nam fdp :SERVICE: nam.c

pid udp :SERVICE: uid.c

dbm tcp :SERVICE: dbm.c -ldbm

-ldbm : .DONTCARE
```

:SERVICE: abstracts the directory naming conventions, the libraries that must be linked, and any installation-time service registration. The *lhs* of :SERVICE: is the service name and protocol type (fdp—local stream that can pass file descriptors; udp—network datagram; tcp—network stream); and the *rhs* is the same as for the :: operator.

The .DONTCARE attribute on -ldbm allows *nmake* to ignore *-ldbm* if it is not found (otherwise it would complain with *don't know how to make -ldbm* and stop). .DONTCARE also handles a detail glossed over in the calc example above: what appears to be a nonportable reference to -lm. In this case, the base rules probe automatically assigns .DONTCARE to -lm for each compiler that does not support it. The *nmake* user can rely on an abstract compilation model, letting the probes and base rules handle implementation inconsistencies.

The average *ast* makefile is simply a collection of :PACKAGE:, ::, :LIBRARY:, :SERVICE:, and :MAKE: assertions. Makefile assertion operators are comparable to C library function calls in C programs: If the operator is buggy or insufficient, then only the operator must change, not the makefiles that use the operator. But, assertion operators provide much more than convenient build maintenance. Makefiles now abstract software at the source level, and source is the one piece that has a chance of remaining unchanged across different compiler and operating system implementations. This stability makes source the best medium for communicating its semantics: Object files, libraries, and suffix conventions are merely intermediate implementation details that lead from the source to the ultimate targets.

Two examples show the advantage of source assertions. The base rules supply the ciadb rule that generates a *cia* (see Section 6.2) database for the source controlled by the makefile. *cia* generates a .A file for each .c source file and then combines the .As to form the database. ciadb provides a %.A:%.c metarule and generates a list of all .As by collecting all .TERMINAL and generated .c files (for example, *yacc*, *lex*, and *sql* generate .c files) and editing them to a .A list. reference.db is then asserted with the .A list as its prerequisites and reference.db is made.

Source assertions also make code instrumentation a snap. nmake instrument=purify generates *purify*'d executables; instrument=app (see Chapter 5), `instrument=quantify`, and `instrument=sentinel` are also available.

Of course, a source level makefile is only as good as the source it abstracts. The source itself must be careful to factor out *minor* details, such as word size, byte order, supported include files, standard library functions, and so on. *ast* does this at the library level by using *iffe* (described in Section 3.2) to do installation-time feature testing and *probe* to do runtime feature testing.

These examples illuminate an *nmake* principle: Specify information *once* and *correctly*. This principle winds its way through the rest of the software management process.

3.1.2   Test

Testing is part of the compile-edit-debug cycle. It often involves references or modifications to files that have not been officially installed. The main point in this phase is to keep temporary, possibly incorrect, file changes separate from official versions of the files. This is a problem ideally suited to *n-DFS* viewpathing (see Section 3.3.2). *n-DFS* users usually maintain two or more viewpath levels: one for the official source, and at least one for development modifications.

Viewpathing can also keep generated files separate from the corresponding source. This is particularly useful when compilers for different architectures access the same filesystem, either through cross-compilation on a single platform or through cross-mounting on different platforms.

3.1.3   Install

Although an important phase in software management, *ast* installation is trivial because it is provided by default in the *nmake* base rules. There are some exceptions, most notably for headers. Recall that the *proto* program (described in Section 2.2.1.5) allows the *ast* libraries (and thus headers) to be compatible with the K&R, ANSI, and C++ C dialects. Instead of requiring that *proto* be used by all compilers that reference *ast* headers, the *ast* headers are themselves passed through *proto* at installation time. This is done with the `:INSTALLPROTO:` assertion operator:

```
$(INCLUDEDIR) :INSTALLPROTO: header.h
```

With the file details handled by *nmake*, the hardest part of installation is to make sure that the users are prepared for the changes in the newly installed software.

3.1.4   Package

The package and bootstrap phases fall under the control of the *ship* commands found in $INSTALLROOT/ship. Packages are generated by *shipcrate* and *shipout* and contain all of the files required to bootstrap part or all of the software on another system. Individual packages are called shipments. A source shipment contains files that can be installed on any platform that has a C compilation system, whereas a binary shipment contains files that can be installed on binary-compatible platforms.

A source shipment ultimately replicates or generates equivalent versions of the src, bin, lib, and include directories on the recipient host (binary compatible with the recipient, of course). In contrast to the sending host, the recipient host most likely will not have as rich a computing environment. For maximal portability, *ship* must be conservative in the requirements it places on the recipient environment:

- UNIX system V7 compatible shell: *ship* handles shells with broken -e option and no [! xxx] patterns.
- UNIX file system pathname syntax and semantics: "/" separated path components, case sensitive names, 14-character filename limit.
- Traditional C compiler interface: **-c**, **-D**macro, **-I**directory, and **-o** *output* options supported.
- The mv, cp, rm, cmp, sed, sort, comm, tee, grep, ls, and cpio or pax commands.

The *shipcrate* command places all shipment information in the ship directory. The ship directory contains the *ship* system commands and a subdirectory for each *item* (command or library) to be shipped. An item is the smallest unit of software that can be shipped and usually corresponds to a single application or library. The source file directory for an item can be derived from its name: All library items have a lib prefix

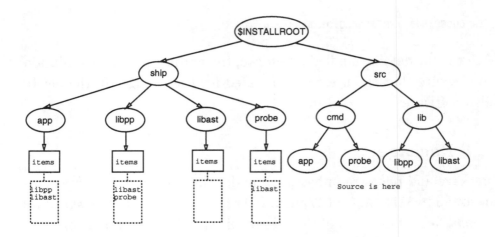

Figure 3.2   Before crating.

and the source is located in **$INSTALLROOT**/src/lib/*item*; commands have no **lib** prefix and the source is located in **$INSTALLROOT**/src/cmd/*item*. The only peculiarity with this scheme is that the source for any command with a **lib** prefix, **library** for example, must be placed in **$INSTALLROOT/src/lib**.

An item may depend on other items to build. For example, most of our tools link with the *libast* library. Item dependencies are expressed as item name lists placed in **ship**/*item*/**items** files. An item with no dependencies must still have an empty **items** file; this distinguishes item directories from others that may appear in **ship**. Figure 3.2 illustrates the **ship** hierarchy before crating.

The *shipcrate* command takes item names as arguments and forms the transitive closure of required items using the **items** files. If no items are specified, then all items with **items** files are crated. For each item in the closure, *shipcrate* generates a *pax* archive (in *cpio* compatible character format) containing:

- Source files
- *nmake* source **Makefile**
- Generated **Mamfile**

The **Mamfile** is a *make abstract machine* file that allows generated files to be built using a shell script rather than by *nmake*, which may not be present on the recipient host, or by *make*, which has many unreliable and incompatible implementations. The most difficult problem to work around is caused by an old but prevalent bug with the Bourne shell -e option. This option, used by *make* to execute its actions (recipes), causes the shell to exit with non-zero status whenever any command it executes exits with non-zero status. Some shell implementations improperly apply -e to commands subject to the shell conditionals (if, elif, &&, and ||), making it impossible to differentiate real errors from those caused by conditional tests. *make* also cannot handle actions containing multiline statements; these are often used to generate compile-time configuration information. *nmake* generates both the source file list and the Mamfile.

n-DFS is often used to join src hierarchies from different users. It is also used to overlay the ship hierarchy on top of src when generating the Mamfiles and shipment archives. Overlaying keeps the ship information disjointed from the src information and provides a simple way to add new items to a shipment.

If the source files have not changed since the last time shipcrate ran, then a new base is not created. Otherwise, the result is a directory ship/*item*/YYMMDD for each item that contains:

- The *pax* archive *base* .
- A copy of the *items* file (since the original may change with future revisions).
- A copy of ship/*item*/message, if it exists, that contains item specific installation information.
- A copy of ship/*item*/owner, if it exists, that contains the mail address of the user responsible for the item (the owner is notified of any build problems encountered on the recipient hosts).
- A copy of ship/*item*/copyright, if it exists, that contains source copyright information—*proto* uses the copyright information to automatically prepend copyright comments to all source files as they are extracted from the shipment archives.

The shipment version naming scheme uses YYMMDD, the current year, month, and day digits, limiting the system to one crate per item per day. This has not been a problem in practice since multiple crates in a single day usually suggests an item that has been shipped before its prime. We have a special command that can generate archives containing only the bytewise changes between a previous archive and the current source file list (**changes** also include file permission changes, file deletion, and file creation). If a previous base archive **ship/**_item_**/YYMMDD/base** exists, **shipcrate** will generate a delta archive **ship/**_item_**/YYMMDD/YYMMDD** by default, rather than a complete base archive. For example, the **base** archive for **931225** is generated by:

```
pax -wf 931225/base files ...
```

and the **delta** archive for **940214** based on **931225/base** is generated by:

```
pax -wf 940214/931225 -z 931225/base  files ...
```

The file-naming scheme itself identifies the base for a given delta: The base for delta **931225** is **931225/base**.

Delta archives are compact. Even for modifications spanning years, delta sizes are typically less than 10 percent of the size of the original base. _nmake_ has been in the _ship_ system since June 1989, and 36 deltas have been generated with a total size of 783K bytes. This number compares favorably with the current _nmake_ base archive size of 776K bytes (the _nmake_ source has changed significantly since 1989). Figure 3.3 illustrates an **$INSTALLROOT** hierarchy after **shipcrate**. Note that on the recipient side, only the most recent base and delta are retained (**931225** and **940214** in Figure 3.3).

When the delta size exceeds a threshold, 20 percent of the base size by default, **shipcrate** automatically generates a new base along with the delta. This new base can be generated from the previous base and new delta, so previous recipients need only be sent the new delta. Because delta archives must be read by the new _pax_, **shipcrate** automatically adds _pax_ to each shipment closure.

A crated shipment contains all the files needed to build its constituent items, even in the absence of _ksh_, _nmake_, and _pax_. This allows us to use crated shipments to record our software change history and allows us to restore any item from any previous shipment.

A major headache for a software researcher is keeping track of software that has been sent to other users: What version? What system? What items? Was there good feedback? Did the installation work? Did they even try it? Should an update be sent? One method posts the software

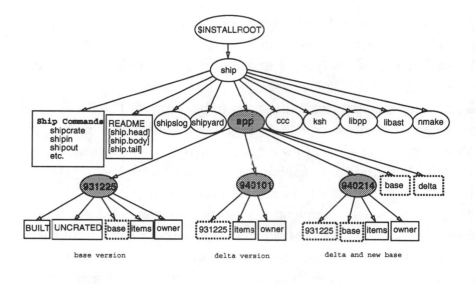

Figure 3.3 After crating.

to a global repository (a directory on an anonymous *ftp* host) and leaves software update management up to the recipients. *ship* takes a different approach by assuming control of the recipient `ship` directory, updating this directory with each new shipment. The updates are such that obsolete files are deleted, preventing the accumulation of old, unused files. By controlling the `ship` directory, *ship* can maintain a database of recipient items and versions. As long as the recipient `ship` directory remains intact, a minimal amount of information can be transported for updates.

Recipients are identified by electronic addresses appropriate to the transport method:

- *uucp* recipients are identified as *host!recipient*.
- *rcp* recipients are identified as *recipient@host:installroot*.
- Source *ftp* recipients are identified as *archive%src* (generates an installation message file and a compressed archive of source files for all items).
- Binary *ftp* recipients are identified as *archive%bin* (generates an installation message file and a compressed archive of generated files for all items).

The recipient database uses <address><item><type> keys to access <YYMMDD><date><shipper> data, where<YYMMDD> is the crated version, <date> is the date the item was shipped, and <shipper> is the user id of the person who shipped the item. <type> is either `base` or `delta` and identifies the type of item shipped. The *shipout* command takes both a recipient list and an item list as input, and uses the recipient database to determine the items that need to be shipped. The database is updated as new items are shipped. Database update is done using a single database server so that *shipout* may run concurrently on any host on the local network. An important aspect of this is that multiple shippers can share a single `ship` directory (and recipient database).

As mentioned above, recipient addresses determine the transport mechanism. Most transports are flexible, but some impose limitations on the number and size of files that can be sent; for example, some *uucp* implementations have a 160K byte size limitation. *shipout* generates a single virtual file for each recipient. This virtual file is split into physical chunks sized for the individual transport. Split shipments are staged on the recipient host and reassembled by *shipin*, described in the next section. Other transport mechanisms, such as `ftp` and `rcp`, have their own peculiarities, and these are also handled by *shipout* and *shipin*.

Accompanying each shipment is a mail message that explains the shipment contents. The message, generated by *shipout*, also includes instructions for uncrating, building, and reshipping.

Since the recipient `ship` directory is a replicated version of the sending `ship` directory, the recipient may use *shipout* to pass shipments on to other recipients. Many of our recipients are system administrators and they prefer to receive shipments on a single host. Once satisfied with the shipment contents, they then use *shipout* to move the shipment to other hosts in their administrative domain. *shipout* modifies the `owner` files at each stage, so the original owner is still notified of installation problems.

3.1.5   Bootstrap

Once *shipout* has completed, all actions are controlled by the recipient via the *shipin* command. The first-time recipient must choose a suitable (and empty) `$INSTALLROOT` directory, create an `$INSTALLROOT`/ship subdirectory, and copy the *shipin* script there. Running `nohup ship/shipin &` in the `$INSTALLROOT` directory, builds and installs all the shipped items.

shipin only modifies the directory hierarchy under $INSTALLROOT and does not require special user privileges to run.

shipin is by far the most complicated part of *ship*—first, because it avoids recipient interaction by generating and running programs to check local features, and, second, because it is designed to restart after intentional or unintentional build interruptions. Each item version has a state, and *ship* acts as a state machine that moves each item from its initial to its final state. The file $INSTALLROOT/*item*/YYMMDD/STATE means that the item is in or has passed through state STATE. If no state file exists for an item, then it is in the START state. If more than one state file exists, then the item is in the highest-numbered state from the list below:.

1. START: No actions have been taken.
2. UNCRATED: Source files have been read from shipment archive and put in $INSTALLROOT/src/cmd/*item* or $INSTALLROOT/src/lib/*item*.
3. GENERATED: The current base archive was generated from a previous delta and base.
4. BUILT: The *installed* files were correctly built and installed.
5. ERROR: An error occurred during some part of the shipment—the item will not be built until after an update shipment arrives from the item (the -E option to *shipin* ignores ERROR files).
6. BYPASS: Prevents further action on the item until BYPASS file is removed.

Figure 3.4 illustrates the shipment states and transitions.

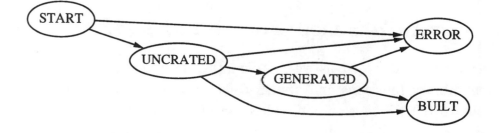

Figure 3.4   Shipment states.

3.1.5.1   Software Portability

So far, all that has been said about the shipment items is that each item can be generated on the sending host. This does not guarantee that the item will build on the recipient hosts. In preparing source for **ship**, designing and coding for portability takes the most time by far. As a general rule, we rely on published standards whenever possible. All programs are coded in a subset of C that is compatible, modulo **extern "C" { ...}** linkages, with C++. ANSI C, POSIX, and X/OPEN library and header interfaces are used before private ones are invented. Except for one basic library (*libast*), all other items are coded in this style.

Not all systems provide standard interfaces and compilers; we leave it up to **ship** to configure the source and to provide the missing (or broken) parts of the standards. This is done as a two-step process. First, just before *shipin* reads in the **src** archives, it checks if the local C compiler handles ANSI C. If not, then it applies the *proto* filter to each *.[chly] file that contains the statement **#pragma prototyped**. The input to *proto* is a valid ANSI C file; the output is a file that simultaneously compiles under the classic K&R, ANSI, and C++ dialects. This is done by inserting **#ifdefs** and macros in places where the three dialects differ. *proto* is also used on the sending host, but is automatically applied by *nmake* as a part of the normal compilation process by *nmake*. *Libpp cpp* detects **#pragma** prototypes and applies the *proto* algorithm as a discipline.

The second and more involved part of the porting process deals with the *iffe* command and accompanying coding style. This is discussed in the following section.

3.2   Feature Based Portability

Many critical parts of *ast* as well as our other software tools must use different library functions and system calls on different platforms. For example, to tell whether or not a file descriptor is ready for I/O, on a BSD-derived system, one should use the **select()** system call, while on newer System V systems, the **poll()** system call is required. The problem is compounded by the fact that there are many hybrid systems, some from the same vendor, that provide mixed services. In another dimension, most systems come with standard libraries, such as string and mathematical packages, but some are implemented better than others. An extreme case is the VAX family of machines that come with hardware instructions for certain string and character look-up operations that are more efficient than any handcrafted software. In such cases, we would like to take advantage of local features to optimize our software. Of course, in all cases, we have to be certain that the platform feature that we use does what it is supposed to. In sum, the porting problem is this: How can we certify that a particular feature exists on a local software/hardware platform and that it does what is required?

3.2.1 A Programming Style for Portability

Traditionally, the porting problem is solved by embedding `#ifdef selector` in the code to select different implementations. Here, `selector` is a predetermined token that somehow guarantees that the respective implementation will work. Typically, `selector` must be supplied by a local knowledgeable user. This usually means that `selector` must define fairly broad categories, such as `SUN` or `SGI` for hardware and `BSD` or `SYSV` for operating systems. With the existence of hybrid systems, this can miss the mark and lead to the construction of bad code.

We solve this problem by applying a programming style and a tool, *iffe*, that supports the programming style. It is best to show this with an example. Consider the following code fragment:

```
1: #include      "FEATURE/vfork"
2: #if _lib_vfork
3: #undef fork
4: #define fork     vfork
5: #if _hdr_vfork
6: #include      <vfork.h>
7: #endif
8: #endif
```

This code is taken from the source of the `sfpopen()` function of the *sfio* library. Line 1 includes a file `FEATURE/vfork` that may define two tokens, `_lib_vfork` and `_hdr_vfork`. Line 2 determines if `_lib_vfork` is non-zero, indicating the existence of a system call `vfork()` that can be used in place of `fork()`. Like the traditional `fork()` system call, `vfork()` is a BSD system call to create a new copy of the current process. It is faster than `fork()` since it does not create a separate copy of the data section for the new process. This works well for `sfpopen()` because the requested command will immediately overlay the new process anyway. However, there is a major problem on SUN SPARC machines where registers modified by a child process get propagated back to its parent. SUN solved this problem by providing a header file `vfork.h` that contains a compiler pragma that generates code to avoid this bug. This fact is tested on line 5 using the token `_hdr_vfork`.

In the preceding example, the parameterization of system requirements is done in a single file. Where such requirements span more than one module, it is possible to create a single header file for all parameterizations. Now, to complete the picture, we need to see how the tokens `_lib_vfork` and `_hdr_vfork` can be correctly and automatically generated. This is done via the *iffe* language and system. The reader may have noticed that a subdirectory, FEATURE, is used to store the file `vfork` that contains the definitions of the required tokens. This file is generated from a specification file, `vfork`, in a parallel directory, `features`. The contents of `features/vfork` is:

```
lib vfork
hdr vfork
```

The line `lib vfork` determines if `vfork()` is a function provided by the standard libraries by compiling and linking a small test program that contains a `vfork()` call. Similarly, the line `hdr vfork` determines if the header file `vfork.h` exists by compiling a small program containing the line `#include <vfork.h>`. The output file FEATURE/vfork for a SUN SPARC follows. Note that to prevent errors with multiple inclusions the generated symbols are automatically wrapped with the wrapper `#ifndef` and `#endif` which is generated from the base name of the feature test file `features/vfork` and `sfio`, the parent directory of `features` and package name. By the way, FEATURE does not have an S to parallel `features` so that the two directories can be kept distinct on operating systems such as Windows NT where cases are indistinguishable in directory and file names.

```
#ifndef _def_vfork_sfio
#define _def_vfork    1
#define _lib_vfork    1    /* vfork() in default lib(s) */
#define _hdr_vfork    1    /* #include <vfork.h> ok      */
#endif
```

Actually, we are a little trusting in the preceding example, since compilability is not equivalent to execution correctness. For complete safety, *iffe* can specify programs that must compile, link, and execute successfully. The following example is a *iffe* specification to test for the register layout of a given VAX compiler. If the program compiles and runs successfully, we know that the register layout is as expected and certain hardware instructions can be used for optimization.

```
tst vax_asm note{ standard vax register layout }end exec{
    main()
    {
#ifndef vax
        return absurd = 1;
#else
        register int    r11, r10, r9;
        if(sizeof(int) != sizeof(char*))
            return 1;
        r11 = r10 = r9 = -1;
        asm("clrw    r11");
        if(r11 != 0 || r10 != -1 || r9 != -1)
            return 1;
        asm("clrw    r10");
        if(r11 != 0 || r10 != 0 || r9 != -1)
            return 1;
        asm("clrw    r9");
        if(r11 != 0 || r10 != 0 || r9 != 0)
            return 1;
        return 0;
#endif
    }
}end
```

The preceding code will compile and run correctly only on a VAX with a proper compiler. If that is the case, the output would be as follows and we would know that the register layout is as expected so that certain hardware instructions can be used safely for optimization.

```
#define _vax_asm 1    /* standard vax register layout */
```

iffe specifications can be integrated with **makefiles** in the obvious fashion. *nmake* does this automatically: It first determines the required **FEATURE** files by scanning the source code for any implicit header file prerequisites (a.k.a. `#include` dependencies). Then, the base metarule

```
FEATURE/% : features/% .SCAN.c (IFFE) (IFFEFLAGS)
    $(IFFE) $(IFFEFLAGS) run $(>)
```

provides the action to generate the **FEATURE** files. Note that *oldmake* makefiles generated by *nmake* contain all header dependencies including the generated **FEATURE** files.

To summarize, the programming style that we adhere to is:

1. Determine needed features that may have platform-specific implementations.
2. Write *iffe* probes to determine the availability and correctness of such features.
3. Instrument `makefiles` to run such *iffe* scripts to create header files with properly defined configuration parameters.
4. Instrument C source code to include **FEATURE** header files, and use `#define` symbols in these files to select code variants.
5. Restrain **FEATURE** file proliferation by limiting use to libraries when possible.

By following the preceding steps during any port of a software system, porting knowledge is never forgotten. Indeed, such knowledge is coded in a form that is readily *reusable* in different software systems. In extreme cases, **FEATURE** files generated on one platform may be used to bootstrap software on another; this is how the initial Windows NT port was done (*iffe* would not work with the NT shell, so we started with **FEATURE** files from a mostly ANSI/POSIX system and edited them as problems arose, eventually getting *ksh* up and running, at which point we could rebuild with *iffe*).

3.2.2   The *iffe* Language

A *iffe* input file consists of a sequence of statements that define comments, options, or probes. A comment statement starts with # and is ignored by *iffe*.

An option statement is of the form:

    set *option* [value]

Option statements are used to customize the execution behavior of the *interpreter*, such as `cc` to change the compiler or `debug` to change debugging levels.

A probe statement is of the form:

    type name [header ...] [library ...] [block ...]

where `type` names the type of probe to apply, `name` names the object on which the probe is applied, `header` and `library` are optional headers and libraries to be passed to the compiler (ignored if they do not exist), and `block` is optional multiline blocks of text of the form:

    label line ... end

`type` and `name` may be "," separated lists, in which case, all `types` are applied to all `names`. The default output for a successful probe is statement of the form:

```
#define _type_name 1          /* comment */
```

and the entire output file is wrapped by:

```
/* :: generated from input-file by iffe version 07/17/94 :: */
   #ifndef _def_name
   #define _def_name 1
```

> *iffe probe output*

```
   #endif
```

where *name* is derived from the directory and base name of the input file or the name of the first probe type if input is from the standard input. Unless otherwise noted, the standard output and standard error of each probe is redirected to `/dev/null` and the standard input is redirected from `/dev/null`.

`block` labels are selected from a predefined list and indicate actions done following the result of a probe. A few examples are:

fail: If the probe fails, then the block is evaluated as a shell script and the output is copied to the output file.

pass: If the probe succeeds, then the default output is suppressed and the pass block is evaluated as a shell script and the output is copied to the output file.

compile: The block is compiled as a C program.

execute: The block is compiled and linked as a C program and is then executed; the output is ignored.

output: The block is compiled and linked as a C program, and is then executed and the output is copied to the output file.

cat: The block is copied to the output file.

The sense of a block test is inverted by prefixing the block label with **no**. If **run**, **preprocess**, **compile**, **link**, **execute**, and **output** blocks are not specified and type is one of the predefined types, then default code templates will be generated and tested. A probe is successful if it exits with status 0. Inside the fail and pass blocks, $m expands to the default macro name for **type** and $v expands to the normalized identifier for **name** (that is, **name** converted to a valid C identifier). Examples of most commonly used predefined types are:

hdr: Checks if #include <name.h> is valid.

sys: Checks if #include <sys/name.h> is valid.

lib: Checks if **name** is a function in the standard libraries.

For example, the following code checks to see if the functions **bcopy()** and/or **memcpy()** are available:

```
lib bcopy,memcpy
```

On an old BSD system, the output of this probe is likely to be:

```
#define _lib_bcopy 1    /* bcopy() in default lib(s) */
```

This can be used to mimic or replace **memcpy** () as follows:

```
#if _lib_bcopy && !_lib_memcpy
#define memcpy(to,from,size) bcopy((from,to,size), (to))
#endif
```

3.2.3   The *iffe* Interpreter

As *iffe* is used in building the base libraries, it is important that the interpreter can be run before any of our tools are built. For this reason, *iffe* is written in the Bourne shell language, which is supported on all known UNIX systems. The *iffe* interpreter has one option. If the first argument is "–", then the probe output is written to the standard output rather than the default **FEATURE**/*name*. The remaining arguments are interpreted as probe statements, where a ":" argument is the statement separator. Typical invocations are:

```
iffe run feature/lib
iffe set cc CC : run feature/stdio.c
```

Queries can also be entered at the shell prompt:

```
iffe - lib,sys socket
```

3.2.4   Discussions

As stated at the start of this section, the portability problem boils down to finding out from a platform exactly which of its features are required and whether such features perform as expected. Any scheme of answering this question based on a broad classification of platforms (for example, BSD vs. SYSV or SPARC vs. MIPS) is doomed to fail. This is mostly because many modern UNIX systems are hybrids. But, even when a required feature is available, a bane of programmers is that its implementation quality can vary greatly from platform to platform. For example, the `mmap()` system call is a good alternative to `read()` for reading disk data on many modern UNIX systems because it avoids a buffer copy. But, on certain platforms, the performance of `mmap()` can be much worse than `read()`. This can make it hard to implement high-quality software, such as the buffered I/O library *sfio*. The *iffe* tool and the accompanying programming style described in this section provide a good solution by enabling programmers to target specific platform features and perform a variety of tests to determine their acceptability. From an organizational point of view, the most important attribute of this approach is that it provides a mechanism to record porting knowledge in a form that is easily shared among software developers.

3.3   Versioning and Viewpathing

3.3.1   Introduction

Two ingredients for the success of the UNIX system for software development are its process model and its file system. The process model makes it easy to connect simple tools together to perform complex tasks. The file system is simple to understand, has relatively few limitations, and encourages the sharing of information. This has led to the creation of a rich set of software development tools, such as, *nmake.*

However, using the UNIX File System for configuration management has several drawbacks. There is no intrinsic capability to store multiple versions of the same file. This has led to the creation of software database management systems, such as SCCS and RCS, to store revisions of each source file by encoding the changes into a file. Because SCCS and RCS are not an integral part of the file system, new commands are needed to first extract the information from the database before using source files. In addition, both SCCS and RCS are not able to capture the relationship between revisions of multiple files. To build a configuration, it is necessary to get a revision for each of the required files.

Several developers may be required to make changes to the software project simultaneously. With the standard UNIX file system, only the last version of the changes will be kept. SCCS and RCS provide for locking of portions of the source database to prevent the same source file from being changed by different developers at the same time. The traditional solution to dealing with concurrent access problems is to build a configuration management system on top of SCCS and RCS. A notable example of such a system is Sablime [Cic88].

Another direction that has become popular recently is to store source code for programs in object-oriented databases. Each language token may be represented as an object within the database and a given configuration of the software can be thought of as a view of the database. Changes to code are database transactions. Special-purpose editors are often provided to trigger database updates and changes are made. There is no need for the *make* or *nmake* utility, because an update to the database triggers the actions needed to keep the object code up to date.

While the object-oriented database approach offers certain advantages, it has some disadvantages. Object-oriented databases are usually tied to a language, which makes them hard to use for projects that use more than one language. Often, documentation must be maintained separately. Object-oriented databases tend to require a lot more disk space than storing source as UNIX files. They often have trouble dealing with source code that is generated. Perhaps the biggest drawback is that these configuration management systems tend to be closed.

We are strong believers in open and extensible systems. Coupled with a powerful tool to build releases, *nmake*, we believe that the advantages to our approach outweigh the benefits of the object-oriented program database approach. On the other hand, configuration management systems, such as Sablime, are too monolithic.

The facilities of *n-DFS*, described in Section 2.5, provide a rich environment to embed a software configuration management system into UNIX-like file systems. Through *n-DFS*, it is possible to handle revisions of the same file directly in the file system name space. It is possible to name configurations and have different users access different configurations simultaneously. The viewpathing feature of *n-DFS* makes it possible to create user views so that users can make changes to the system and test these changes without having to make a complete copy of the code. Finally, *n-DFS* makes it possible to generate file system events that can be handled by YEAST, described in Chapter 9, to provide a level of synchronization and control.

3.3.2   Viewpathing Service

A user view is created by mounting one file tree onto another. The result is that the top file tree now virtually contains the union of files from both trees. It is as though each file in the bottom tree that was not in the top tree was copied to the top tree. The user can now work in this merged top file tree. Only the top layer is writable; all other layers are read-only. So, when the user modifies a file located below on the top layer, the desired file is copied to the top layer before it is accessed. Files from the bottom tree that have the same name relative to the root of the tree as a file on the top tree are obscured. However, files on the layer underneath can be

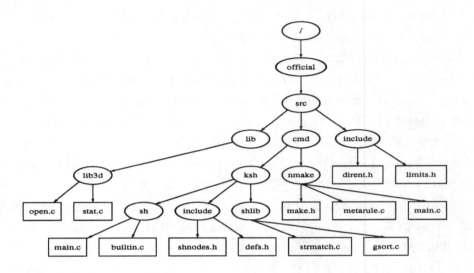

Figure 3.5   Official source.

referenced with the special filename "...". The effect of "..." is to remove the top layer, exposing files that are covered.

Unlike ordinary mounts, these mounts are visible only to the current process and its descendants. Trees are mounted pair-wise. It is possible to mount **a** on **b**, and **b** on **c**, to get viewpathing effects equivalent to setting the **VPATH** environment variable to **a:b:c**, a technique introduced by *build*.

For example, consider a software project where the released source files reside in an official area (see Figure 3.5). After software bugs are found and fixed, but before another release, the changed files are left in a separate directory tree controlled by system testers (see Figure 3.6). To add a new feature or fix a bug, a user creates a *working area* to modify files as shown in Figure 3.7. The user may construct his/her own view of the project by viewpathing the private working area on top of the system tester area, which is, in turn, viewpathed on top of the official area; Figure 3.8 shows the three-dimensional view of the system through the user's working area. The user can then modify and build the system

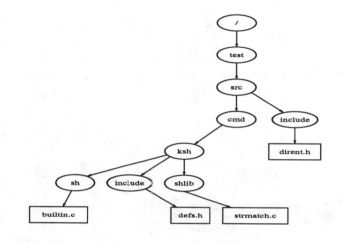

Figure 3.6   Tester's source.

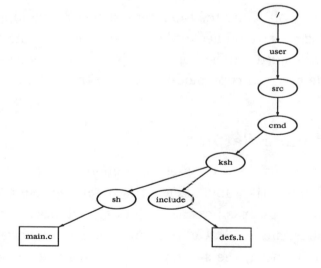

Figure 3.7   User's workspace.

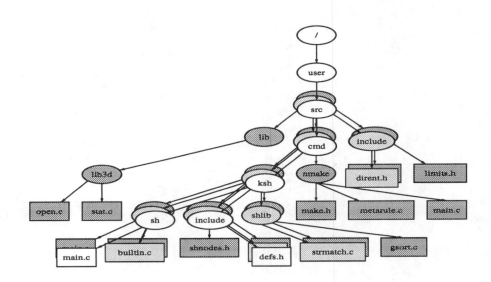

Figure 3.8   Three-dimensional view.

using conventional tools. Only the top layer—the user's working area—is writable. When the user modifies a file located below on the top layer, the desired file is copied to the top layer before it is accessed. After modifications, the user can copy modified files to the system tester area.

3.3.3   Versioning Service

A *version* file is a new type of file used to support multiple *instances* of a logical file, all under the same name. It is organized like a directory, with instances as entries. It is possible to browse instances using regular directory commands, such as *ls*. Unlike regular directories, however, when a version file is referenced, the system returns a reference to one of its instances rather than to the version file itself; it may actually invoke operations to check out the desired instance from the version file. Each instance is named by one or more version names, and users are able to specify search paths of instances on a per-directory basis. We use a byte-oriented, block-move algorithm to compute the delta of an instance

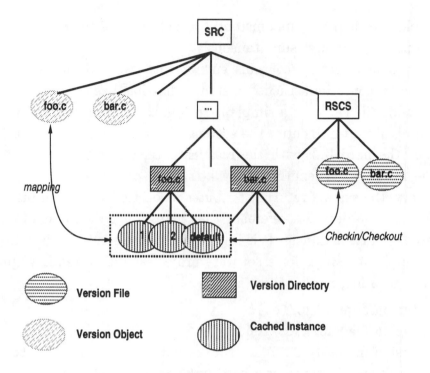

Figure 3.9 Versioning.

related to a common base and to store the delta in the version file. A central server is used to handle checking out (in) instances from (to) the version file using the corresponding delta.

The system contains *version files*, *version directories*, and *version objects*. A version file is implemented as a regular UNIX file, containing a base and sets of delta. When checking in an instance, the system generates a new delta by computing the difference of the instance and the base in the version file, and appends the delta to the end of the version file. The system also stores the instance information: an instance name, file attributes from the system call *stat*, and the predecessor instance name. When checking out an instance, the desired instance is regenerated using the base and the corresponding delta. Original attributes of the instance, such as, ownership, access control, and timestamps are restored. Each version file is append-only and immutable. A newly appended delta replaces the old ones with the same instance name. With this immutable feature, it is easy to handle the case where version files are replicated on multiple sites and multiple instances are checked in to the same version file from different sites simultaneously.

A version directory contains entries with available instance names. Each entry could be a cached instance that has been checked out from the version file early, or a simple hard link to the version file. Whenever accessing a hard-link entry, the system performs check-out operations to replace the hard link with the real instance, and returns the reference of the instance. Whenever listing attributes of entries under a version directory, the system returns attributes associated with each instance.

A version object is a reference that maps a generic name of a logical file to one of its instances. It is implemented as a symbolic link. Consider an example of sources for a software project as illustrated in Figure 3.9. For a logical file, `foo.c`, there are:

- A version object `SRC/foo.c`
- A version file `SRC/RSCS/foo.c`
- A version directory `SRC/.../foo.c` containing instances of `foo.c`, either a cached instance or a hard link to the version file.

The link of the version object `SRC/foo.c` is `../.../foo.c/default` originally, where the last component is dynamically replaced by a user-specified instance name. For example, a user can specify the instance name to access via the command `vmap`:

```
$ vmap  SRC/foo.c  1
```

The system then replaces `default` with 1, and therefore the version object points to `../.../foo.c/1` instead.

3.3.4   Event Notification Service

Many aspects of configuration management can be modeled as the occurrence of events that require additional actions. For example, the upgrade of a library module is an event whose occurrence triggers several actions, such as, rebuilding all systems of which the library is a component. Instead of a daemon polling the file system, *n-DFS* provides an alternative: event notification. Users specify interesting events in the context of system calls. *n-DFS* detects these events and notifies an external server, YEAST (Chapter 9), which, in turn, triggers the proper actions.

4

Tool- and Application-Building Languages

David Korn, John Snyder, and Kiem-Phong Vo

4.1 *ksh*–A Tool-Building Language

4.1.1 Introduction

One common thread among many of the tools described in this book is their use of the shell, *ksh* specifically. The actions in *nmake* (Section 3.1.1) and YEAST (Chapter 9) are *ksh* commands. The *ship* (Section 3.1.4) system is written entirely in *ksh*. The *cia* (Chapter 6) queries are written as *ksh* shell scripts that invoke the C query language command, *cql*, for database access.

A user writing *ksh* scripts can tap into all the runtime facilities offered by *ksh*. In this way, the shell is a service whose purpose is to interpret the script it is sent. *coshell* (see Section 2.2.6) turns this service into a network service by providing a mechanism to invoke shell commands on appropriate machines in a network based on a variety of scheduling constraints. *ksh* is a reusable asset.

In addition to being a reusable asset, *ksh* itself has been built using many of the reusable assets contained in *libast* (see Section 2.2.2). It uses a library for line editing and history that is also reusable. This library has been used with several other interactive tools to provide the same facility to other tools.

ksh uses the portability services provided by *proto* and *iffe* (Section 3.2) to make it highly available. *ksh* runs on virtually all UNIX systems as well as Windows and Windows NT. High availability across a wide variety of platforms fosters reuse, because scripts do not need to be rewritten when moving to a new platform.

This section presents a brief history of UNIX system shells. It then describes how the needs of other tools have contributed to the evolution of the language. After describing how *ksh* is currently being used, we describe some of the significant new features that are in *ksh-93*, the latest version of *ksh*. To help illustrate the potential for reuse, a list of possible extensions for *ksh* is presented. Finally, we describe the pros and cons of using *ksh* as a common scripting language, rather than other scripting languages, such as *awk* [AWK88], *perl* [WS90], or *tcl* [Ous94].

4.1.2   History

The original UNIX system shell was a simple program written by Ken Thompson at AT&T Bell Laboratories as the interface to the new UNIX operating system. It allowed the user to invoke single commands, or to connect commands together by having the output of one command pass through a special file, called a *pipe*, and become input for the next command. The Thompson shell was a command interpreter, not a programming language. While one could put a sequence of commands in a file and run them, that is, create a shell script, there was no support for traditional language facilities, such as flow control, variables, and functions. When the need for some flow control surfaced, the commands /bin/if and /bin/goto were created. These were separate commands, not part of the shell itself. The /bin/if command evaluated its first argument and, if true, executed the remainder of the line. The /bin/goto command read the script from its standard input looking for the given label, and set the seek position at that location. When the shell returned from invoking /bin/goto, it read the next line from standard input from the location set by /bin/goto.

Unlike most earlier systems, the Thompson shell command language was a user-level program that did not have any special privileges. This meant that new shells could be created by any user, which led to a succession of improved shells. In the mid-1970s, John Mashey at AT&T Bell Laboratories extended the Thompson shell by adding commands so that it could be used as a primitive programming language. He made commands, such as `if` and `goto` built-ins, for improved performance, and he added shell variables.

At the same time, Steve Bourne at AT&T Bell Laboratories wrote a version of the shell using programming language techniques. A rich set of structured flow control primitives was part of the language, and the shell processed commands by building a parse tree and then evaluating the tree. Because of the rich flow control primitives, there was no need for a `goto` command. Bourne also introduced the notion of a *here document*, whereby the contents of a file are inserted directly into the script for processing by the shell. One of the often overlooked contributions of the Bourne shell is that it helped to eliminate the distinction between programs and shell scripts. Earlier versions of the shell read input from standard input, making it impossible to use shell scripts as parts of a pipeline.

By the late 1970s, each of these shells had sizable followings within AT&T Bell Laboratories. The two shells were not compatible, leading to a division as to which should become the standard shell. Steve Bourne and John Mashey argued their respective cases at three successive UNIX user group meetings. Between meetings, each enhanced its shell to have the functionality available in the other. A committee was set up to choose a standard shell. It chose the Bourne shell as the standard.

At the time of these "shell wars," we needed to build a form entry system. We decided to build a form interpreter, rather than writing a separate program for each form. Instead of inventing our own new language, we were able to modify the Bourne shell by adding built-in commands and use it as our form scripting language. We added a built-in to read form template description files and create shell variables, and a built-in to output shell variables through a form mask. We also added a built-in named *let* to do arithmetic using a small subset of the C language expression syntax. An array facility was added to handle columns of data on the screen. Shell functions were added to make it easier to write modular code, since our shell scripts tended to be larger than most shell scripts at that time. Because the Bourne shell was written in an Algol-like variant of C, we converted our version of it to a more standard K&R version of C. We removed the restriction that prevented I/O redirections for built-in commands, and added `echo`, `pwd`, and `test` as built-in commands for improved performance. Finally, we added a capability to run a command as a coprocess so that the command that processed the user-entered data and accessed the database could be written as a separate process.

At the same time, at the University of California at Berkeley, Bill Joy created a new shell called C shell. Like the Mashey shell, it was implemented as a command interpreter, not a programming language. While the C shell contained flow control constructs, shell variables, a better command interface, and an arithmetic facility, its primary contribution was job control. It introduced the idea of a history list and an editing facility so that users didn't have to retype commands that they had entered incorrectly.

The first version of *ksh* was created from the form scripting language by removing some of the form-specific code and adding features from the C shell, such as history, aliases, and job control. In 1982, the UNIX System V shell was converted to K&R C, `echo` and `pwd` were made built-in commands, and the ability to define and use shell functions was added. Unfortunately, the System V syntax for function definitions was different than that of *ksh*. In order to maintain compatibility with the System V shell and preserve backward compatibility, *ksh* was modified to accept either syntax.

The popular inline editing features (*vi* and *emacs* mode) of *ksh* were created by two software developers at AT&T Bell Laboratories. Each had independently modified the Bourne shell to add these features and both were in organizations that wanted to use *ksh* only if *ksh* had their respective inline editor. When it became clear that line-editing was not going to move into the terminal driver, both line-editing modes were integrated into *ksh*. Each of them was made optional so that they could be disabled on systems that provided editing as part of the terminal interface.

As more and more software developers at AT&T switched to *ksh*, it became the *de facto* standard shell at AT&T. As developers left AT&T to go elsewhere, external demand for *ksh* led to AT&T making *ksh* source code available to external customers via the UNIX System Toolchest, an electronic software distribution system. For a one-time fixed cost, any company could buy rights to distribute an unlimited number of *ksh* binaries. Most UNIX system providers have taken advantage of this and now ship *ksh* as part of their systems. The wider availability of *ksh* contributed significantly to its success.

As use of *ksh* grew, the need for more functionality became apparent. Like the original shell, earlier uses of *ksh* were primarily for setting up processes and handling I/O redirection similar to that of the original shell. Newer uses required more string handling capabilities to reduce the number of process creations. The 1988 version of *ksh*, the one most widely distributed at the time this was written, extended the pattern-matching capability of *ksh* to be comparable to that of the regular expression matching found in *sed* and *grep*.

In spite of its wide availability, *ksh* source is not in the public domain. This has led to the creation of *bash*, the Bourne again shell, by the Free Software Foundation, and *pdksh*, a public-domain version of *ksh*. Unfortunately, neither is compatible with *ksh*.

In 1992, the IEEE POSIX 1003.2 and ISO/IEC 9945-2 shell and utilities standard [IEE93] was ratified. This standard describes a shell language that was based on the System V shell and the 1988 version of *ksh*. The 1993 version of *ksh* is a superset of the POSIX shell standard. With few exceptions, it is backward-compatible with the 1988 version of *ksh* as well.

The *awk* command was developed in the late 1970s by Al Aho, Peter Weinberger, and Brian Kernighan of AT&T Bell Laboratories as a report-generation language. A second generation *awk* developed in the early 1980s was a more general-purpose scripting language but lacked some shell features. It became common to combine shell and *awk* to write script applications. For many applications, this had the disadvantage of being slow because of the time consumed in each invocation of *awk*. The *perl* language, developed by Larry Wall in the mid 1980s, is an attempt to combine the capabilities of shell and *awk* into a single language. Because *perl* is freely available and performs better than combined shell and *awk*, *perl* has a large user community, primarily at universities.

The need for a reusable scripting language was recognized in the late 1980s by John Ousterhout at the University of California at Berkeley. He invented an extensible scripting language named *tcl*, an acronym for tool control language. Rather than being a command, *tcl* is written as a library that can be embedded into any command to give it scripting capability. The *tcl* language has gained a sizable following, primarily because of a window programming interface that is provided by an adjunct *tk*. With *tk*, it is possible to write X Window System applications as *tcl* scripts.

At the same time as *tk* was invented, Steve Pendergrast from the UNIX Systems Laboratory created *wksh*, a program that extends *ksh* for X Window System programming. The extensions were added as a collection of built-in commands to create and manipulate widgets. Callback functions are written as shell functions. A version of *ksh* for X Window System programming similar to *wksh*, *xksh* was developed by Moses Ling at AT&T and is used in several applications. While *wksh* and *xksh* are excellent examples of reuse, they also created new demands on *ksh* and were a major influence for the new features that have been added to *ksh-93*. A new windowing desktop shell, *dtksh*, based on *ksh-93* and *wksh*, has been developed by Novell and will be part of the Common Desktop Environment (CDE) that was defined by Common Operating System Environment (COSE).

4.1.3   How *ksh* Evolved for Reuse

As mentioned in the previous section, *ksh* was created as part of a form entry system. The intent was to extend and reuse the shell language. Features initially added for the form application were useful in other contexts and became part of the language. In this section, we show how the needs of other tools and applications led to new *ksh* features, which enhanced its reusability.

The C language library routines, `system()` and `popen()`, have made it easy to use shell services. These routines are the method that tools, such as *make*, use to execute each line in an action block.

While this approach is simple and often adequate, it has some drawbacks. First, executing a command in this manner has traditionally required at least two processes to be created: the shell and the command(s) that are invoked by the shell. Recent versions of *ksh* have been able to optimize this by recognizing when it is possible to overlay *ksh* by the command given as an argument to `system()`, and eliminating a process creation.

A second drawback to this approach is that each shell invocation is separate so that no state information can be carried across invocations. An alternative C to *ksh* interface can be created by thinking of the shell as a service. Rather than invoking `system()` for each command invocation, a shell service is invoked that is capable of running one or more commands. Each command is carried out by sending a message to the shell containing the command that needs to be executed. Because the shell runs as a server process, rather than having to reinitialize for each message, it is able to maintain state between messages.

The approach of using *ksh* as a service was first used in the original version of *nmake*. A library interface was written to make it easy to use this interface without having to understand and deal with difficulties, such as the handling of signals. The implementation of this library led to one simple modification to *ksh*. The *make* program traditionally uses the -e option when invoking the shell to cause the current action to terminate when an error was encountered. The current *nmake* can continue to run and may perform additional actions. To simulate this behavior using *ksh* as a shell service required that there was some means to terminate an action without terminating the *ksh*. A trap named ERR was added to *ksh* for this purpose.

Several major benefits resulted from this approach. First, for large makefiles, the memory size for *nmake* may be large, and the time to *fork* *nmake* to run an action might not be negligible. Because there was state, it was possible to send functions to *ksh* and have *ksh* do more of the work. For example, the execution trace of commands with *nmake* is performed by *ksh*, not by *nmake*. With the server model, it is easy to see that it is better to send a complete action block at a time, rather than running each command separately as old *make* does. This change makes it easy to write complex action blocks that allow any possible *ksh* command. The line-at-a-time approach does not allow *here documents* to be used in action blocks.

Perhaps the biggest benefit to the new interface is that parallel execution is easy to add. The reason for this is simple. The shell already knows how to run commands in parallel; just put an & after the command. By having the library send a block, such as { *command ;* } & reply $! to the *ksh* server, the process that uses the service can continue to compute as the shell is carrying out its commands.

Thinking of the shell as a reusable service led to the creation of a network shell service, *coshell*, which is described in Section 2.2.6. The idea behind *coshell* is to have a server, which looks like a shell to each of its clients, but which carries out its work by distributing the commands it receives to shells that it keeps running at different hosts in the network.

To implement this, it is necessary for the shell to be able to send its standard output and its standard error back to the process that invoked the service. However, *ksh* had no way to connect its output to a network socket or stream. Rather than create a special server program that would have to be present on each machine, a simple extension to *ksh* that enabled it to connect to a network socket was added. The code, about 25 lines in C, enabled a script to make a *tcp* or *udp* connection to a socket, using the existing shell redirection operators. *ksh* checks for filenames of the form **/dev/tcp/***machine/port* or **/dev/udp/***machine/port* and makes a socket connection, rather than trying to open the given file. Through this mechanism, the *coshell* server is able to establish network connections to shells whose standard output and standard error are redirected to the appropriate places. See Section 2.2.7 for additional details of connect-stream syntax.

This simple change, driven by the needs of a new tool, is typical of the evolutionary changes to *ksh*. The change, while necessary to the original tool that required it, is useful in its own right. Because of the change required by coshell, it is easy to write shell scripts as clients to existing services, particularly when the service is line-oriented.

Another example of a tool that has led to a change to *ksh* is *n-DFS*, described in Section 2.5. With *n-DFS*, each process can set up a name space by invoking mount(). The mount() calls affect the current process and child processes, but do not affect the parent process. Without a change to *ksh*, there would be no way to modify the *n-DFS* services in the current shell environment. A similar situation exists with cd, which is why cd is a built-in command. The built-in commands vpath and vmap were added to handle the original *3DFS* services of creating views and setting version mapping. These commands were extended for *n-DFS* so that all mount() operations could be invoked through this interface. Adding these commands to *ksh* solved the immediate problem, but it also made it clear that it would be useful to have a mechanism to add new built-in commands to *ksh* without having to modify the language. This was one of the many changes described below that were made for *ksh-93*.

Many of the changes for *ksh-93* have been driven by the needs of windows based programming. Here again, the changes that have been added to meet these needs are also usable by many of the other tools that use *ksh* services. These changes are described below.

4.1.4   How *ksh* Is Used

The most frequent use of *ksh* is as an interactive command language. In this context, most users learn the basics of redirection and pipelines. The most important feature for this use is command-line editing and history interaction. A second common use of the shell is for writing scripts that combine several commands into a single command. These scripts are usually placed into the user's private bin directory, and are customized to the individuals needs and usually not designed for reuse.

A third common use of the shell is as an embedded scripting language. In addition to library calls popen() and system(), tools such as *make* and *cron*, have used shell as their specification language. *nmake* and YEAST also use *ksh* this way. A fourth use of *ksh* is for writing administrative scripts. Since all UNIX systems are delivered with scripts written in the shell language, system administrators need to be able to read and write scripts to do their job. The most important features for these applications are the ability to generate and test files and to invoke pipelines.

A fifth use for *ksh* programming is for the generation of front ends. *ksh* provides a coprocess mechanism that makes it easy to run a process that is connected to a shell script via pipes. The script interacts with a user, and then generates commands to send to the coprocess to carry out most of the work. With *wksh* and *dtksh*, the front ends can be graphical.

A sixth use of *ksh* is for program generation. Scripts can be written that produce code for compiled languages, such as C and C++, or for script languages, such as *ksh*. For this use, the ability to handle arbitrary strings and patterns is essential. The *here document* feature is well suited for program templates, as used by *iffe* (Section 3.2).

The final use for shell programming is for writing programs. In this context, the shell does virtually all the work without relying heavily on other utilities. This is the area in which shells have traditionally been weakest and the reason that languages, such as *perl* and *tcl*, were invented. The new version of *ksh*, *ksh-93*, is intended to eliminate this weakness.

4.1.5   New Features in *ksh-93*

ksh-93 is the first major revision to *ksh* in five years. It was revamped to meet the needs of a new generation of tools and graphical interfaces. Much of the impetus for *ksh-93* was *wksh*, which allows graphical user interfaces to be written in shell, just as *tk* allows one to write graphical user interfaces in *tcl*. The intent was to provide most of the *awk* functionality as part of the language, as does *perl*. Because *ksh-93* maintains backward compatibility with earlier versions of *ksh*, older *ksh* and System V shell scripts should continue to run with *ksh-93*. This section describes several important new features introduced in *ksh-93*.

4.1.5.1   Floating Point Arithmetic

Applications that required floating point arithmetic no longer have to invoke a command, such as *awk* or *bc*. The comma operator, the ?: operator, and the pre- and post-increment operators were added. Thus, *ksh-93* can evaluate virtually all ANSI-C arithmetic expressions. An arithmetic `for` command, nearly identical to the `for` statement in C, was added, as were functions from the math library.

4.1.5.2   Associative Arrays

Earlier versions of *ksh* had one-dimensional indexed arrays. The subscripts for an indexed array are arithmetic expressions that are evaluated to compute the subscript index. Associative arrays use the same syntax as indexed arrays, but the subscripts are strings; they are useful for creating associative tables. However, because the list of subscripts is not easily determined, a shell expansion was added to give the list of subscripts for an array. Because associative arrays reuse the same syntax as indexed arrays, it is easy to modify scripts that use indexed arrays to use associative arrays.

4.1.5.3 Additional String-Processing Capabilities

Shell patterns in *ksh-93* are far more extensive than in the Bourne shell, having the full power of extended regular expressions found in *awk*, *perl*, and *tcl*. In addition, *ksh-93* has new expansion operators for substring generation and pattern replacement. Substring operations can be applied to aggregate objects, such as arrays.

4.1.5.4 Hierarchical Namespace for Shell Variables

One of the lessons learned from the UNIX system is that a hierarchical name space is better than a flat name space. With *ksh-93*, the separator for levels of the hierarchy is . (dot). It is possible to create compound data elements (data structures) in *ksh-93*. Name references were added to make it easier to write shell functions that take the name of a shell variable as an argument, rather than its value. With earlier versions of *ksh*, it was necessary to use *eval* frequently inside a function that took the name of a variable as an argument.

Shell variables in *ksh-93* have also been generalized so that they can behave like active objects rather than simple storage cells. This was done by allowing a set of discipline functions to be associated with each variable. A discipline function is defined like any other function, except that the name for a discipline function is formed by using the variable name, followed by a . (dot), and the discipline name. Each variable can have discipline functions defined that get invoked when the variable is referenced or assigned a new value. This allows variables to be active rather than passive. At the C library level, variables can be created that allow for any number of discipline functions to be associated with a variable. These functions can be invoked in an application-specific way: An X Window System extension can associate each widget with a shell variable, and the user can write callback functions as discipline functions.

4.1.5.5 Formatted Output

One of the most annoying aspects of shell programming is that the behavior of the `echo` command differs on various systems. The lack of agreement of the behavior on `echo` in the POSIX standard led to the requirement of `printf`. In *ksh-93*, `printf` is a built-in command that conforms to the ANSI-C standard definition with a few extensions. The two most important extensions are the `%P` format conversion which treats the argument to be converted as a regular expression, and converts it to a shell pattern; and the `%q` format conversion which prints the argument quoted so that it can be input to *ksh* as a literal string. These two simple extensions make it much easier to correctly write scripts that generate scripts.

The implementation of `printf` relies heavily on the *sfio* library of *libast*, which allows extension to the underlying `sfprintf()` function. *ksh-93* does not have to interpret the format string.

4.1.5.6 Runtime Built-in Commands

With *ksh-93*, a user can add built-in commands at runtime on systems that support dynamic linking of code. Built-in commands have much less overhead to invoke, and unless they produce side effects, they are indistinguishable from nonbuilt-in commands. Each built-in command uses the same argument signature as `main()`, and returns a value that is its exit status. Complete applications can be written in *ksh-93* by writing a library that gets loaded into *ksh-93* for the application-specific portion.

To give an example of the performance improvement that arises from having a command built in, the following script takes roughly 20 seconds to run on a Silicon Graphics workstation when `cat` is not a built-in command, versus 0.2 seconds when `cat` is a built-in.

```
for ((i=0; i < 1000; i++))
do    cat
done < /dev/null
```

4.1.5.7   Support for Internationalization

The earlier version of *ksh* was 8-bit transparent and had a compile option to handle multibyte character sets. The behavior of *ksh-93* is determined by the locale. In addition to the earlier support for internationalization, *ksh-93* handles:

- Character classes for pattern matching: One can specify matching for all alphabetic characters in a locale-independent way.
- Character equivalence classes for pattern matching: One can specify matching for all characters that have the same primary collation weight.
- Collation: The locale determines the order in which files and strings are sorted.
- String translation: One can designate strings that can be looked up in a locale-specific dictionary at runtime by preceding the string with a $; for example, $"hello world".
- Decimal point: The character representing the decimal point for floating point numbers is determined by the current locale.

4.1.5.8   Usability as a Library

ksh-93 has been rewritten so that it can be used as a library and called from within a C program. This makes it possible to add *ksh*-compatible scripting capabilities to any command, just like one can with *tcl*.

4.1.6   Requirements for a Reusable Scripting Language

The primary requirement for any language is that it enables one to easily specify what one wants. Also, a scripting language should be able to run without requiring a separate compilation system. Since strings are a basic element of any general-purpose programming language, the language must be able to handle arbitrary-length strings automatically.

We list the additional requirements that we had for a general-purpose scripting language.

A general-purpose scripting language should be simple to learn. There is no easy way to measure how simple a language is to learn, but the time to learn a language can be reduced by making the language similar to one that users already know. For instance, arithmetic computations should use familiar notation and operators should have conventional precedences.

The language should be widely available and well documented in order to achieve wide usage. Programmers do not want to spend time learning a language that will not be available to them wherever they work. Also, because no single document is right for everyone, there should be several documents for different types of users.

In addition to performing arithmetic, a script language should have string and pattern matching capabilities. The details of memory management of variable sized objects should be handled by the language, not by the user. Many applications require the handling of aggregate objects. Even though very high level languages require fewer lines of code, real world applications are likely to be large; thus, a good script language needs to have a method to write procedures or functions that have automatic variables and that can return arbitrary values.

Applications coded in the language should have performance comparable to that of the application if it were written in a lower level language. This means that the overhead for interpretation must be amortized by the useful work of the application. The lower the overhead for interpretation, the larger the class of applications for which the language will be useful. Some applications are short-lived and will be dominated by the time they take to start up.

For many applications, the language should interface simply with the operating system. It should be possible to open or create files and network connections, and to read and write data to these objects. It must be possible to extend the language in application-specific domains to achieve high reuse.

Finally, the language should make it easy to write portable applications. One should be able to write scripts that do not depend on the underlying operating system, file system, or locale.

4.1.7   Pros and Cons of Using *ksh*

There are several advantages to using *ksh*. Many of these stem from the fact that *ksh* is upward-compatible with the Bourne shell. This reduces the learning curve and makes it possible to reuse the many thousands of existing scripts. Because of the large number of Bourne shell users, there is a large community who already know how to use *ksh*.

Because *ksh* is compatible with the Bourne shell, there is no limit to the length of variable names, the length of strings, or the number of items in a list. File manipulation and pipeline creation are simple, and *here documents* allow script applications to be packaged into a single file.

Compatibility with the Bourne shell makes *ksh* a better interactive language than most other high level scripting languages. Having the same language for interactive use as for programming has several advantages. First of all, it reduces the learning curve since everything learned for interactive use can be used in programs and vice versa. Secondly, interactive debugging is simpler since it uses the same language as do the programs.

Using *ksh*, rather than the Bourne shell, has many additional advantages other than improved performance. The inline editing feature makes *ksh* friendlier to interact with. Since the inline editing feature can be enabled by scripts that are read from the terminal, interactively debugging *ksh* scripts is easier.

The Bourne shell is notorious for its lack of arithmetic facility. The **expr** command is both slow and awkward. The string processing capabilities are inferior to languages that are based on regular expressions. *ksh* uses ANSI-C style arithmetic and a pattern matching notation that is equivalent to regular expressions.

ksh has a better function mechanism than the Bourne shell or POSIX shell. Large applications are difficult to write with the Bourne shell or POSIX shell because of an inadequate function facility. Bourne shell and POSIX shell functions do not allow local variables. In addition to allowing local variables, *ksh* allows functions to be linked into an application when they are first referenced, making it possible to write reusable function libraries. *ksh* is also more suitable for larger applications because it has better debugging facilities.

One advantage of using *ksh* is that it has been around for several years and has a large user community. The result is that *ksh* is well documented. There are several books on *ksh*, including [BK89], [BK95], [Olc91], and [Ros93].

There are some drawbacks to using a Bourne shell-compatible shell as a programming language. One drawback, the unfortunate choices in the quoting rules, makes it harder to write scripts that correctly handle strings with special characters in them. The use in *ksh* of the $(...) syntax in place of `...` is a big improvement that allows easy nesting of command substitution. Another Bourne shell mistake that remains is that ANSI-C sequences are not expanded inside double quoted strings. This makes it hard to enter non-printable characters in a script without sacrificing readability. It also leads to the different behaviors of the `echo` command on different systems. With *ksh-93*, any single quoted string preceded by $ is processed using the ANSI-C string rules.

A second problem with using a Bourne shell compatible language is that field splitting and filename generation are done on every command word. In purely string processing applications, this is not the desired default, thus these operations are better left to functions as with *perl* and *tcl*. With *ksh* it is possible to disable field splitting and/or filename generation on a per function basis, which makes it possible to eliminate this common source of errors.

A third drawback is that scripts depend on all the programs they invoke, and these programs may not behave in the same way on all systems. In addition, there are variances in the versions of the shell that exist on different systems. To overcome this obstacle, we have written versions of many of the standard utilities that we ship along with *ksh*. The scripts that are needed to build *ksh* and these standard utilities are written in the Bourne shell, and use features of the Bourne shell known to exist in all implementations so that they are easy to port.

A fourth drawback is performance. On many UNIX systems, the time to invoke command that is not built-in is about 100 times more than the time to run a built-in command. This means that, to achieve good performance, it is necessary to minimize the number of processes that a script creates. To overcome this problem, *ksh* has much more built-in functionality so that more operations can be performed without creating a separate process.

4.1.8 Alternatives

At the time most of the tools described in this book were developed, there were few options for choosing a scripting language. The only widely available alternative for scripting was *awk*, and a standard version of *awk* was not widely available. In addition, *awk* does not have some of the shell capabilities. By the time the *perl* language became available, *ksh* already had many of the *perl* facilities as built-ins. In addition, because of the syntax, many users find *perl* harder to read and write than *ksh*. We have seen several examples of scripts written in *ksh* that are about 10 percent shorter than in *perl* and have approximately the same performance.

The *tcl* language has a somewhat simpler syntax than *ksh*. However, because most of the script isn't expanded until used, it is difficult to find certain syntax errors until runtime. *tcl* doesn't appear to offer any functional advantages over *ksh-93*.

One major advantage to *perl* and *tcl* is that they are available as freeware, whereas *ksh* is not. However, since our focus has been software development within AT&T, this has not been a problem. Since *dtksh* is a standard part of CDE, the Common Desktop Environment, interpreters for *ksh-93* scripts are more likely to be installed on the machines than *perl* or *tcl*.

4.1.9 Possible Reuse Extensions

In this section, we describe several extensions that could be written for *ksh* and added at runtime. The intent of this list is to demonstrate how *ksh* can be reused.

4.1.9.1 Graph Drawing

In Section 11.2, we describe the *lefty* language that is used as an interactive tool with *dot* as a coprocess to perform graph layouts. While *lefty* is an excellent language for this purpose, one might ask why not use *ksh* instead? Had the new features in *ksh-93* been available at the time *lefty* was first created, it would have been a logical choice. We are considering creating a runtime extension for *ksh-93* that will enable *dotty* applications to be written in *ksh* rather than in *lefty*.

4.1.9.2   Writing Servers

A second possible extension is a connection-stream library (see Section 2.2.7) that would make it simple to write servers in *ksh*. The addition of **/dev/tcp** ... and **/dev/udp** ... with redirection already allows clients to be written as *ksh* scripts. A built-in command could be added to *advertise* the service and to associate this service with a variable. Callback functions that handle message events could be written as discipline functions for this variable. A second built-in command would then process events received by the server and invoke the appropriate discipline function. To write servers of *n-DFS*, it is necessary to process *n-DFS* protocol messages. A built-in command can be added for this purpose.

4.1.9.3   Persistence

A built-in command could be added that declares that a portion of the variable name space of a script be persistent. The built-in would take a second argument that maps this store onto the file system. Each assignment to a variable under this part of the variable name space would also cause the file system to be updated.

4.1.9.4   Object-oriented Database Manipulation

Built-in commands can be added to read and write objects stored in an object-oriented database. The objects can be represented as shell variables, and the methods as shell discipline functions.

4.1.10   Conclusion

ksh has proven to be a good choice as a scripting language. It has the capabilities of *perl* and *tcl*, yet it is upward-compatible with the Bourne shell. *ksh* scripts of sizes up to 25,000 lines have been written for production use. Because it uses the libraries described in Section 2.2.2, *ksh* is very portable. This means that *ksh* scripts are very portable. Finally, because *ksh* is extensible, new, reusable components are likely to be implemented as *ksh* libraries.

Finally, because *ksh* is extensible, new reusable components are likely to be implemented as *ksh* libraries. Extensions for graphical user interface programming provided by *dtksh* are likely to be widely available. Additionally, it may be possible to use *ksh* with *tk* for graphical user interface programming. For a detailed description of the new features in KornShell the reader is referred to the second edition of the KornShell book [BK95].

4.2 EASEL–An Application-Building Language

4.2.1 Introduction

A major class of applications are so-called end-user applications, which are systems usable by users who are not very sophisticated in certain aspects of computing. This section focuses on the End-User Application System Encoding Language, EASEL, a language and system to write end-user applications based on interactive constructs, such as windows, forms, menus, and hypertexts. Similar to *ksh* discussed in the last section, EASEL is built on top of other reusable assets discussed in Chapter 2: *curses*, *libdict*, *sfio* and *vmalloc*. In fact, as we shall discuss later, these libraries grew along with EASEL's development.

Over the past ten years, hundreds of projects in AT&T have used EASEL, including several current network management products, each supporting hundreds of users daily. Because of its *curses* heritage, EASEL is character-based. Even with the advance of bit-mapped graphics, for many cases, such as offices with expensive embedded equipment, this is still a desirable solution. However, EASEL's internal design separates high-level interactive constructs from display manipulations. The execution of high-level constructs is negotiated by a display library that, in turn, calls lower-level display functions, such as *curses*. Thus, with some additional work on the display library, EASEL can be made to use other screen-handling packages, such as the *X Window System* [Nye90].

The remainder of this section discusses the challenges in building end-user applications; how EASEL meets such challenges; the current state of the EASEL language; how its approach to system construction encourages software reuse; how language macros help build a higher abstraction level;

some experiences in building end-user applications with EASEL; and some of our own experiences in building reusable software tools.

4.2.2   Challenges in Building End-user Applications

An end-user is a user who needs to perform some computing functions but may not be well-acquainted with the underlying theories and mechanics. In this sense, even an expert computer user can be an end-user in some application domain. An end-user application is a software system designed to be used by end-users. As such, the primary characteristic of an end-user system is an interface that is easy to use, directly addresses users' needs, and hides any complexity in the solution methods. As computing techniques become more diverse and complex while the cost of computing machinery becomes cheaper, the market for end-user applications gets larger. This is particularly true in business computing, where combinations of techniques from networking, databases, statistical analyses, equation-solving, and graphics are routinely required.

Though computing techniques can be complex, there is a multitude of high-quality software tools readily available to solve such problems. From a system-construction point of view, it is desirable to take advantage of such tools in building a new application. Coupled with the requirement of a good user interface, the main challenges in building an end-user application are:

- Designing a system architecture that maps closely to users' needs.
- Building an interface that reflects that architecture.
- Leveraging as much as possible from existing software tools in implementation.

As successful applications often live long and beget others, additional challenges are to ensure that a system is easily evolvable, and to grow the pool of reusable software tools as systems are built. A sign of a successful software development organization is its ability to build families of applications quickly and still provide good maintenance support. This is possible only if:

- The system construction method encourages building reusable tools.

Design Programming	User Interface	Forms, Menus, Text
	System Structure	Tasks and Subtasks
Computation Programming	Computational Functions	Application-Specific Code
	Data Architecture	Application-Specific Data Types

Figure 4.1 Interactive End-User Systems Architecture

- Enough characteristics of an application family can be abstracted into reusable templates.
- A means exists to help the coding and maintenance of such templates.

4.2.3   End-user System Architecture

To see how EASEL helps to build an end-user system, we need to understand the components that comprise such a system. The logical structure of an end-user system can be divided into four layers [Vo90], as shown in Figure 4.1. The top two layers represent *Design Programming*, that is, programming activities focusing on the user interface and high-level tasks as seen from the user's point of view. The lower two layers represent *Computation Programming*, that is, activities focusing on how the high-level tasks are to be implemented and with what data structures.

The *User Interface* layer allows users to manipulate the systems using well-defined and easy-to-use steps. A major function of this layer is to hide all differences and idiosyncrasies in the interfaces of underlying computing tools and techniques. An EASEL application builds this layer using menus, forms, and hypertexts to provide an active interface that guides users in taking appropriate computational steps.

The *System Structure* defines a task partition and relationships among tasks. In the EASEL framework, the design process of an end-user system begins with identification of tasks and subtasks as seen from the user's perspective. The high-level tasks are mapped to objects known as *frames*, which are interconnected in a *frame network*. Each frame defines all user dialogs appropriate to the task, and prescriptions for computing methods necessary to carry out that task. Dialogs can cause transitions to other frames in the frame network, or induce certain low-level computations. For example, a simple electronic-mail application might consist of the following tasks:

- Getting a list of users
- Picking addressees from the user list
- Filling out a mail form
- Sending the mail

Each of these tasks maps to a frame that defines:

- Its own set of relevant parameters
- Mechanisms to obtain the parameters (from the user, from other frames, by running other programs, and so on)
- Appropriate commands to drive lower-level computational processes (such as calling a C function, retrieval from a database, and so on)

Thus, frames focus on high-level activities required to perform a given task. Actual computations are performed at a lower level by invoking applications code, utilities, and other packages.

The *Computational Functions* layer consists of utilities and application-specific code embodying the computational methods to access, transform, and generate the data necessary to accomplish the end-user's tasks as requested. The EASEL language provides for string manipulation, mathematical operations, file input/output, and event handling. In addition, there are several language mechanisms to execute application-specific code that may be in C or some interpretive languages, such as the Korn-Shell [BK89] or `awk` [AWK88].

The *Data Architecture* layer defines the types of data to be manipulated, along with their storage and access methods. Specific data types depend on the application and the tools used to perform the computational functions. Data types may be tuned to support, facilitate, and optimize execution of algorithms and methods at the computational level. Examples include EASEL variables, C and C++ data types and structures, data for relational and object-oriented databases, as well as data types required by specific packages, such as statistical or queuing packages.

The four-layer architecture points out some useful insights on reusability in some broad categories of tools. Traditional UNIX tools are often designed to do single tasks that, in many cases, embody powerful data structures and algorithms. Since their interfaces are geared toward the specific computing methods being implemented, they are not easily usable by end users, although they are immensely reusable. At the other end of the spectrum, many screen-oriented applications based on screen libraries, such as *curses* [Arn84, Vo85], *X*, and various spreadsheets or database packages, are easy to use but offer little reuse, because the computational methods are too intertwined with the implementation of other parts of the system. EASEL bridges this *reuse gap* between general-purpose but hard-to-use tools and application-specific but easy-to-use software.

EASEL's approach to system construction can be summed up as that of *separating Design Programming from Computational Programming*. The EASEL language focuses on expressing the high-level design of a system, including its user interface and task partition. Most computational details in the lower two layers are left out at this level, but enough of the interface to appropriate software components can be specified. In this way, tool reuse is naturally a component of the EASEL's system construction method. As we shall see later, by using a language tool for program design, EASEL enables the reuse of certain high-level tasks, just as software tools improve computational reuse.

4.2.4 EASEL Language for Building End-user Systems

The EASEL programming language is block-structured, where the block types map to certain high-level activities. Some blocks define user interface components and such tasks as:

- `{frame`   – A high-level task
- `{context`   – Grouping of related activities
- `{menu`   – Selections to be decided by users
- `{question`   – A group of questions is a form
- `{write`   – Display text to screen

Other blocks and statements define such computations as:

- `{action`   – Runs the enclosed shell script
- `{process`   – Runs named cooperating UNIX process and sends enclosed text to its standard input
- `~Ccall`   – Calls the named C function
- `~call ~goto ~overlay ~return` – Transition among frames
- `~evglobal ~evlocal`   – Event handling
- File input and output
- String handling
- Mathematical operations and functions

Other language statements provide for managing the scope of variables, manipulating the runtime UNIX process environment, key bindings and macros, and file input/output. Another group of statements is used to modify default display attributes, such as window locations, border styles, colors, and so on.

EASEL variables need not be declared and are initialized as empty strings. Most operations, including those requiring communicating with external processes or subroutines, result in string values. However, in cases where numerical values are required, the mathematical assignment statement `:=` can be used to do arithmetical and other mathematical computations.

EASEL applications are constructed in a network of frames. Each frame is defined in a frame block:

```
{frame  FrameID  ~arg1 ~arg2 ...
   ....
}f
```

Each frame has its own name or frame identifier, may accept arguments, may contain statements and other nested blocks, and may return values to its caller. EASEL variable names (and keywords) begin with the ˜ (tilde) character.

Composite blocks provide grouping of statements and nested blocks:

```
{context   (entry):(exit)
    . . . .
}c
```

Control flow as exemplified above is directed via (*entry*) and (*exit*) conditions. A block or statement is executed only if its (*entry*) condition is true; control loops through the block or statement until its (*exit*) condition is satisfied. An omitted, or null, condition is taken as true.

Rather than examining the EASEL programming language in detail, we will illustrate how to build a system with EASEL using a small example.

4.2.4.1   An EASEL *email* Application

An electronic-mail application serves as a small but realistic example. The main tasks of the application consist of:

- Getting a list of users
- Asking the user to select addressees
- Filling out a mail form
- Sending the mail

The design of the frame network for such an *email* application might then look like Figure 4.2.

Following is the EASEL code for the top level `email` frame. Line 1 begins a frame block for frame `email`. Line 2 calls frame `users` to get a list of users that is assigned to variable ˜`users`. Line 3 calls frame `select` with argument ˜`users` to ask user to make selections that will be assigned to variable ˜`to`. Line 4 calls frame `mform` with argument ˜`to`. This frame will return three values to be assigned to ˜`to`, ˜`subj`, and ˜`mesg`. Line 5 begins with an entry condition that is true only when both ˜`to` and ˜`mesg` are not null; if that is the case, then frame `msend` is called to send the message to the selected people. Line 6 denotes the end of the frame block.

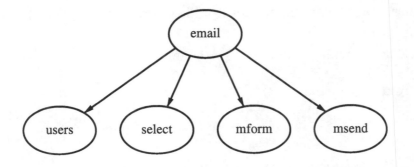

Figure 4.2   The *email* frame network.

```
1: {frame  email
2:     ~call users  >  ~users
3:     ~call select ~users  >  ~to
4:     ~call mform ~to  >  ~to ~subj ~mesg
5:     (~to!=~null && ~mesg!=~null): ~call msend ~to ~subj ~mesg
6: }f
```

The first task or frame called by **email** is **users**. Following is the code
for **users**. Line 2 runs **/bin/ksh** as a cooperating process or coprocess.
Values returned from the coprocess will be assigned to variable ~**logins**.
Line 3 specifies the *end-of-response* and *end-of-commands* protocol delimiters to be used between EASEL and the coprocess. When EASEL is
done sending data to the coprocess (the text on line 5), it sends the
end-of-commands text (**echo ShIsDone\n**). EASEL then starts reading
text returned from the coprocess until it sees the end-of-response text
(**ShIsDone\n**). Line 4 says that the screen will not be disturbed during
this execution, so EASEL will not refresh the screen when it gets back
control from the coprocess. Line 5 is the complete body of text to be
sent to the coprocess; on Suns running NIS (formerly Yellow Pages), this
shell script will generate the current list of logins. Line 6 ends the process
block. Line 7 causes control to return to the calling frame and returns
the value contained in the variable ~**logins**.

```
1: {frame  users
2:     {process  "/bin/ksh"  > ~logins
3:         ~!"ShIsDone\n","echo ShIsDone\n"
4:         ~$
5:         ypcat passwd | cut -d: -f1 | sort -u | xargs
6:     }p
7:     ~return ~logins
8: }f
```

The next task is to ask the user to select the desired addressees from the available list of users. Following is the frame **select** that performs this task. Line 1 begins frame **select**, which has argument ~list. Lines 2 to 8 present the ~list of logins as a menu to the end-user, build a ~to list adding each user selection, and loop until a null choice is entered. The .window statement on line 3 defines a window for the menu. If this is not defined EASEL will construct some default window whose size and placement are designed to make good use of screen real estate. Line 5 provides the list of options to be shown, namely, those stored in variable ~list. Delimiters for the list are specified as space, tab, or newline characters. Line 6 builds a list of the logins selected by the user and stores the result in the variable ~to. This variable is used in the menu's title given in line 4 to give immediate feedback to the user on the current set of selections. Line 9 returns the value of ~to to the calling frame.

```
 1: {frame  select ~list
 2:     {menu  :(~pers == ~null)  ~pers
 3:         .window( x=5, xlen=50, y=0, ylen=10 )
 4:         Mail To: ~to
 5:         {option  ~list  " \t\n"
 6:             ~to  = ~to * ~pers * " "
 7:         }o
 8:     }m
 9:     ~return ~to
10: }f
```

A screen snapshot of **select** is shown in Figure 4.3. Note that the frame stack email:select shows the traversal sequence in the frame network to get to the frame **select**.

The third **email** task is to display a mail form and let the user fill it in. Following is the frame **mform**. The context block beginning on line 2 is used to group the enclosed question blocks so that they will be displayed together as a unit or form. The .form statement on lines 3 to 8 specifies that answer fields should be shown in color 2 (typically underlining on black and white terminals), with attributes set to printable characters. The .form statement also includes a template for the form and indicates which question variables correspond to which answer fields. For example, line 4 indicates that the answer field is the ~To variable, which, in this case, was passed as an argument to the frame. Thus any menu selections made by the user in the **select** frame will be shown on the form as soon as

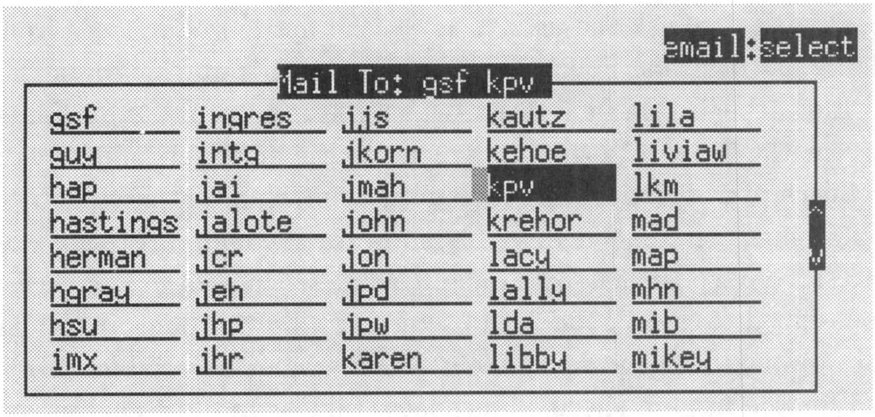

Figure 4.3 The `select` screen.

it is displayed. The user can edit the answer field on the form or move on
to the next field. Lines 10 to 12 provide help text for this form should the
user request help. Although not shown here, help text may include EASEL
variables as well as hypertext links. Lines 13 to 22 are the question blocks
used to build up the form; each provides a variable to collect the user's
response to that question. The `.field` statement in line 20 overrides the
suggested template and specifies that the answer ~Mesg field be repeated
ten times for a ten-line answer. If the user types beyond the tenth line, the
answer field will scroll (unless the answer has been restricted to the length
specified). Although the syntax for specifying a form is a bit verbose with
its `.form` statement and group of question blocks, it saves frame designers
from counting row and column coordinates and allows entry conditions
on question blocks to tailor field access dynamically. Line 24 returns the
values in ~To, ~Subj, and ~Mesg back to the calling frame. Figure 4.4
shows a screen snapshot of the form.

```
 1: {frame   mform    ~To
 2:      {context
 3:          .form( c=2, a=p,
 4:          To: <_____ $ ~To
 5:          Subj: <_____ $ ~Subj
 6:
 7:          Mesg: <_____ $ ~Mesg
 8:          )
 9:          Mail Form
10:          {descript
11:              Some HELP for the form
```

```
                                                    email:mform
                        ─Mail Form──────────────────────────────
To: gsf kpv
Subj: cpp macros


Mesg: Can we get together Tues
      after lunch to discuss
      name=value macros for cpp and EASEL?
```

Figure 4.4 The **mform** screen.

```
12:            }d
13:            {question  ~To
14:                 To:
15:            }q
16:            {question  ~Subj
17:                 Subj:
18:            }q
19:            {question  ~Mesg
20:                 .field( r=10 )
21:                 Mesg:
22:            }q
23:      }c
24:      ~return ~To ~Subj ~Mesg
25: }f
```

The final task, if the user has provided non-null text for the addressees and the message, is to send the user's e-mail, as coded in the following frame **msend**. Line 2 gets the current value of the environment variable $LOGNAME and stores it in the EASEL variable ~LOGNAME (for use in the mail message body). Lines 3 to 14 communicate with the same coprocess /bin/ksh as was set up in the frame **users**. This time, what is being sent to the shell is a multiline mail command that is parameterized by several EASEL variables. The variable ~e~sdate in line 8 is an EASEL read-only variable containing the current date as a string, for example, `Sat May 21 01:40:10 EDT 1994`.

```
 1: {frame  msend  ~To ~Subj ~Mesg
 2:     ~getenv ~LOGNAME
 3:     {process  "/bin/ksh"
 4:         ~!"ShIsDone\n","echo ShIsDone\n"
 5:         ~$
 6:         mail ~To <<!!
 7:         Subj: ~Subj
 8:         Date: ~efsdate
 9:
10:         ~Mesg
11:
12:         Thanks! ~LOGNAME
13:             !!
14:     }p
15: }f
```

The actual text for the mail command, as sent to the shell, follows. In prototyping and early testing of a frame, the process block for the mail command in lines 3 to 14 might be enclosed in a write block (to the screen or to a file) to simply write out the mail command as it would be sent to the coprocess to let the command be checked without sending any unnecessary mail.

```
mail gsf kpv <<!!
Subj: cpp macros
Date: Sat Apr 30 01:40:10 EDT 1994

Can we get together Tues
after lunch to discuss
name=value macros for cpp and Easel?

Thanks! jjs
!!
```

That has been a quick look at EASEL as a language and system to build end-user systems. As the *email* application shows, the application design process starts with identifying tasks from the user's perspective. These tasks can be quickly prototyped in the EASEL language without lower-level computations. In this way, the tasks can be tested out with users to see if they are suitable. In parallel to or with user testing, computational tasks can be implemented and tested. This cycle continues until the system is complete. Figure 4.5 shows this system construction method.

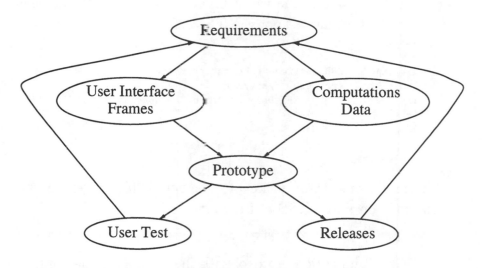

Figure 4.5 EASEL frame system development cycle.

4.2.4.2 Building Higher-Level Abstraction with Macros

The availability of a language suitable for design programming enables design reuse in the traditional style of building macro templates and code libraries. It is clear how frames parallel traditional library functions and can be reused as such. In many projects where families of applications are built, higher levels of reuse can be achieved by defining macro templates. Such templates are useful because they:

- Reduce programming time of repetitive tasks
- Standardize the look and feel of the user interface
- Standardize the access to lower level computational functions

For example, consider the task of obtaining a list of logins in frame **users** of the *email* application. The shell communication can be abstracted to the actions of:

- Sending the shell a set of commands
- Reading responses from the shell
- Assigning responses to an appropriate EASEL variable

Following is a macro definition of this task in an extended C preprocessor language [KR78, Fow88]. The macro KSH_get takes two arguments,

Cmd and Var, that define the command to be sent to the shell and the
variable to store any responses. The default values for Cmd and Var are
the string echo ok and the variable name ksh_out.

```
1:   #macdef KSH_get(Cmd="echo ok", Var=ksh_out)
2:           {process  "/bin/ksh"     > ~Var
3:               ~!"ShIsDone\n","echo ShIsDone\n"
4:               ~$
5:               Cmd
6:           }p
7:   #endmac
```

The following instantiation of the macro KSH_get generates the equivalent code on lines 2 to 6 of frame users:

```
KSH_get(Var=users, Cmd="ypcat passwd | cut -d: -f1 | sort -u | xargs")
```

The communication protocol with the shell, as defined in this example,
is relatively simple. For other tools, it can be much more complex. By
using macro templates, frame developers can focus directly on *what* needs
to be performed without having to worry about *how* it is performed, which
helps avoid inadvertent errors.

The same technique can also be applied to the menu task in the select
frame. Following is the macro template to do that. Here, macro parameters are used to describe the main components of a menu block. In this
example, the menu window is constrained to always appear with the top
left corner at location x=5 and y=0 and dimensions xlen=50 and ylen=10.
This is somewhat contrived (by default, windows are automatically sized
and placed by a best-fit rule) but it serves to show how interface constraints can be standardized using macro templates.

```
1:   #macdef Menu_list( Title=Selections, List=list, Sel=sel, Ans=ans)
2:           {menu  :(~Sel == ~null)  ~Sel
3:               .window( x=5, xlen=50, y=0, ylen=10 )
4:               Title: ~Ans
5:               {option ~List  " \t\n"
6:                   ~Ans = ~Ans * ~Sel * " "
7:               }o
8:           }m
9:   #endmac
```

For completeness, the following instantiation of Menu_list generates
the same code for the menu block on lines 2 to 8 of frame select:

```
Menu_list(Title=Mail To, Sel=pers, Ans=to)
```

4.2.5   Experience with Building an Application Family with EASEL

Within AT&T, several projects have successfully used EASEL to build sophisticated network management applications. In particular, a project that we shall call Project D made extensive use of EASEL to generate families of end-user applications for a variety of end-users, including:

- Switch engineers–to monitor, forecast, plan, and equip switches to handle traffic loads efficiently
- Operations support staff–to monitor and evaluate operator services throughout a network
- Service planners–to conduct traffic analyses of specialized services and provide reports

Much of the raw data for these systems is generated automatically by the switches themselves in the telephone network. Portions of this data are periodically downloaded onto UNIX servers and stored in relational databases for use by applications. These applications are often written in C with embedded SQL calls. The C code can be complex, sophisticated, and not easy to use by non-experts. But to better serve telephone customers, it is becoming more and more important to make such capabilities readily available to end-users.

When Project D first started, it recognized the needs to reuse existing C code and to provide friendly user interfaces. They found lots of literature on user interfaces, such as [Sch87], and a variety of user interface packages inspired by the early work at Xerox PARC [Gol84], including Apple Macintoshes and PCs with Microsoft Windows; but what was needed was to wrap a friendly user interface around large existing C applications running on UNIX systems. EASEL was chosen for this task.

In building applications, Project D's architects recognized that there were many tasks that are repeated again and again, such as:

- Obtaining information from the database
- Formatting data for display to end-users
- Collecting end-user responses via menus and forms
- Providing hypertext help

- Storing new information into the database
- Time-stamping and posting messages to end-users

This led Project D architects to layer their code as follows:

- A library of high-level objects
- EASEL frame code
- Application-specific libraries, including database access utilities (C and SQL)
- A relational database

The high-level objects currently number about 70 and are implemented as macros that expand into EASEL code (using awk and cpp). Code generated by the macros reference a library of about 90 utilities, written both in EASEL and C, many of which interface with the database. As new reusable objects or object attributes are found and defined, EASEL code and database access utilities can be expanded as needed.

To date, Project D has built nearly a dozen different end-user systems, each consisting of hundreds of EASEL frames. During the initial phase of the project, many new objects were discovered, implemented in macros and, as necessary, supported by new low-level C functions and/or database transactions. Application architects have said that the capability to write new macros and new code at any level avoids hitting "brick walls" and makes this approach based on EASEL even more powerful than a typical 4GL. Recent applications have been built entirely out of predefined macros. The expansion of common macros can be "personalized" to meet particular requirements of particular customer sets.

A typical Project D source code file written with macros averages about 100 to 200 lines long, which, after macro expansion, averages about 1,000 lines of EASEL source code. Thus, use of the macros reduces code size roughly by a factor of 5 if compared to straight EASEL code. It is not as easy to get a similar comparison between EASEL code and equivalent code in C, but it is not hard to conclude that the code size reduction would be much larger than that. Project D developers have estimated that programming in EASEL alone (without macros) offers a 10 to 1 advantage in terms of implementation time over writing the same end-user system in C.

This high-level of software reuse has allowed Project D to employ small teams to interact with customer focus groups, design, test, and rapidly refine prototypes, using customer feedback to flesh out features for production releases. The end results for Project D are customers who feel that they are getting what they really want. Finally, from an organizational point of view, an important aspect of having high-level macro objects is that they are easily learned by developers new to the project. New Project D developers typically can begin to build screen objects within a few days of training.

4.2.6   Reuse Experiences in EASEL's Evolution

EASEL has grown and matured significantly over the years, thanks to two complementary forces. One has been feedback from designers and developers using EASEL to build end-user systems. Many discovered leading-edge ways to use EASEL, pushing at its frontiers and suggesting new features. The other has been continued involvement and interaction with other software engineering researchers. Discussions frequently led to the recognition of common problems, some of which eventually lent themselves to common solutions to the benefit of more than one project.

An example of users' feedback is the recent addition of an interactive frame builder `efb`. For many years, EASEL provided a language and environment to program and execute end-user systems. We have discussed the benefits of having a language suitable for implementing the high-level design of such systems. However, an aspect of user interface design that cannot be easily addressed by a textual language is that of experimenting with different screen layouts. The frame builder `efb` addresses this need by allowing users to write EASEL code and lay out the screen interactively. It is interesting to note that `efb` itself is implemented in the EASEL language as a frame system consisting of about 150 frames and three coprocesses written in C.

EASEL is based on a number of standard libraries; the original list included: *curses*, for screen manipulations, *malloc* for memory allocation, *regex* for regular expression matching [KP84], and *stdio*, the standard input/output library. In the course of EASEL's evolution, we found that some of these libraries needed improvement and that new libraries were needed.

The earliest version of EASEL, around early 1982, was based on the original *curses* library on the BSD4.1 UNIX System. Aside from a number of bugs, this version of *curses* also suffered from lack of features (such as hardware scrolling) and from poor performance. After much consideration, *curses* was rewritten to improve code quality and efficiency. The new library, *screen* (Section 2.2.4), remains upward-compatible with *curses* and includes new features, such as screen editing, menu display, and mouse support. It is also fully internationalized and supports multiple international multibyte character sets. Because of *screen*, EASEL is perhaps the only current application construction system that enables applications that run transparently in multiple countries using different character code sets across Asia and Europe.

EASEL uses the *malloc* package for dynamic memory allocations. Early in its development, it was discovered that standard *malloc* implementations, both on System V and BSD UNIX systems, had severe deficiencies, either in terms of space fragmentation or time performance or both. This prompted a 1985 study by Korn and Vo [KV85] to compare all available *malloc* implementations. At that time, a new *malloc* package based on the best-fit strategy was also implemented. The study found that this package provides the best trade-off in both time and space. This version of *malloc* is now part of the standard System V UNIX distribution. More recently, we found that certain large EASEL applications may have hundreds to thousands of users running concurrently on the same server. This indicates that there is much to be gained by using shared memory for storing frames online. Coupled with certain other needs, this prompted a generalization of *malloc* to *vmalloc* (Section 2.3.4).

When event-handling was added to EASEL, it was discovered that signals could cause the screen to be only partially updated. The bug was tracked down to the *stdio* library, which drops data if a `write` system call is interrupted by a signal. This and other shortcomings of *stdio* led to the writing of *sfio*, a faster, safer I/O library (Section 2.3.1).

Along the way, it was found that several pieces of software in the department, including EASEL, would benefit from a library for online dictionary management–for example, to access variables in a symbol table. A flexible dictionary library, *libdict*, was written to handle both ordered and unordered objects using binary trees or hash tables (Section 2.3.3).

The need to distribute low-level libraries that depend on system calls and other environmental parameters for a wide range of hardware and software platforms led to the development of an installation tool to automate the process. The tool, called *iffe* [FKSV94], probes and then configures the software automatically without human intervention (Section 3.2).

4.2.7   Alternatives

The first version of EASEL, called IFS [Vo90], was first developed in the early part of 1982. At that time, there were few alternative languages for building end-user applications. Within AT&T, the best-known tool for form-based applications was FE, a form-entry system [Pri85]. As FE focused on forms, it could not be used for more general applications requiring menus or windows. More recently, there are a number of commercial character-based packages with comparable functionality to EASEL. Most notable are the FMLI package distributed with UNIX System V and the JAM package [Jya94]. FMLI is based on the *curses* library and uses a syntax similar to the shell language enhanced with constructs to write forms and menus. The heavy reliance on separate scripts for forms and menus makes FMLI cumbersome to use. JAM runs on both PC and UNIX systems and is based on proprietary software for screen handling. JAM relies more on an interactive screen builder to prototype screens than on a language to write applications. Though this makes it easy to build single applications with few screens, it can become cumbersome when families of applications must be built along the line of Project D, as discussed in Section 4.2.5. In fact, Project D developers investigated both JAM and EASEL and decided to use EASEL because its open-ended architecture makes it easy to add new functionality at any number of architectural levels, such as, high-level macros, EASEL's code, processes, or C routines. On the bit-mapped graphic side, the `tcl/tk` language and toolkit is compatible to EASEL in the basic approach to tool and application design. In fact, it would be interesting to rewrite the display library of EASEL based on `tcl/tk` or a similar toolkit. An advantage of doing this is that

EASEL-based applications could run transparently on character terminals and graphical workstations.

4.2.8 Conclusion

We have described EASEL as a language and system for building end-user systems. From an application builder's point of view, the success of EASEL derives directly from its philosophy of separating *Design programming* from *Computational programming* by providing a programming language suitable for design implementation. This enables a style of system development that focuses on partitioning tasks as seen from users' perspectives and increases the chance of matching users' expectations. Having a high-level language for design programming brings in traditional reuse techniques, such as code libraries and templates. In addition, by defining precisely a small number of standard interfaces to external code, EASEL encourages the construction of reusable code. We described experiences with a project where a family of end-user applications were built based on these ideas. In this case, the application builders themselves claimed at least a factor of 5 reduction in code size and corresponding productivity improvement.

We have also touched on our own experiences of software reuse in the construction and evolution of EASEL. The total size for EASEL and associated libraries stands at a little over 60,000 lines of C code. For many years, this body of code was maintained and enhanced by essentially a single person (Vo). This is not normally feasible but for the high-level of reusability in the internal code. As the software evolves, we gradually abstract pieces of it into reusable libraries. The construction of such libraries has sometimes led to new and interesting theoretical problems. For example, early in the rewrite of the *curses* library, it was recognized that screen scrolling is best modeled by a string-matching problem in which matches have weights. This led to the development of a new heaviest common subsequence algorithm [JV92]. Recently, new algorithms and heuristics for memory allocation were developed in building the *vmalloc* library. Thus, reuse permeates our way of building software and drives the interplay between theory and practice.

5

Self-Checking Programs and Program Instrumentation

David Rosenblum

5.1 Introduction

Assertions are formal constraints on software system behavior, which are commonly written as annotations of a source text. The primary goal in writing assertions is to specify *what* a system is supposed to do, rather than *how* it is to do it. Assertion features are available today as programming language extensions, as programming language features, and in complete high-level formal specification languages. The C programming language [KR88] has traditionally provided a simple assertion facility as an `assert` macro, which is expanded inline into an if-statement that aborts the program if the assertion expression evaluates to zero. Extensions have been proposed for other languages, such as C++ [Str91], that originally provided no higher-level assertion capability [Gau92, CL90]. Still other programming languages, such as Turing [HC88] and Eiffel [Mey88], provide assertion features as part of the language definition. Such languages can be used to specify system behavior at the design level. These uses of high-level formal specifications offer a practical alternative to mechanical proof of correctness.

APP is an Annotation PreProcessor for C programs developed in UNIX-based programming environments. APP has been designed to be easily integrated with other UNIX development tools. In particular, APP was designed as a replacement for the standard preprocessor pass of C compilers, making the process of creating and running self-checking programs (that automatically check their own assertions) as simple as building unannotated C programs. Furthermore, APP provides complete flexibility in specifying how violated assertions are handled at runtime and how much checking is to be performed each time a self-checking program is executed. In addition to assertion checking, it has been natural to extend APP to support other kinds of instrumentation. All of the instrumentation capabilities that APP provides to a program are controllable at program runtime through a UNIX shell environment variable called APP_OPTIONS; this way, the program need not be recompiled whenever a modification in the instrumentation behavior is desired. APP does not require complete specifications for its correct operation, and the assertions one writes for APP typically are not complete specifications in any formal sense.

This chapter begins with a brief description of the features and operation of APP. It then describes the architecture of APP and its construction from reusable components described in previous chapters. It finishes with some thoughts on how the work on APP has contributed to the improvement of reusable components on which APP is based, and to the development of tools that use APP as a component.

5.2   Assertion Constructs

In an empirical study by Perry and Evangelist, it was shown that most software faults are interface faults [PE85, PE87]. Hence, APP was initially designed to process assertions on function interfaces, as well as assertions in function bodies. APP also supports a number of facilities for specifying the response to a failed assertion check and for controlling the amount of checking that is performed at runtime.

APP recognizes assertions that appear as annotations of C source text. In particular, the assertions are written using the extended comment indicators /*@ ... @*/. Informal comments can be written in an assertion region by writing each comment between the delimiter // and the end of the line, as in C++.

Each APP assertion specifies a constraint that applies to some state of a computation. The constraint is specified using C's expression language, with the C convention that an expression evaluating to zero is false, while a non-zero expression is true. To discourage writing assertion expressions that have side effects, APP disallows the use of C's assignment, increment and decrement operators in assertion expressions. Of course, functions that produce side effects can be invoked within assertion expressions, but such expressions should be avoided except in the rarest of circumstances, since assertions should simply provide a check on the computation rather than be a part of it.

APP supports two enhancements to the C expression language within assertion regions. First, the operator **in** can be used to indicate that an expression is to be evaluated in the entry state of the function that encloses the expression. Second, bounded quantifiers can be specified using a syntax that is similar to C's **for**-loop syntax. Both of these extensions are illustrated below.

APP recognizes four assertion constructs, each indicated by a different keyword:

- **assume**—Specifies a precondition on a function.
- **promise**—Specifies a postcondition on a function.
- **return**—Specifies a constraint on the return value of a function.
- **assert**—Specifies a constraint on an intermediate state of a function body.

The first three kinds of assertions are associated syntactically with function interface declarations, while the last kind is associated syntactically with statements in function bodies. The **assert** construct corresponds to the **assert** macro found in many C implementations, in the sense that it constrains only the state of the program at the place of the **assert**.

Note that an assumption for a function is a constraint that the calling environment must satisfy in order for the function to satisfy any of its postconditions. APP generates runtime checks in such a way that postconditions are checked independently of preconditions. Thus, a failed precondition check on a function call reveals a fault in the program, even

```
int square_root(x)
int x;
/*@
    assume x >= 0;
    return y where y >= 0;
    return y where y*y <= x && x < (y+1)*(y+1);
@*/
{
    . . .
}
```

Figure 5.1   Specification of function **square_root**.

in the presence of successful checks for all postconditions for the same call. However, information from failed postcondition checks may not be reliable in the presence of a failed precondition check for the same call.

To briefly illustrate these four constructs, consider first a function called **square_root** that returns the greatest positive integer less than or equal to the square root of its integer argument. Such a function can be specified in the manner shown in Figure 5.1. The first assertion is a precondition of **square_root**, as indicated by the keyword **assume**. It states that the implementation of the function assumes it is given a non-negative argument; if this precondition is not satisfied at runtime, nothing can be guaranteed about the behavior of the function. The remaining two assertions are constraints on the return value of **square_root**, as indicated by the keyword **return**. Each return constraint declares a local variable (called **y** in the return constraints of this example) that is used to refer to the return value of the function within the constraint. The first return constraint states that the function returns positive roots. The second one states the required relationship between the argument and the return value. It is, of course, possible to conjoin these two **return** constraints into a single one; however, it is often useful to separate constraints not only for the sake of clarity, but especially when using APP's severity-level and violation-action features (described later in Section 5.3). Note that all of these assertions merely state what the function does, not how it does it.

```
void swap(x,y)
int *x, *y;
/*@
    assume x != 0 && y != 0;
    assume x && y;   // equivalent to the first assumption
    assume x != y;
    promise *x == in *y;
    promise *y == in *x;
@*/
{
    *x = *x ^ *y;
    *y = *x ^ *y;
    /*@
        assert *y == in *x;
    @*/
    *x = *x ^ *y;
}
```

Figure 5.2 Specification of function **swap**.

Consider next a function called **swap** that swaps two integers without using a temporary variable. The function takes as arguments a pointer to each of the two integers, and it performs the swap through the pointers using a series of exclusive-or operations on the integer values. The function can be specified and implemented in the manner shown in Figure 5.2. The first two assumptions are equivalent (as indicated by the informal comment), and they state the precondition that the pointers **x** and **y** should be non-null. The first assumption states this explicitly by saying that the pointers should not be equal to zero. The second assumption states the same thing using the C convention that a non-zero expression value is interpreted as the value *true*; this convention provides a very convenient way of specifying nullness and non-nullness constraints on pointers. The third assumption states the precondition that the pointers **x** and **y** are not equal to each other. The two postconditions, indicated by the keyword **promise**, use the operator **in** to relate the values of the integers

```
int* sort(x,size)
int size, *x;
/*@
    assume x && size > 0;
    return S where
        S &&  all (int i=0; i < in size-1; i=i+1)
                    S[i] <= S[i+1]
          &&  all (int i=0; i < in size; i=i+1)
                    (some (int j=0; j < in size; j=j+1)
                        x[i] == S[j])
              &&  card(S[i], S, in size) ==
                        card(S[i], x, in size);
@*/
{
    ...
}
```

Figure 5.3 Specification of function **sort**.

upon exit from the function to their values upon entry. In particular, the first promise states that the exit value of the integer pointed to by **x** should equal the value pointed to by **y** upon entry, while the second promise states the reverse. The assertion in the body of **swap**, indicated by the keyword **assert**, states an intermediate constraint on the integers at the point where one of the promises must become satisfied.

As a final example, consider a function **sort** that sorts two arrays of integers. The specification shown in Figure 5.3 describes its required behavior at a level of abstraction that allows the use of any sorting algorithm to implement its body. In this function, **x** is the unsorted input array, and **size** is the number of elements in the array. The function returns a pointer to the sorted result. The specification of **sort** uses quantifiers to state both the obvious ordering requirement of the result, as well as the requirement that the result must be a permutation of the input array. Note that the return constraint of **sort** uses the name **S** to refer to the *pointer* returned by **sort**; thus, each occurrence of **S** is treated as a pointer, including the first conjunct, which requires **S** to be non-null.

An APP quantifier can be thought of as a sequential iterator over a set of values, with the quantified expression evaluated for each element in the set; these individual evaluations are combined in the obvious way for the particular kind of quantifier. Syntactically, a quantified expression resembles a **for**-loop in C. Indeed, APP expands each quantified expression into a **for**-loop that performs the specified iteration and evaluations, with nested quantifiers expanded into appropriately nested **for**-loops.

As shown in Figure 5.3, an APP quantifier specification contains the existential specifier **some** or the universal specifier **all**, followed by a parenthesized sequence of three fields separated by semicolons. The first field is a declaration of the variable over which quantification is to be performed, including its name, type, and the initial value of the set. The second is a condition that must be true in order for the iteration to continue. The third is an expression that computes the next value in the set. Thus, the first universally quantified expression in the return annotation says that each element of the result but the last must be less than or equal to its successor element. The second universally quantified expression contains a nested, existentially quantified expression to state that for every element of the input array **x**, there exists an equal element of the result array. The second universally quantified expression uses a cardinality function **card** (definition not shown) to further state that each element of **S** must occur the same number of times in both arrays.

5.3   Violation Actions, Predefined Macros, and Severity Levels

APP converts each assertion to a runtime check, which tests for the violation of the Boolean condition specified in the assertion. If the check fails at runtime, then the additional code generated with the check is executed in response to the failure. The default response code generated by APP prints out a simple diagnostic message, such as the following, which indicates the violation of the first promise of function **swap**:

```
promise invalid:   file swap.c, line 6, function swap
```

```
promise *x == in *y
   {
      printf("out *x == %d, out *y == %d\n", *x, *y);
   }
```

Figure 5.4   Violation action for promise of function **swap**.

```
promise *x == in *y
   {
      printf("%s invalid: file %s, ", __ANNONAME__,
             __FILE__);
      printf("line %d, function %s:\n", __ANNOLINE__,
             __FUNCTION__);
      printf("out *x == %d, out *y == %d\n", *x, *y);
   }
```

Figure 5.5   Enhancement of the violation action of Figure 5.4.

The default response provides a minimal amount of information needed to isolate the fault that the failed check reveals. However, the response to a violated assertion can be customized to provide diagnostic information that is unique to the context of the assertion. This customization is done by attaching a *violation action* to the assertion, written in C.

For instance, in order to determine what argument values cause the first promise of **swap** to be violated, the promise can be supplied with a violation action, as shown in Figure 5.4 (using C's library function **printf** for formatted output). Using some preprocessor macros that are predefined by APP, this violation action can be enhanced, as shown in Figure 5.5, to print out the same information that is printed out by the default violation action.

The macros __ANNONAME__ and __ANNOLINE__ expand to the keyword of the enclosing assertion and to the starting line number of the enclosing assertion. The macros __FILE__ and __FUNCTION__ expand to the name of the source file in which the enclosing assertion is specified, and to the name of the function in which the assertion is specified.

In addition to violation actions, APP supports the specification of an optional severity level for each assertion, with 1 being the default and

```
1: assume x >= 0;
2: return y where y >= 0;
1: return y where y*y <= x
               &&  x < (y+1)*(y+1);
```

Figure 5.6 Severity levels for assertions of function **square_root**.

indicating the highest severity. A severity level indicates the relative importance of its associated constraint and determines whether the assertion will be checked at runtime. Severity levels can be used to control the amount of assertion checking that is performed at runtime without recompiling the program to add or remove checks. For example, the assertions on **square_root** can be given severity levels, as shown in Figure 5.6. Under level-1 checking at runtime, only the assumption and the second return constraint would be checked. If one of these assertions were violated at runtime, it might then be desirable to re-execute the program under level-2 checking in order to additionally enable checking of the first return constraint and obtain more information about the cause of the assertion violation. Level-0 checking disables all checking at runtime. Severity levels are useful for implementing the *two-dimensional pinpointing* method of debugging [LST91]. The mechanism for controlling the checking level at runtime is described in Section 5.4.

The macro __DEFAULTACTION__ expands to the default violation action, while the macro __DEFAULTLEVEL__ expands to the default severity level. Both of these macros can be redefined to alter the default processing of APP.

5.4   Generating and Running Self-Checking Programs

APP has the same command-line interface as *cpp*, the standard preprocessor pass of *cc*, the C compiler. In particular, APP accepts the macro definition options −D and −U and the interface or *header* file directory option −I, and it performs all of the macro preprocessing of *cpp* in addition to its assertion processing. Hence, to compile an annotated C source

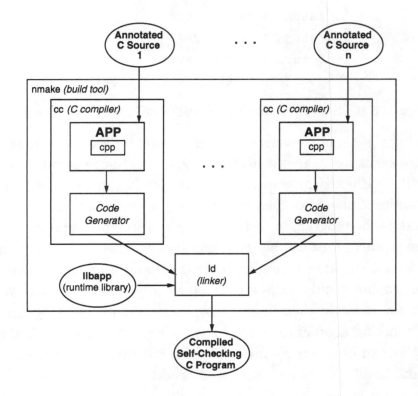

Figure 5.7   Generating self-checking C programs with APP.

file, APP is simply invoked through *cc* by using appropriate command-line options that tell *cc* to use APP as its preprocessor pass; such options are a standard feature of every C compiler. Furthermore, standard build tools, such as *make* [Fel79] and *nmake* (see Chapter 3), can be used to build executable self-checking programs, with only slight modifications to existing *makefiles* or build scripts. These processing techniques are illustrated in Figure 5.7, which depicts *nmake* compiling the *n* source files of some program with APP and then linking the resulting object files together into a self-checking executable. This method of integrating assertion processing with standard C development tools greatly simplifies the generation of self-checking programs and requires almost no change to one's customary use of UNIX and C programming environments.

As shown in the figure, self-checking executables must be linked with a runtime library called *libapp*. This library provides a variety of runtime support, including generation of diagnostic output for assertion violations, generation of function trace messages (Section 5.5), control of assertion checking according to the desired severity level, and freeing of heap memory that is allocated as a result of evaluating an assertion expression.

Once a self-checking program has been created, it can be executed, with checking performed according to the severity level specified in a field of the environment variable APP_OPTIONS (or at the default level if the field is undefined). Note that a self-checking program can be treated like any other program in a C programming environment. For instance, a self-checking program can be run inside a symbolic debugger, such as *dbx*. The debugger can be used to set breakpoints at assertions, single-step through them, trace their execution, and so on, all relative to the contents and line numbering of the original source files in which the assertions were specified.

5.5   Instrumentation for Tracing

Because APP is essentially a program-instrumentation tool, it has proven highly desirable and quite easy to enhance APP to perform other, more traditional kinds of instrumentation that can be implemented independently of programmer-supplied assertions. In particular, APP was enhanced to allow instrumentation of programs for tracing of their function call activity.

Programs that are instrumented for function tracing generate four kinds of messages during their execution. Figure 5.8 depicts these four kinds of messages. As shown in the figure, both function calls and function bodies are instrumented for tracing. At the place of a call, a **Call** (or **C**) message is generated immediately prior to the call, while an **End-of-call** (or **E**) message is generated immediately following the call. Within a function body, an **Invocation** (or **I**) message is generated upon entry to the function body, while a **Return** (or **R**) message is generated upon exit from the function body. Each generated trace message is a single line of text containing the name of the function; the name of the file in which the call or body appears; the number of seconds (to a precision of 1 microsecond) since execution began; the number of seconds (to a

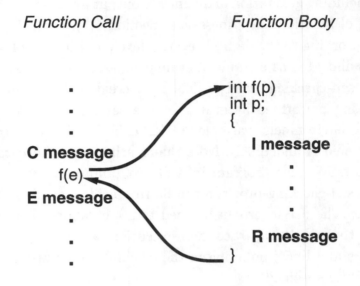

Figure 5.8   Function tracing with App.

precision of 10 milliseconds) of CPU and system time; and other useful information.

Because of the execution complexities introduced by the functions `setjmp` and `longjmp`, the beginnings of calls to `setjmp` and `longjmp` are represented by **S** and **L** messages, respectively, rather than by **C** messages. Furthermore, each such **S** and **L** message contains the address of the `jmp_buf` involved in order to aid matching of corresponding `setjmps` and `longjmps` during processing of the trace output.

Tracing is carried out in one of three modes:

1. *Full tracing* produces **C**, **S**, **L**, **I**, **R**, and **E** messages for every call to every instrumented function call and function body. This kind of tracing is used to support *Xray* (see Section 11.4).

2. *Body tracing* produces all **I** and **R** messages for every call to every instrumented function.

3. *Summary tracing* produces **I** messages for the first call to every instrumented function. This kind of tracing is used to support TESTTUBE (see Section 11.3).

Generation of the trace and selection of the tracing mode are controlled

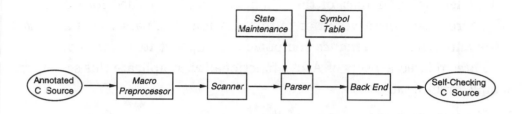

Figure 5.9 The architecture of APP.

at runtime by fields in the environment variable APP_OPTIONS that specifies where the trace is to be stored; if this option is not present, the trace will not be generated. The trace can be piped directly to another application for analysis in real time, or it can be saved in a file for post-mortem processing.

Of course, programs that run for a long time and call a large number of functions can generate enormous traces. While text-processing tools such as **awk** and **sed** can be used to filter large traces, there still exists the problem of storing the trace on disk prior to filtering. To avoid the problem of storing large traces on disk, it is possible to have *libapp* perform the filtering prior to generation of the trace. This is achieved by specifying one or more filter files in a field of the environment variable APP_OPTIONS, each such file containing a list of functions that are to be filtered out of the trace. Whenever a **C**, **S**, **L**, or **I** message for one of the filtered functions is encountered during generation of the trace, the trace is suspended until after the corresponding **E** or **R** message is encountered.

5.6   The Architecture of APP

Figure 5.9 presents a top-level view of the architecture of APP. The architectural style of APP is a unidirectional pipeline of analysis components akin to those of typical compilation and source-to-source transformation systems. The *scanner* breaks the input stream into tokens, the *parser* checks the token sequence for syntactic and semantic validity, and the *back end* produces the instrumented output. The *macro preprocessor* component is an artifact of the C language and is needed for expansion of preprocessor directives prior to tokenization. The parser uses a *symbol table* and *state maintenance* component to support its operation.

Three related aspects of APP's functionality complicate this seemingly simple architecture:

1. *The need to reorder pieces of the input.* Function interface assertions appear syntactically *before* their associated function body, yet the run-time checks generated for function interface assertions must be inserted at different places *within* the function body. In addition, **in**-expressions appearing in assertions require the generation of temporary variables for their evaluation, and these temporary variables must be placed at the beginning of the function body to ensure that the entry values of these expressions are evaluated before any computation takes place within the function body. Thus, pieces of input text must be periodically saved in a number of in-memory buffers until it is appropriate to output them.

2. *The need to parse comments.* Because APP assertions are written within C comment fields, it is necessary to trap the processing of comments by the scanner and force their tokenization at the appropriate place in the input stream.

3. *The need for the parser to communicate with the scanner and macro preprocessor.* It is necessary for APP to dynamically alter the behavior of the scanner and macro preprocessor, depending on the current input context. For example, C++-style comments must be recognized within assertion regions but not outside of them.

Figure 5.10 presents an enhanced view of the architecture of APP, showing in boldface those additional components and component interactions that are required because of the complications previously discussed. The *output buffers* component is used to provide temporary storage for reordering pieces of the input stream, and two-way communication is supported between the *parser* and the *scanner*.

Four reusable components were available to support the implementation of APP: *libpp*, *sfio*, and the hash table and stack facilities of *libast*. *libpp* provides all of the functionality needed by the *macro preprocessor* and *scanner* components, including support for the special handling of

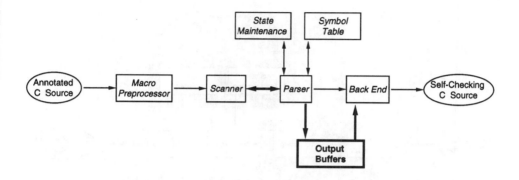

Figure 5.10   Enhanced view of the architecture of APP.

comments described earlier. The *sfio* library provides facilities for the *output buffers* component. In particular, *sfio* supports manipulation of in-memory buffers as output streams, which allows APP to generate its output in a uniform manner independently of which piece of the input stream it is processing. *libast*'s hash table system is a convenient facility for implementing the *symbol table* component of APP, providing quick storage and retrieval of information associated with program symbols, as well as separation of this information into name spaces as defined by the semantics of C. *libast*'s stack system provides the necessary functionality for the *state maintenance* component, which helps the *parser* track the traversal of nested scopes and regions of visibility during parsing. Besides these reusable components, the *parser* is generated with *yacc*, using the same C grammar specification that is used in the parser of CIA (see Chapter 6).

Figure 5.11 presents a final view of the architecture of APP, showing the incorporation of reusable components.

5.7   Contributions to Reuse

The quick development of APP was made possible by the availability of *libpp*, which provided a complete C preprocessing capability in a form that was highly suited for development of a language-processing system, such as APP. In return, the experience in developing and using APP led to a number of modifications of *libpp* itself. For instance, it was neces-

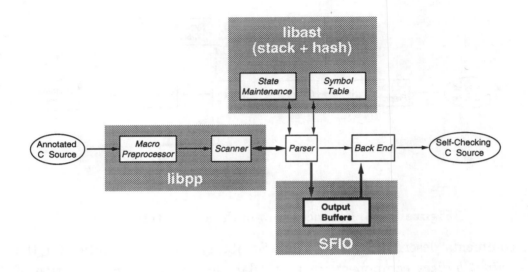

Figure 5.11 The architecture of APP with its reusable components.

sary to split *libpp*'s C++ tokenization option into two separate options, one for tokenization of C++-style comments (needed by APP to allow informal comments within assertion regions) and one for tokenization of C++ keywords (not needed by APP). *libpp* was also modified to support compilers that allow only eight characters in identifier and macro names (treating all names with the same eight-character prefix as being equivalent). And it was necessary to enhance *libpp*'s treatment of comments and input buffers in order to fully support APP's need to rescan and parse comments. But the most noticeable change to *libpp* was in the way it exports terminal token types.

In attempting to port APP to many different computing platforms, two conflicting situations were frequently encountered. On the one hand, it became apparent that there was no limit to the creativity of C compiler writers to invent new, nonstandard keywords to support architectural or environmental oddities (such as the keywords **near** and **far** for declaring pointers in Intel segmented memory architectures). On the other hand, the versions of *yacc* that were used on these platforms to generate APP's parser were typically built with a limit of 127 on the number of different terminal token types. Because each of the nonstandard keywords that were encountered on these platforms required a corresponding token type definition in *libpp*'s interface, the prevalent limit on token types in *yacc* was quickly reached. The solution to this problem was to group non-standard keywords into a meta-token type called NOISE (or NOISES for nonstandard grouping constructs) so that the number of token types exported by *libpp* would always be less than 127. Of course, because *libpp* also provides the string representation of every token that it scans, applications that need to distinguish among the different NOISE tokens need only look at their string representations.

In a way, APP can be viewed as providing two architectural services, program instrumentation and fault detection, that are inserted into an application at build-time and controlled at runtime. APP's cpp-like command-line interface was a natural by-product of using *libpp*, and this interface makes APP a natural mechanism for hooking into the program build process to support dynamic analysis of programs.

Furthermore, the ease with which APP could be modified to support instrumentation for tracing led to the rapid development of two trace-based dynamic analysis tools, and to an increased interest in instrumentation technology within the department. APP's ability to provide monitoring of the runtime workings of a program naturally complemented *cia*'s ability to discover static relationships within a program. *cia* had already been integrated with *dag* (later *dot*; see Section 11.2) to provide static views of program relationships. What was needed to support graphical display of dynamic data was the ability to animate graphs, such as those produced by *dag* for *cia*. The arrival of *lefty* (also described in Chapter 11) and its integration with *dag* led to the development of *Xray*, which required only small enhancements to APP's back end to support instrumentation for runtime tracing. *Xray* was quickly followed by the system TESTTUBE for selective regression testing. *Xray* and TESTTUBE are discussed in Chapter 11.

5.8   Conclusion

This chapter has described a tool called APP, an assertion-processing and instrumentation tool for C programs. APP was designed for seamless integration with C programming environments, allowing it to serve as a replacement for the standard C preprocessor. The implementation of APP exploits reusable components that provide much of the complex functionality of a C language front-end, plus other components that support complex manipulation of I/O buffers and other data structures. The ease with which APP fits into C programming environments has not only made programming with assertions more practical than before, but it has also engendered the development of tools that use program instrumentation to support dynamic analysis of program behavior.

6

Reverse Engineering

Yih-Farn Chen

6.1 Introduction

Chikofsky and Cross [CI90] define reverse engineering as a process of analyzing a subject system to find its components and their interrelationships, followed by creating representations of the system in another form or at a higher level of abstraction. This chapter describes CIA, the C Information Abstraction System [CNR90, Che89] designed to facilitate this process. CIA partitions a C program into a set of entities, analyzes their dependency relationships according to an *entity-relationship* model [Che76], and stores the structure information in a program database. A set of reverse engineering tools then accesses the database and the tools build on each other to provide successively higher levels of C structure abstractions.*

Figure 6.1 shows the reuse architecture of CIA as a dependency graph, where the CIA tools are shown in oval nodes, the program database and libraries in boxes, and non-CIA tools in diamonds. Edges between nodes represent dependency relationships. Reusable components that do not belong to the CIA proper are shaded.

The evolution of this architecture, where new members are added constantly, is guided by two major forces:

---

*We use CIA to refer to the C Information Abstraction System, which consists of *cia*, the C information abstractor, and related tools.

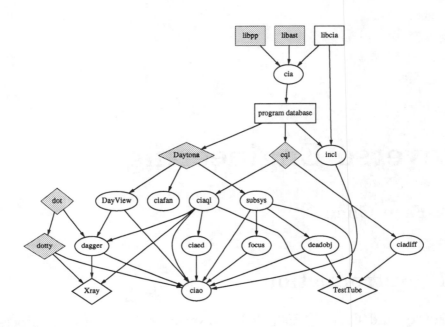

Figure 6.1 The reuse architecture of CIA.

- *Minimize the code size* so that the code complexity can be managed realistically.
- *Unify tool interaction styles* so that users can master and connect new CIA tools quickly.

Both call for heavy software reuse at library and tool integration levels. Most CIA tools are built as reusable *ksh* (Section 4.1) scripts that invoke or connect other plug-compatible query, graphics, or analysis tools. If performance or algorithm requirement of a tool dictates a C implementation, then portable C libraries are used wherever possible, to reduce code size.

CIA tools can be partitioned into the following categories:

- *Database Construction Tools*: *cia*, the C information abstractor, parses a C program to produce a database. It uses *libast* (Section 2.2.2) for maximal performance and portability, and the tokenizing preprocessor in *libpp* (Section 2.2.9) to integrate the preprocessing and parsing phases in a single process. Section 6.2 describes the CIA program database model and how CIA databases are constructed and maintained with *nmake* (Section 3.1.1).

- *Query Tools*: Instead of having each CIA tool access the program database directly, we provide a layer of basic query tools as building blocks that can be parameterized and reused in many scripts. The CIA database can be loaded by most well-designed database management systems. This feature allows us to provide users with two sets of query tools, each with its own unique merits: *ciaql*, based on *cql* [Fow94], a flat-file database query interpreter, and *DayView*, based on *Daytona* [Gre94], a complete database management system. When constructing new tools, C programmers find *cql* pleasant to use because of its C-like database schema and query expressions. Database programmers like to take advantage of *DayView*'s powerful query constructs for SQL-like manipulations. However, *ciaql*, *DayView*, and all CIA tools maintain the same consistent style of user interfaces. Section 6.3 describes how the CIA query tools can be used to explore program entities and relationships.

- *Program Visualization Tools*: *dagger* [Che94] is a CIA tool that visualizes   program structures with directed graphs. It uses CIA query or analysis tools to retrieve a subset of program relationships, maps the set to a directed graph, and then passes it to *dot* for automatic layout. Section 6.4 describes the CIA program visualization process and its associated tools.

- *Program Analysis Tools*: The entity-relationship information stored in the CIA program database enables the construction of several C analysis tools in substantially reduced   efforts. *subsys* performs reachability analysis to help package reusable software components and is used by *deadobj* to detect unused program entities. *incl* [VC92] analyzes reference relationships in the include hierarchy to detect unnecessary include files. For optimal performance, *incl* implements a special graph construction and search algorithm in C directly. *ciadiff* computes program differences at the entity level and allows users to query the results using *cql*. Both *subsys* and *ciadiff* were used to construct TESTTUBE (Section 11.3), a system for selective regression testing. Section 6.5 briefly describes the capabilities of these analysis tools.

The large number of CIA tools, some not shown in Figure 6.1, makes it difficult for users to remember what tools are applicable to what program entities or relationships. *ciao*, an open graphical front-end based on *dotty*, a customizable graph editor, provides easy access to all the CIA tools through a mix of table-based and graph-based interfaces. The consistent CIA user interfaces and data exchange formats make it possible in *ciao* to connect CIA tools in orthogonal ways to produce various textual, relational, and graphical views. Section 6.6 describes the basic architecture of *ciao* and uses a sample session to demonstrate its use.

In terms of the four reuse layers described in Chapter 1, the CIA system uses libraries in the substrate for maximal portability and better performance. CIA also uses several base tools: *ksh* to provide tool communications and construction, *nmake* to help construct and maintain program databases, *cql* and *Daytona* to provide query services, and *dot* and *dotty* to provide visualization services. CIA itself provides many standalone tools that build on each other and are also reused by other connected tools, such as *Xray* (Section 11.4) and TESTTUBE. Section 6.7 reports how the CIA reuse architecture has evolved through the years to become the picture shown in Figure 6.1.

One reuse experience in CIA that is probably not shared as much by other tools described in this book is its *reuse through a database or repository*, which encapsulates the entity-relationship information shared by all CIA applications. Section 6.8 concludes by proposing a new architecture style, *Aero*, based on our design and implementation experience of CIA. *Aero* is an attempt to generalize the architecture of all repository-based reverse engineering tools. We hope reuse guidelines for this architecture style can help significantly reduce the design and implementation efforts of all similar systems.

6.2   An Entity-Relationship Model for C

All CIA tools deal with three main concepts: entities, attributes, and relationships. A C program is partitioned into a collection of C programming entities referring to each other. CIA recognizes five kinds of C entities: *file*, *type*, *function*, *variable*, and *macro*. Each entity and relationship kind has its own set of attributes. For example, consider the following C program:

```
/* file ftable.c */
#include "coor.h"    /* defines types COOR and struct coor */
#define TBLSIZE 2
extern COOR *rotate();
extern COOR *shift();
typedef COOR *(*PFPC)();
static PFPC ftable[TBLSIZE] =  { rotate, shift };
```

After processing this piece of code, *cia* records nine entity declarations in the database:

file: **ftable.c** and **coor.h**
function: **rotate** and **shift**
type: **PFPC, COOR,** and **struct coor**
variable: **ftable**
macro: **TBLSIZE**

Nine relationships between these entities are also recorded by *cia*. For example, **ftable** refers to the macro **TBLSIZE**, the type **PFPC**, and two functions, **rotate** and **shift**, which, in turn, refer to the type **COOR**. In addition, the attributes (storage class, data type, definition/declaration, and so on) of each entity declaration are recorded. The complete database for the above piece of code can be easily mapped to a directed graph, as shown in Figure 6.2, where files and functions are shown in boxes, types in diamonds, variables in ellipses, and macros in plain text.

In summary, the job of *cia* is to selectively map program source text to an entity-relationship database, complete at its abstraction level, by ignoring certain details, such as data and control flow information involving only local variables.

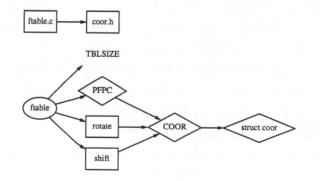

Figure 6.2   The complete graph of a small C program.

The use of an entity-relationship database, where language-specific information is encapsulated as much as possible in the database model, allows CIA tools to achieve a strong degree of language independence. For example, although the CIA model for C++ [GC90] incorporates additional relationship kinds, such as *inheritance* and *friendship*, program database tools for both C and C++ share the same style of query interface.

The process of creating a CIA database is similar to the process of compiling and linking C programs. The main difference is that *cia* creates a database file (.A), instead of a .o file, for each source file to store the corresponding entity-relationship information. For example, the following commands build a simple CIA database **peek.db** from three C source files:

```
$ cia -c -Iliblist peekf.c
$ cia -c -Iliblist view.c
$ cia -c xmalloc.c
$ cia -o peek peekf.A view.A xmalloc.A
```

The similarity allows us to create the *ciadb* rule for *nmake* by reusing the C compilation rule with minor adaptations. Projects that already use *nmake* can build a CIA database automatically by simply running the following command without any changes in their Makefiles:

```
$ nmake ciadb
```

Most query examples and program graphs presented in this chapter are derived from the CIA program databases of three tools: *peek*, a simple tool that retrieves sets of lines in a file; *incl*, a tool that detects unnecessary include files; and *xgremlin*, an X11 version of a graph drawing tool called *gremlin* [OTC86]. The last two programs have many users and have evolved over the years to meet user demands. Some metrics on the complexity of these three programs are shown in Table 6.1. The numbers include all the user and system header files used by these programs, but they exclude the source files of libraries used. Both source and database sizes are measured in the number of bytes.

While we were able to visualize the complete software structure for the simple piece of code shown earlier, for any real and complex programs, we must rely on queries to selectively retrieve subsets of the entities and relationships to study slices of programs. The next section presents the

Table 6.1   Complexity Metrics for Program Database Examples

Program	Lines	Source Size	db Size	Entities	Relationships
peek	749	19,760	6,491	114	122
incl	1,957	49,963	26,416	392	517
xgremlin	24,582	620,726	390,430	4,842	6,634

basic queries used by many CIA tools to build successively more complex tools.

6.3   Query Tools

The two CIA query systems, *ciaql* and *DayView*, share the same style of user interface. In this section, we shall focus on *ciaql*, the query system based on the C-like query language *cql* [Fow94]. *Ciaql* consists of two basic query commands that retrieve relational views:

- *cdef* retrieves attributes of C entities
- *cref* retrieves relationships between C entities

These two commands are the major building blocks used by tools in the following two categories:

- *Entity query tools*: Each tool in this category uses *cdef* to retrieve a set that matches an entity specification, and then applies an operation to that set.
- *Relationship query tools*: Each tool in this category uses *cref* to retrieve a relationship set that matches a (parent entity, child entity) set specification, and then applies an operation to that set.

Typical operations include closure computation, fanin/fanout computation, graph-drawing, analysis, and other filtering tasks. The result of an operation is frequently another set of entities or relationships, possibly with additional attributes that are application-specific. The uniform tool interface and data exchange paradigm allow CIA tools to be connected easily with each other and with many standard UNIX tools.

The following two sections describe the two basic queries *cdef* and *cref* and some of their derivatives in more detail. All query examples are derived from the CIA database for *peek*, the first tool listed in Table 6.1.

6.3.1   Entity Query Tools

A simple entity query retrieves entities that match an *entity pattern* in the
form of *entkind entname*, where an entity name is a *ksh* pattern or a wild
card in the form of "–". An entity pattern can be further characterized
with a set of selection clauses in the form of *attr=value*.

For example, the following *cdef* query retrieves all static variable declarations:

```
$ cdef var - sclass=static
file                          name sclass dtype          def     bline eline
==================== ============ ====== ============== ======= ===== =====
view.c                          fp static struct _iobuf  def     13    13
view.c                     srcfile static char *         def     14    14
xmalloc.c                      msg static char []        def     19    19
```

The entity-based specification of *cdef* allows users to retrieve program
entities without knowing where they are located. This is especially crucial for large software projects, where thousands of source files scatter in
complex directory hierarchies.

Most CIA tools are designed as reusable components or filters for building more complex tools. To facilitate further processing, an unformatted
form of data representation is provided by both entity and relationship
query tools for exchanging data. The following *cdef* query shows all the
attributes of the function `viewline` in the unformatted form:

```
$ cdef -u func viewline
97;viewline;function;0;view.c;void;static;28;29;45;def;3514062;
```

Writing tools that operate on this standard entity data exchange form
is an easy task. For example, to count the number of static variable definitions, simply use:

```
$ cdef -u var - sclass=static def=def | wc -l
      3
```

If we pipe the raw data to a filter that uses the location information of
each entity to retrieve its corresponding source text, then we get the *vdef*
command. For example, to view all static variables in `view.c`, simply use:

```
$ vdef var - sclass=static
static char *srcfile;
static FILE *fp;
static char msg[]    = "storage allocator out of space";
```

The same information can be used to build *ciaed*, an *entity editor*. The
following *ksh* script shows its simple implementation, where an editor is
invoked to place its cursor on the definition of any specified C entity:

```
# Usage:  ciaed entkind entname
EDITOR=${EDITOR-emacs}
set $(cdef -u "$@" def=def | cut -d ;' -f5,8 | sed -e 's/;/ /')
# $1 now set to file and $2 set to bline
$EDITOR +$2 $1
```

For example, a user can edit the function definition of `viewlines` by
simply invoking:

```
$ ciaed func viewlines
```

All entity tools in CIA, including *cdef, vdef, ciaed, ciafan, subsys, deadobj, focus*, and so on, share the same basic interface style to retrieve entity
sets, thus greatly reducing the user's learning and the author's implementation efforts.

6.3.2   Relationship Query Tools

cref is the fundamental relationship query tool for examining program
relationships. It takes a *relationship pattern*, which is the concatenation
of two *entity patterns* that represent the parent and child of a specified relationship. Once a user becomes familiar with entity queries, relationship
queries come naturally.

For example, the following query finds all functions that start with
`view` and refer to static variables (the letter p stands for a C procedure,
that is, function):

```
$ cref func 'view*' var - sclass2=static
k1 file1                 name1             k2 file2             name2
== ================= ================ == ================= ================
p  view.c                viewlines         v  view.c             fp
p  view.c                viewlines         v  view.c             srcfile
p  view.c                viewline          v  view.c             fp
p  view.c                viewline          v  view.c             srcfile
```

As with *cdef*, some interesting new C tools can be created by using the
data exchange form of *cref*, which is the concatenation of the *cdef* data
exchange records of the parent and child with associated attributes of the

specified relationship. The CIA visualization tool, *dagger* (Section 6.4), is one example that processes the *cref* data exchange form further to generate directed graphs.

As a simpler example, we can construct a pipeline to compute the *file-fanout* of `view.c`; that is, the number of files that it includes:

```
$ cref -u file view.c file - | wc -l
       4
```

ciafan is a more general CIA tool for computing various fanins and fanouts for a set of specified entities. The tool is interesting because it first uses *cdef* to retrieve a set of entities, and then uses *cref* to compute their fanins and fanouts. For example, we can use *ciafan* to obtain the complete set of fanin and fanout numbers for the function definition of `viewlines`:

```
$ ciafan func viewlines def=def
file               name         ifu ofu oma ity oty iva ova ifi ofi itot otot
================   ===========  === === === === === === === === === ==== ====
view.c             viewlines      1   8   1   0   1   0   2   0   0    1   12
```

Here, *ifu* stands for the number of functions that refer to `viewlines` (fanin functions), *ofu* stands for the number of functions that `viewlines` refers to (fanout functions), and so on. *ciafan* also shows the total fanin (*itot*) and fanout (*otot*) numbers. The total fanin is the sum of *ifu, ity, iva,* and *ifi.* The total fanout is the sum of *ofu, oma, oty, ova,* and *ofi.*

cref is also ideal for performing module-dependency analysis. In the following discussion, we define a module as a logical program unit that imports and exports some entity definitions. In the case of C programs, a module can consist of a single file or a set of files (such as all files that make up a library). By simply setting the two file attributes to patterns that correspond to the modules of interest, we can use *cref* to study various module dependencies. For example, we can find out how dependent the functions in module `peekf.c` are on external entities by first counting all references from functions defined in `peekf.c` to any entity *not* defined in that file. The following query shows that there is a total of 30 external references originating from functions in `peekf.c`; three of the references go to external variables:

```
$ cref -u func - - - file1=peekf.c file2!=peekf.c | wc -l
     30
$ cref -u func - var - file1=peekf.c file2!=peekf.c | wc -l
      3
```

As we can see from the fanin/fanout and module-dependency computations, it is frequently easy to use *cref* to write software metrics tools that deal with entity dependencies. For example, the reuse numbers in column 3 of Table 1.1 were generated with a set of scripts that use *cref* and *subsys* (see Section 6.5.1) to calculate the numbers of entities and source lines in each library reused by a tool.

Similar to the correspondence between *vdef* and *cdef*, *vref* displays text of selected references that correspond to the same *cref* query. For example, we can retrieve the text of all references in **peekf.c** to list-handling functions:

```
$ vref -n func - func '*_list' file1=peekf.c
000103;   insert_list(pairs_list, (VOID *)p);
000111;   insert_list(pairs_list, (VOID *)p);
000115;   } else insert_list(pairs_list, (VOID *)p);
000095;   pairs_list=init_list();
```

Examples presented in this section attempt to demonstrate that the power of *cdef* and *cref* lies in their simple and flexible query patterns. The set of possible queries that can be created by mixing different kinds, symbol patterns, and selection clauses on different attributes, coupled with different filters that can be applied to the retrieved sets, represents a large tool space that most other existing C tools cannot fill. The next section presents examples on how a visualization tool, which is also built on top of *cref*, was used effectively to map programs to graphs.

6.4 Program Visualization Tools

Roman and Cox define program visualization as a process of mapping programs to graphical representations and give a comprehensive survey on its various forms [RC92]. This section presents a program visualization approach that focuses on automatically generating abstractions of the static code structure. The visualization process consists of a sequence of selective mappings. First, a parser analyzes the source of a program and

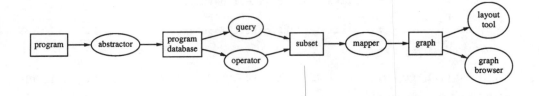

Figure 6.3 The process of generating program graphs.

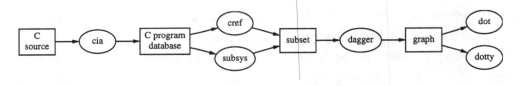

Figure 6.4 An instantiation of the graph generation process for C.

maps it to a program database, according to an entity-relationship model. Next, a *query* or *operator* retrieves a subset of the database, which is then mapped to a directed graph. Finally, the graph specification is passed to layout tools or interactive graph browsers. The complete graph generation process is diagramed in Figure 6.3.

This process is largely language-independent because of its focus on entities and relationships. Our instantiation of this process for C includes *cia* as the abstractor, *cref* as the query tool, *subsys* and other analysis tools (see Section 6.5) as the operators, the C version of *dagger* for mapping the subset to a directed graph, *dot* to layout the graph automatically, and *dotty* for browsing the graphs (see Section 11.2). By changing a set of mapping functions, *dagger* can easily adapt to different entity-relationship databases and automatic layout tools. Figure 6.4 shows an instantiation of the graph generation process for C.

dagger generates a large variety of C and C++ program graphs, including header file hierarchy, entity dependency, module binding, type inheritance, and *focus* graphs (Section 6.5.1). By default, *dagger* invokes the *cref* tool to obtain a subset of relationships. For example, Figure 6.5 shows the type dependency graph of a C program generated by *dagger* and drawn by *dot* with the following simple command pipeline:

```
$ dagger type - type - | dot -Tps
```

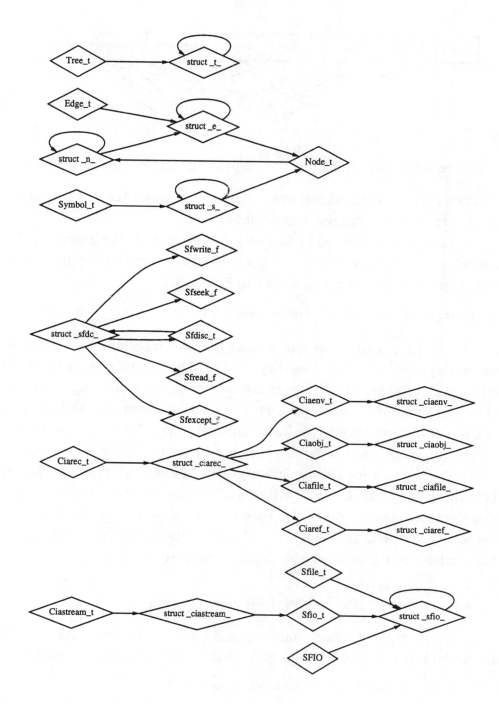

Figure 6.5 A type dependency graph generated by *dagger* and drawn by *dot*.

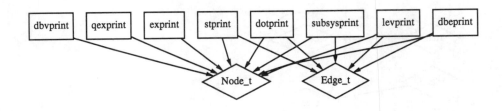

Figure 6.6 All printing functions depend on Node_t, Edge_t, or both.

The picture reveals several cyclic dependencies and the relative structural complexity of **Ciarec_t** and **Symbol_t**.

dagger inherits the complete query power of *cref*. For example, the following command retrieves a subset of function-to-type relationships and maps them to the graph shown in Figure 6.6:

```
$ dagger -R func '*print' type - | dot -Tps
```

The diagram shows the connections between functions whose names end with **print**, and the types they refer to. The picture reveals an interesting structural fact that is not as obvious in the corresponding relational view: All functions that depend on **Edge_t** also depend on **Node_t**, but not the other way round. We later confirmed that this structural fact is preserved across many programs that use the same pair of data types.

As an example for C++ program graphs, Figure 6.7 shows a typical type inheritance graph generated from a C++ program database using the same process. The graph is also generated by *dagger*, with the language set to C++ and with the relationship kind to inheritance (**rkind=i**). Note that virtual inheritance relationships are properly labeled.

```
$ export CIALANG=CC
$ dagger type - type - rkind=i | dot -Tps
```

As an example of more complex graphs, Figure 6.8 shows the include hierarchies in *xgremlin* that are generated by the following command:

```
$ dagger -F file - file '!(icons/*)' | dot -Tps
```

The diagram has been simplified by using a *negation* operator in the child name pattern to ignore all include relationships involving header files stored in the **icons** subdirectory. Unfortunately, the picture is still

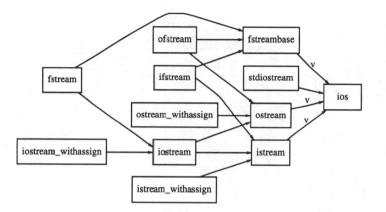

Figure 6.7 A C++ type inheritance graph.

too difficult to read on a single page. What the user frequently wants is a single include hierarchy rooted at a particular source file, with all other include relationships ignored. We shall see how this problem can be resolved in the next section.

While the labels in Figure 6.8 are hard to read, the function reference graph in Figure 6.9, generated by the following command, seems to be beyond comprehension:

```
$ dagger -F func - func - | dot -Tps
```

The diagram does show some interesting facts, though. The first observation is that a few functions have very large fanins. Identification of and further studies on these functions can be performed with the CIA tool *ciafan* (see Section 6.3.2). Another observation is that many functions do not seem to be on any of the reference paths from **main** (the root function at the lower left corner). There are two possibilities:

- These are dead functions that never get exercised. The CIA tool *deadobj* does detect 11 dead functions in *xgremlin*.
- These are functions indirectly invoked through variables. In this case, both function-to-function and variable-to-function relationships must be drawn to complete the static dependency picture. *Xgremlin* indeed has many functions defined in a variable array for menu selections. Section 11.4 discusses how dynamic function reference relationships

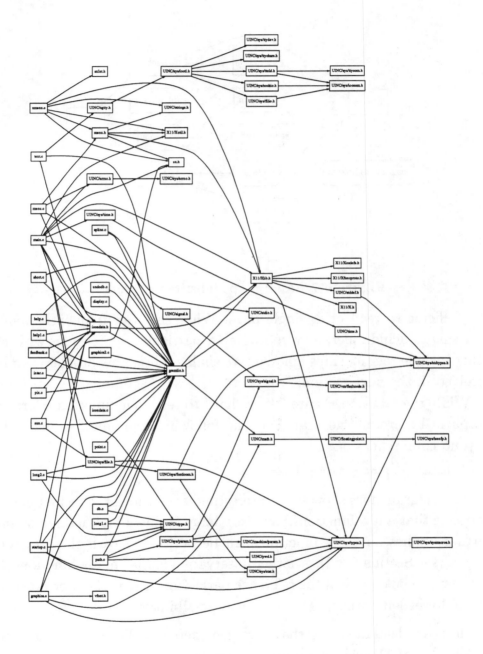

Figure 6.8 The simplified include graph of *xgremlin*.

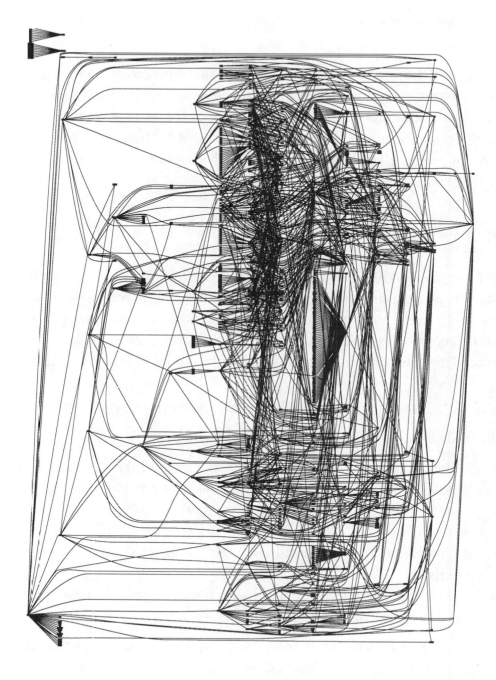

Figure 6.9 The complex function reference graph of *xgremlin*.

can be captured during program execution to supplement the static ones.

A brute-force way to solve the graph complexity problem is to blow up the diagram. Magnifying complex graphs, however, is usually not satisfactory because the number of edge crossings increases substantially and they become a major distraction. In the next section, we show how a closure operator can work in tandem with *dagger* to help manage graph complexity.

6.5   Analysis Tools

This section discusses three program analysis tools that provide good abstractions encapsulated in operators: *subsys* performs reachability analysis, *incl* detects unnecessary include files, and *ciadiff* compares programs at the entity level. These operators provide reusable components that other CIA tools can build on in addition to the basic query operators.

6.5.1   *subsys*: A Tool for Reachability Analysis

Typical software maintenance tasks might require:

- Finding all program entities that an entity depends on directly or indirectly. This information is particularly useful for partitioning complex program graphs and for packaging software components for reuse in other projects.
- Finding all program entities that might be affected by the change of an entity.
- Displaying a *focus* graph that shows a few layers of relationships centered around a particular node.

The CIA closure operator *subsys* is designed to answer these questions by computing all entities and relationships reachable from selected entities. The reachability computation can be done in either the forward or backward direction. For example, the following command retrieves all data types that `Symbol_t` depends on directly or indirectly:

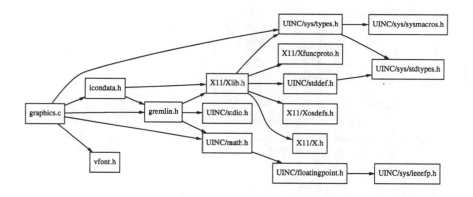

Figure 6.10   The include hierarchy rooted at `graphics.c`.

```
$ subsys t Symbol_t
file                        kind      name
========================== ===== =================
incl.h                     type         Symbol_t
incl.h                     type        struct _s_
incl.h                     type           Node_t
incl.h                     type        struct _n_
incl.h                     type        struct _e_
```

subsys can also retrieve the reachable relationship set (rather than the reachable entity set) and present the set to *dagger* to generate reachability graphs. The include hierarchy of `graphics.c`, shown in Figure 6.10, can be extracted by the following command pipeline:

```
$ subsys -u -e file graphics.c | dagger -i | dot -Tps
```

In the previous example, only file-to-file relationships are traced. However, it is frequently necessary to compute a *complete* reachable set, where all kinds of relationships are considered. For example, *subsys* can generate a complete subsystem rooted at the function `mustuse` of *incl*, shown in Figure 6.11. If the function `mustuse` is to be reused in a different software project, then all the entities present in this reachable set must also be available in that project to avoid missing references during the compilation of `mustuse`.

The set of graphs generated by *dagger* can be further extended by mixing an interesting collection of standard *cref* data exchange records and presenting the resulting set to *dagger*.

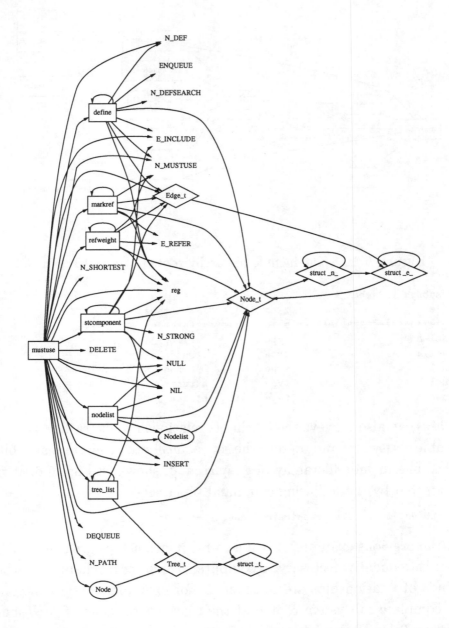

Figure 6.11 A complete subsystem graph rooted at the function `mustuse`. (Functions are shown in boxes, types in diamonds, variables in ellipses, and macros in plain text.)

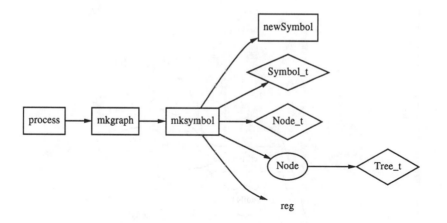

Figure 6.12 A five-layer focus graph centered at the function `mksymbol`.

The following simple shell script concatenates the output of two *subsys* commands and generates a *focus* graph with the specified entity at the center. The first *subsys* command traverses the graph starting from the root in a forward direction, and the other one traverses backward.

```
# a simple version of focus
(subsys -u -e "$@"; subsys -u -e -r "$@") | dagger -i | dot -Tps
```

In general, *focus* can go as many levels deep as the user desires. Figure 6.12 shows a focus graph centered at the function `mksymbol`. The graph traversals were limited to only two levels deep in each direction.

Even the reachable set of a selected entity may be so complex that further simplifications are necessary. One common technique is to recursively partition a reachable set into trackable pieces. During the generation of a subsystem, we can stop the graph traversal at certain selected nodes, ignore their subhierarchies, and later expand these nodes as necessary. For example, Figure 6.13 shows the subsystem of the *xgremlin* function `GRArc` by ignoring the relationship hierarchy rooted at `GRVector`.

As soon as *subsys* became available, a CIA user took advantage of it to implement a script that detects dead functions. The basic idea is simple: Use *subsys* to find out all functions reachable (including those through variable initializations) from `main`, and then compare that list with the list of functions stored in the database; the difference is the set of *dead*

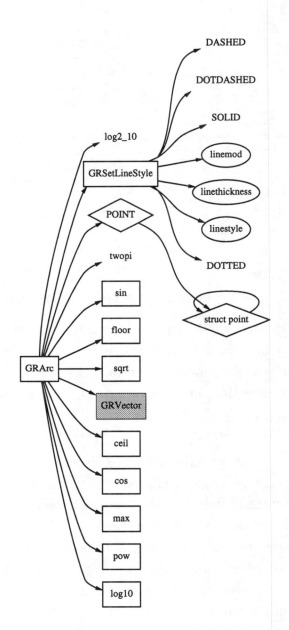

Figure 6.13 A partial subsystem graph rooted at the *xgremlin* function
GRArc.

functions. The script has evolved to become *deadobj*, which takes general entity patterns to narrow down the focus. For example, we can restrict the detection of dead entities to only those macros that end with either ERR or `err`:

```
$ deadobj m '*ERR|*err'
/usr/include/stdio.h macro _IOERR
/usr/include/stdio.h macro clearerr
```

6.5.2   *incl*: A Tool to Analyze Include Files

incl is a tool that analyzes C include hierarchies to:

- Detect unnecessary include files
- Show the include and reference relationships among include files in graphical or textual forms
- Provide mechanisms to remove or skip unnecessary include files

By default, *incl* lists unnecessary header files included directly or indirectly by a source file. The following command shows that six header files under the include hierarchy of opendb.c were detected to be unnecessary:

```
$ incl -l opendb.c
opendb.c
        /usr/include/stdio.h
        /usr/include/ctype.h~
        hdr/db.h+
            hdr/dir.h+
                /usr/include/sys/stat.h~
                    /usr/include/sys/types.h~
                        /usr/include/sys/stdtypes.h~
                        /usr/include/sys/sysmacros.h~
        hdr/cdb.h~
        hdr/error.h
```

incl classifies files into three categories and tags them differently in the output:

- *used*: The ones that are necessary for the compilation of the source file. These files are not tagged.
- *unused*: The ones that do not have any declarations that are referred to, directly or indirectly, by the source file. These files are tagged with the "~" character; for example, /usr/include/ctype.h in the previous example.

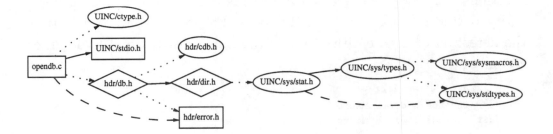

Figure 6.14 A graphical view of the include hierarchy of `opendb.c` with analysis results.

- *onpath*: The ones that are necessary simply because they are on one of the paths to the **used** ones. Those files referred to directly or indirectly by *onpath* files are also marked as *onpath*. All these files are tagged with the "+" character; for example, `hdr/db.h`.

We can also create a graphical view of the *incl* analysis result The following drawing conventions are used in drawing the graph: used files are drawn in *boxes*, onpath files are in *diamonds*, and unused files are in *ovals*. A *dotted edge* means that the tail file directly includes the head file but does not refer to any declarations in the head file; a *dashed edge* indicates that the tail file does not directly includes the head file but contains references to the head file; finally, a *solid edge* indicates that the tail file both directly includes and makes use of declarations in the head file.

There are two ways to deal with unnecessary include files:

- *Delete* them: This is usually feasible with the first-level include statements only because nested include files may be shared with other source files. We can easily generate an *ed* script to remove the first-level include statements.

- *Skip* them: This is achieved by using *nmake*'s *cpp* to read *incl* results and skip those during the C preprocessing and compilation stages.

We have seen significant compilation-time reductions in many software projects, by simply skipping unused files detected by *incl*. Usually between 10 and 35 percent of includes files are unused. More importantly, the *incl* analysis helps programmers to understand and clean up their include architecture.

6.5.3 *ciadiff*: A Tool for Program Differencing

Traditional text-differencing tools are not satisfactory for studying changes in program structures because they present inadequate abstractions. Attempts have been made to do fine-granularity syntactic program differencing based on parse-tree comparisons with only a limited degree of success [Yan91]. We have implemented efficient program differencing tools for C by comparing program databases of corresponding versions to detect changed, deleted, and added program entities. A C++ version has been implemented with various enhancements [Gra92].

As an example, the following query finds all macro differences in the file `trans.c` between versions v1 and v2 of the same program:

```
$ export CIAOLDDIR=v1
$ export CIANEWDIR=v2
$ ciadiff macro - file=trans.c
    tag kind              file              name    chksum
======= ======== ================= ================= ========
deleted macro             trans.c                    DELTA 5e291185
changed macro             trans.c                    FNUM  8185185
  added macro             trans.c                    UNIT  38e6811a
```

Both *ciadiff* and *subsys* have been used successfully to implement TESTTUBE (described in Section 11.3), a system for selective regression testing. Our experience with TESTTUBE on several projects has suggested that it has the potential to reduce the set of test cases that need to be rerun for typical maintenance changes [CRV94].

Following a similar derivation path from *cdef* to *vdef*, we can show the textual differences between two versions of a program entity using *vdiff*, which is built on top of the CIA *vdef* command and the standard UNIX *diff* command. It compares the text of selected entities:

```
$ vdiff type 'struct coor'
2,3c2
<       int refpoint[DIM];
<       int curpoint[DIM];
---
>       int point[DIM];
```

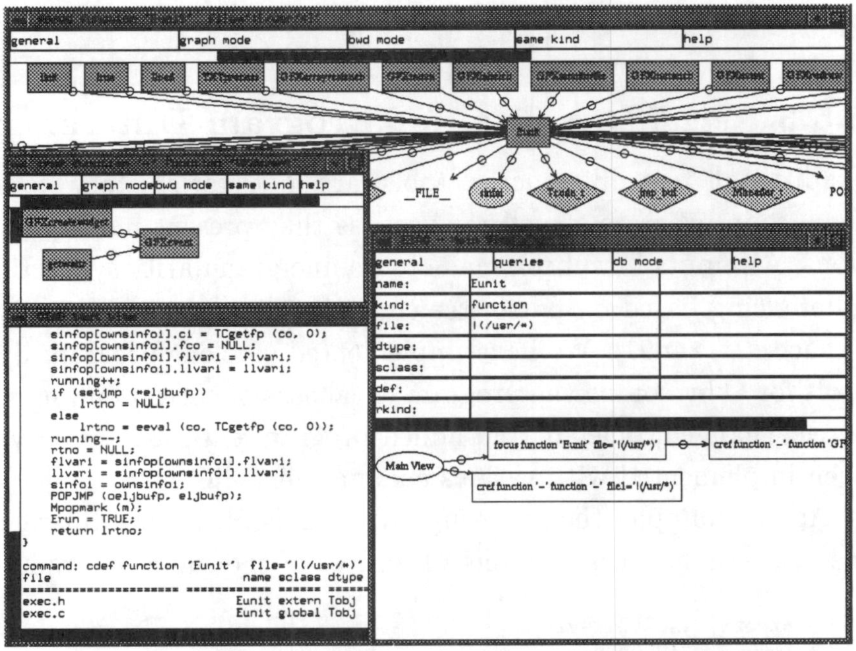

Figure 6.15   A snapshot of *ciao*.

vdiff is interesting and useful because it allows a programmer to compare two versions of an entity without specifying their corresponding source files and line numbers. Such information is usually not readily available to the programmer.

6.6   *ciao*: A Graphical Navigator for C and C++

ciao [KN94] is a graphical front-end to CIA tools described in previous sections. Built on top of *dotty* (Section 11.2), a customizable graph editor, *ciao* connects CIA query and analysis tools in UNIX pipes elegantly through a mix of graph-based and table-based interfaces. Programmers can use *ciao* to selectively generate a sequence of graphical, relational, or textual views to explore the structure and contents of a program.

Figure 6.15 shows the snapshot of a *ciao* session. Users interact with *ciao* through either a query table or a graph. The query table shown in the right of the snapshot helps the user to formulate entity or relationship queries without memorizing the database schema. Each formulated query retrieves a set of entities or relationships. The user then decides what *operator* to apply to that set to produce a desired view. The separation of query formulation and data representation allows users to generate multiple views on the same slice of code by using a single query followed by different filters. As an example, the query table in the snapshot formulates the following query: Retrieve all function declarations of `Eunit` not defined in a system header file under `/usr`. Several views were generated from this query: The `text view` window in the left of the snapshot shows both the scrollable source text and formulated database records of `Eunit`. In addition, a graphical view showing all the interactions with `Eunit` was created first with the *focus* operator, which collects all relationships centered at `Eunit`, followed by applying the *dagger* operator, which maps that set of relationships to a directed graph using the automatic layout tool *dot*. This *focus* graph identifies all the functions that refer to `Eunit` and all entities that `Eunit` depends on. Focus graphs are used heavily during the navigation of a program's static structure, because they provide quick access to entities related to a focal point. In the *ciao* graphs, functions and files are mapped to boxes, types to diamonds, variables to ovals, and macros to plain text–all in different colors—to help distinguish between different kinds of entities in the same graph.

After a directed graph is created, each node in the graph becomes an interactive point with *ciao*. A pop-up menu is attached to each node, listing only the legal operators that can be applied to the corresponding entity. For example, the *incl* operator can be applied only to file nodes, while the *cref* operator, which shows references to and from a particular entity, can be applied to any entity. Operators may generate more graphs for further interactions. For example, the graph window on the left of the snapshot with the caption "cref function - function GFXevent" was created by applying a *reverse cref* operator to the GFXevent node in the focus graph, followed by an application of the *dagger* operator.

Because many graphs can be generated easily from *ciao* and the user may lose control over what has been generated, a *navigation* graph under the query table shows the derivation of all the open graph views.

Menus attached to the nodes in this graph allow the user to bring the corresponding graphs to the foreground or kill them directly.

Graphical programming environments, such as ObjectCenter [MM93], SMARTsystem [Par91], and Energize [Wol93], have become more available recently. However, unlike *ciao*, they usually lack the abstraction and query power needed to selectively visualize facets of complex structures in large software projects. Moreover, *ciao* inherits the ever-increasing graph drawing capabilities of *dot*, and enjoys the extensible and customizable interface provided through *dotty*. New CIA tools can be easily incorporated by modifying the interface description file. As the requisite technologies mature, we expect programmers to rely more heavily in the future on graphical programming environments, such as *ciao*, to explore and improve their software structures.

6.7   Reuse Experience

This section summarizes our years of reuse experience with the design and implementation of CIA tools. We shall focus on the following areas: C dialects, database and query systems, reachability analysis, and program visualization.

- *C Dialects*: The initial implementation of *cia* faced two major problems:

  How to handle C programs written in different C dialects, including variants of C preprocessors

  How to integrate preprocessing, tokenization, and parsing all in a single process so that references to macros do not get lost after C preprocessing

  The first problem was originally solved by inserting undesirable #ifdef statements, and the second by an awkward modification of Reiser's C preprocessor followed by postprocessing the *cpp* output. The resulting tool was fragile and inaccurate in many cases. The problems were later solved by using the tokenizing preprocessor library *libpp* (see Section 2.2.9), which was developed to solve similar problems in dealing with various dialects of C and *cpp* on many platforms. CIA's adoption of *libpp* has also helped enlarge the library's existing user base and made some contribution to its robustness and generalization.

For example, when we first used *incl* to detect unnecessary include files in several large software projects, we realized that those files had to be *skipped* (see Section 6.5.2) rather than removed, because they may be used by other source files. The natural place to perform the skipping is during C preprocessing. Instead of making the preprocessing library handle just the *incl* output, a general *file-ignore* operation was implemented in *libpp*, since it is likely to be used in other applications.

- *Database and Query Systems:*

Initially, CIA used a simple version of *InfoView* [CNR90] that the author wrote exclusively for CIA use. When CIA had to start dealing with large program databases for a project that includes nearly a million lines of code, Charles Hayden, a developer in that project, rewrote *InfoView* to use a B-tree library to get better performance. However, when we started building a version of CIA for C++ programs, instead of making major revisions to *InfoView*, we decided to switch to general-purpose database languages and systems, such as *cql* and *Daytona*, so that both C and C++ program databases can be supported.

While both *cql* and *Daytona* have served the purpose of implementing several CIA query and analysis tools, we also found out that C programmers who are not familiar with database terminologies prefer writing shell scripts rather than detailed database queries. To encourage new tool construction, we had to provide parameterized query commands so that programmers can combine these query tools easily with other existing tools in shell scripts to build successively more complex tools. To make this approach practical, basic queries that serve as fundamental building blocks must run efficiently. The current CIA query tools and their underlying systems have gone through extensive optimizations to achieve a level of performance that is practical for daily use in software projects that involve millions of lines of code.

As an example, for a typical project that includes 6,228 files and 861,939 lines of C code, the CIA database, including over 70,000 program entities and 46,000 relationships, is 6.3 megabytes. Both the database and its indices are roughly 47 percent of the source size, which is 13.4 megabytes. A typical use of the CIA relationship-retrieval query *cref*, which finds all functions that refer to a particular data type, was run on the database. The query took 0.51 CPU seconds (user and system time combined) on an SGI Indy R4400 workstation running IRIX 5.2 to retrieve the 129 function entities that match the specification.

- *Reachability Analysis:* We have repeatedly found the need to perform reachability analysis using an efficient closure operator, which is not a widely available query construct. Currently, we have different implementations embedded in *incl* and *subsys*. The new version of *subsys* employs the closure construct in the *Daytona* database management system to obtain an efficient implementation that can be generalized for use by other tools. Tools that perform reachability analysis have been received enthusiastically by both developers and managers because they help clean up existing software architectures.

- *Software Visualization:* Selectivity is essential to successful visualization of complex software structures. Our initial naive attempt in generating complete program graphs failed miserably for even medium-size projects. Labels were illegible and edge-crossings cluttered up most of the space in blown-up graphs that could cover a complete wall. We have learned to manage the complexity by using database queries to retrieve only slices of the program graph, and by using closure operators to selectively ignore and expand subgraphs.

  Initially, CIA uses *dag*, the predecessor of *dot*, to generate only passive displays of program structures. The new *dot* graph format, which allows user-defined attributes to be carried along with each graph node, makes it easy to attach CIA attributes to the *dot* graphs that *dagger* produces. The attribute information has been used in *ciao* to customize each node menu so that only proper operators that are applicable to a CIA entity are listed. The *file* attribute information is used in *Xray* to help cluster function nodes that belong to the same file or module to reveal module dependencies.

The interactions between CIA and other libraries and tools have benefited both sides. CIA is both a consumer and a producer. The author of CIA selects the best reusable libraries and tools available (in his own opinion and criteria) to assemble the CIA system. Because CIA has a large user base, the adoption by CIA helps increase the user base and robustness of a reusable component. On the other hand, the increasing applications of CIA reusable tools in a project (for example, *subsys* in *Xray* and TESTTUBE), helps offset and justify the overhead introduced by creating a CIA database. It is such a *Free Market* (see Section 1.2) that drives each reusable component used and produced by CIA to achieve its current state and moves it toward greater reusability.

6.8   Conclusion

Advances in software and hardware technologies have made the generation of program databases and presentations of various abstractions of software structures an inexpensive reality. Our years of research and development experience with CIA, a set of reverse engineering tools that help explore software structures, have demonstrated the feasibility of this repository-based approach. We are beginning to reap the benefits of these tools, which have now been put in use in many large software projects.

We are currently exploring the integration and configuration management of program databases for multiple languages, including C, C++, *ksh*, *nmake*, and *yacc*, so that we can complete the software structure picture for many of our own projects. Since the design of CIA is largely language-independent because of its emphasis on entities and relationships, we would like to maximize the reuse of CIA experience in the new efforts.

Our first step was to define an architecture style, *Aero*, for repository-based reverse engineering tools. *Aero* stands for *attribute, entity, relationship, and operator*. The style consists of an *abstractor* that converts a software document according to its entity-relationship model into a database; a *query subsystem* that employs a database service to provide basic entity and relationship query tools that produce exchangeable data formats; a *visualization subsystem* that employs a visualization service to map relationship query outputs to directed graphs; and an *operator subsystem* that builds successively higher levels of operators using a script tool to connect basic query tools and other operators. Note, again, that the main concepts behind all the CIA operators–*subsys, deadobj, incl, ciafan, focus,* and *ciadiff*–are simply entities, attributes, and relationships; therefore, the algorithms behind these tools can be generalized to handle many other kinds of software documents.

We hope a reusable architecture style, such as *Aero*, would help fuel further research work in reverse engineering, configuration management, software visualization, and all other technologies that *Aero* depends on. In return, we expect the *Aero* architecture style to help produce highly reusable components that find exciting applications in other software engineering projects.

7

Security and Software Engineering

Steven Bellovin

7.1 Introduction

The program understanding tools *app* and *cia*, described in Chapters 5 and 6, provide a means to analyze software. The analysis is, however, at an intra-software entity level, that is, the relationships among the program entities. Beyond such relationships, certain dynamic aspects of the program are crucial in many applications. Two of the important criteria of computer programs are security and high availability. This chapter focuses on the security aspect, while the next chapter will discuss high availability.

One does not have to be an expert in the field to know that computer programs are often buggy. Any regular newspaper reader has seen countless stories to that effect. Of late, though, the stories have focused on computer security problems that are often the result of bugs in the design or implementation of software systems.

To some extent, security holes can be reduced or eliminated by the same techniques that are used to eliminate other bugs; but there is one crucial difference: System penetrations are generally the result of deliberate attacks. In other words, someone is *trying* to trigger the bugs. In the security field, you are dealing with an active enemy; more than the usual amount of care is needed.

7.2   Keeping It Simple

It is a truism in the software engineering business that large programs are much buggier than small ones, and that bugs increase roughly as the square of the size of the program. It follows, therefore, that security-critical programs should be as small as possible.

The *remote shell* protocol (`rsh`) provides a good example. The `rsh` command is used to run commands on different systems. Users often invoke `rsh` directly; the same protocol is also used by such commands as `rcp` and `rdist`. We will discuss the security-critical aspects of the protocol here.

The caller creates a *socket* with a local port number below 1024. Access to such low-numbered ports is restricted to *root*. The calling process transmits the identity of the calling user. This information is believed, since only *root* could have created that socket. The target machine compares the name of the calling machine against two lists of authorized callers, one system-wide and one per-user. If everything checks out, the call is accepted and the user's command is executed.

What are the options for an application wishing to use this protocol?

The first answer, of course, is to have it invoke the `rsh` command itself, with pipes for input and output. This is the simplest and cleanest answer, and for many situations it is the right answer. But it suffers from a serious shortcoming: It is inefficient if large amounts of data are being passed to or from the remote program, since all input and output must be passed through the pipes and, hence, take an extra trip to the kernel and back. Accordingly, there are some programs, such as `rcp` and `rdist`, that attempt to emulate `rsh`. Predictably, these attempts have been disastrous from a security viewpoint.

The issue is one of simplicity. In `rsh`, there are less than 100 lines of code between where the connection is set up and where the program exits. Virtually all of it is concerned with input and output on the file descriptors set up earlier; almost none of it executes in privileged state.

While some of the code is rather delicate, it is not security-sensitive; in particular, there are almost no operations performed that will cause any sort of access-control checks and, hence, there are almost no openings for attack. (The one minor exception–a call to `kill()`–is easily seen to be correct.)

In contrast, `rcp` and `rdist` do complex things after opening the connection. In particular, many files are opened, and the names of these files are under user control. The programs attempt to do the right thing, but that's a tough job–and there have, in fact, been security problems with both of them, as documented in advisories from the Computer Emergency Response Team.

The point here is not that the design itself is bad (though in fact it is; see the following section); rather, the problem is that some of the *implementations* of it are too complex to be verifiable. Privileges should be extended only to code worthy to *wield* them.

A better approach would be to design a simple privileged module that initiated the connection and transmitted authentication data, and then handed off control to a completely unprivileged program. The privileged program could be short enough that it was easily verifiable; additionally, it would be reusable. There are several possible ways to implement such a function; the simplest would be a command that created the connection and then `exec()`ed the actual command.

7.3   Assumptions and Interface Design

If it is impossible to make large programs secure, the only solution is for security-sensitive programs to be small. But, that alone is not a full solution; the privileged operations must still take place, and we must still ensure that the small privileged programs cannot be tricked by their callers. Accordingly, the design of the interfaces to privileged programs is quite important.

We must also be explicit about the input assumptions. That is, any program is invoked in a certain environment; if the actual environment differs from the one assumed, security breaches can result. The best defense here is to make the assumptions explicit; that way, the privileged module can verify its inputs and either take corrective action or abort.

For a case study, we will use the aforementioned `rsh` program. Let us list the obvious assumptions made by the target's `rshd` daemon.

1. The calling machine is one with the concept of a privileged *root* account.

2. Only *root* can create low-numbered ports.
3. *Root* can be trusted to identify the calling user correctly.

The first assumption states that the machine is one that has multiple states of trust. On a single-user PC, this is not generally the case. The second assumption concerns the behavior of the TCP on the remote machine. Not all TCP implementations restrict access to low-numbered ports; indeed, such a restriction is not required by the TCP specification. The target, then, must believe that the caller is running a particular kind of operating system, one with certain properties that are not universal. If this trust is misplaced and a nonconforming machine is listed as authorized, a security breach can occur. This could happen in a number of ways, including replacement of a trustable machine by one that can't safely carry out the protocol.

The third assumption is more subtle. If the calling machine has been subverted—or if one of its privileged users has been subverted—then the target *should not* trust it. Of course, there is generally no way of knowing this *a priori*. This is the assumption that fails most often in the real world. Computer break-ins spread this way; a single machine is penetrated by whatever mechanism; following that, any machine that trusts it is likely to fall in short order because of a pattern of trust.

It follows from these observations that trust should not be granted casually. The person responsible for granting trust must ensure that all three assumptions hold; but the third may fail without warning, possibly as a result of inadequate care taken by the calling machine's administrator. It is reasonable, then, to restrict the ability to grant trust. The machines under a system administrator's control may not all be secure; however, they are more likely to be run at roughly equivalent levels of security and, hence, share the same risk of penetration. Thus, there is little incremental risk to trusting them.

Unfortunately, most versions of `rshd` permit the *user* to grant trust as well. In other words, the human interface here can lead to violations of our security assumptions.

The `rsh` system actually makes more assumptions that do not always hold. First, for `rsh` to transmit the user's identity to the server, it must know the user's name. On UNIX systems, this generally entails a call to the `getpwuid()` function. Is that call reliable and secure? On standalone systems, it was; on modern distributed systems, `getpwuid()` often consults a network-resident database, in which case, its integrity is open to question. It is perfectly reasonable to decide that the incremental risk to `rsh` from attacks on the user name database is low, since an attacker who could corrupt access to it could also subvert the login process; but that is not a given. The essential point we are making here is that the correct behavior of `getpwuid()` is essential to the security of `rsh`; this assumption must be stated explicitly.

A related assumption is that the target machine's `rshd` can reliably determine the identity of the caller. This in turn depends on the reliability of the underlying network protocol, and on the routine that maps the network address to a host name. Neither assumption is safe in the presence of a determined opponent; see, for example, [Mor85, Bel89, Sch93].

Bear in mind that these attacks do not mean that `rsh` is hopelessly insecure. Rather, we are saying that *under certain circumstances* it is insecure; it is only by making the environmental assumptions explicit that one can assess its security in any given circumstance.

We applied this methodology to the authentication routine in the *libcs* library (Section 2.2.7). What are its basic assumptions?

Fundamentally, the authentication routine assumes that only the legitimate user could create a file with the specified attributes. That is, only the owner (or the superuser) can set those modes and timestamps for a file. The parenthetical note is important: We are assuming that the administration of the machine is trustworthy. Given networked file systems, the security of the routine therefore depends on further premises: that the file resides on a machine operated by a trustworthy administrator, and that the networked file system connection between that machine and the server is secure.

This realization leads us to an important constraint: that the server, not the client, must specify the name of the file to be created. If the client chooses the name, it can create a file on a machine that isn't trustable, thereby deceiving the server. In fact, the original version of the authentication routine did have this flaw; it was uncovered only when an explicit analysis of assumptions was done.

A security-conscious site should not neglect the question of NFS [SGK+85] (Network File System) security; it is indeed open to question. However, the consequences of failures along those lines are so severe that we will not discuss them further in the context of *libcs*.

There is one more assumption to examine here: that the server can reliably retrieve the attributes of the file. Again neglecting NFS issues, there is still a weak point: If the stat() system call is used instead of lstat(), a client could create a test file on an untrustworthy machine, and create a *symbolic link* to it using the name supplied by the server. The lstat() call will not honor the link, thereby blocking the fraud.

The analysis of the flaws in *libcs* authentication routine point to a more fundamental issue: the ability to establish trust boundaries. Fundamentally, the old routine failed because an indication of trustworthiness–the set-uid bit–could be imported from outside the security perimeter. In its intended meaning (granting privileges upon execution), the operating system does have the ability to disregard it if from an untrusted source. The authentication route overloaded the meaning of the set-uid bit, but could detect the boundary crossing. Alternative semantics for the network file system—deleting this bit on input–would also have solved the problem, had the designers of NFS so chosen. The symbolic link issue also arose because of boundary crossings; again, the server did not have the ability to detect what had happened.

An issue akin to assumptions is validation of input. It is obvious that a program should not trust input from untrustworthy sources. It is less obvious what "trust" means in this context. A properly suspicious program should never rely on untrusted input; similarly, great care must be taken when passing such input to any other programs, since they may not know the source.

The best-known example is the Internet Worm [Spa89a, Spa89b,

ER89, RE89]. One of the ways it spread was by overwriting the input buffer of the `finger` daemon so that the stack frame was corrupted. In particular, the return address was modified to point to code transmitted by the Internet Worm; in turn, that code invoked a shell.

Trust need not be extended in real time. Some attacks can be launched by depositing a trap in some location that will be used later. For example, many systems have clock-driven accounting daemons. If, for example, one of these uses the `sort` command, which is not generally security-sensitive in and of itself, an intruder who replaced it would be able to compromise a system account in a comparatively short period. Similarly, a bogus program deposited in an anonymous `ftp` area is harmless, unless and until someone carelessly executes it.

7.4   Security and Reuse

Given that we cannot trust large, complex programs, and given that developing even a small secure program is a difficult task, it makes sense to put some effort into producing a library of reusable security modules. While the specific design will vary depending on your exact needs, we can lay out certain general classes.

The first, and most important, concerns the security primitives that your code will rely on. A precise definition of their properties and limitations is vital. Consider, for example, the `chroot()` system call on UNIX systems. This call declares a section of the file system to be the entire file system. As such, it is a valuable tool for restricting access to files. But attempting to use it for more general forms of containment is risky.

The problem lies in the abstraction implemented by `chroot()`. Though it blocks access to one set of resources, there are other resources still shared; among these are the machine's network identity and its access to real I/O devices. An intruder who can *execute* a program in this isolated area can still do much damage.

UNIX subsystems that swap internal `uid`'s to implement access controls are exposed to even greater risks under similar circumstances. Again, other resources are not isolated and the relevant system calls do not provide full virtual machines. Furthermore, the same calls that the subsystem uses to change access rights are available to any program that an intruder can execute in this environment.

The problem we see here is not that the primitives are inadequate. Rather, their domain of applicability is limited; attempting to use them for other purposes is chancy. But, within their proper scope, they are quite valuable.

The latter example shows a second rule for security primitives: Implement a function once. The UNIX kernel already has a reliable access control mechanism; attempting to emulate that mechanism at user level is a dangerous proposition. A subsystem that can use this mechanism for its own access controls is more likely to be correct—hence, secure—than one that tries to build its own; and it enjoys the more traditional advantage of hiding an implementation decision: If the host's overall security policy is changed, the subsystem's access decisions will reflect this new policy automatically. This is a very real issue, given the advent of UNIX systems that implement mandatory access controls.

Reuse isn't always a boon. Secure programs need to avoid using some routines that are useful in more benign contexts. *Anything* called from a secure routine must be trustable; if it is not, it can be abused to penetrate the secure system.

An example will make this clearer. Suppose that an automatically invoked resource-use reporting daemon uses a sort command to produce its reports. If this sort command has been booby-trapped, the account under which the management daemon runs will be compromised. Since such accounts are often privileged, the entire system can be subverted.

The problems in this vein are not restricted to maliciously bad programs. Rather, they can be due to ordinary programs being invoked in a hostile environment. If, say, a network server runs a shell script to perform its function, every program invoked by that script becomes security-sensitive. Other programs may have the same flaw as the Internet Worm exploited in the `finger` daemon–but this is irrelevant unless they are invoked by an untrusted party.

For truly sensitive areas, even the development environment needs to be scrutinized. Thompson even showed how examining the source code may not suffice [Tho84]. (Also see [KS74] for an earlier discussion of the problem.)

Reuse of security can have its drawbacks; YEAST (Chapter 9) provides a good example.

The most obvious weakness is that the reused software can be buggy. YEAST uses *libcs* for user authentication, which means that it inherits any problems that *libcs* has. The security flaws in older versions of the library meant that any user of YEAST could have used it to crack any other uid on the system. (Contrariwise, when the library was fixed, YEAST was also secured.)

A second point, though, is that any user of the *libcs* authentication library must satisfy its input assumptions. Thus, since it requires a shared file system between clients and servers, YEAST must as well. This, in turn, constrains how one can deploy YEAST: It is impossible to have a central server without using NFS, which itself has profound security and operational implications.

We thus see the trade-offs. Using an existing authentication mechanism obviated the necessity of writing a new (and possibly buggy) mechanism of its own. On the other hand, it opened up a vulnerability and constrained how YEAST could be deployed.

7.5   Logging and Auditing

Another essential component of any secure system is adequate logging; but great care should be taken in the design of the logging mechanisms or the output they produce will be useless.

Obviously, logs must be accurate. More subtly, they must be complete enough to be useful. Specifically, a log file must give enough information that one can identify the ultimate source of any suspect action. A log file that simply notes that some event has occurred is useless. One that supplies, say, the process id that generated the event may be better, but only if there is an easy link between that field and the user or network connection associated with it. Best of all is a succinct message that identifies the source and the action.

This is illustrated in Figure 7.1, which contains an excerpt from our

```
15:30:05 ftpd[9313]: connection from foo.bar.edu 1.2.3.4
15:30:06 ftpd[9313]: USER anonymous
15:30:06 ftpd[9313]: PASS user@bar.edu
15:30:06 ftpd[9313]: ANONYMOUS FTP LOGIN FROM foo.bar.edu 1.2.3.4, user@bar.edu
15:37:08 ftpd[9313]: file /etc/passwd fetched
```

Figure 7.1 An excerpt from the anonymous FTP log file on our firewall. The source information has been edited.

FTP log file. The first three lines are simply transaction entries; they log events as they happen. The fourth line is a valuable summary line; it ties together the information from the previous lines. But, the really interesting entry is the last line.

Apparently, someone tried to grab /etc/passwd from our anonymous FTP area. This action could be indicative of hostile activity [CB94]; but the only source information in that line is the bracketed process id, [9313]. To use it, one needs to retrieve all lines from that session and, in particular, the summary line. Also, given that process ids can be reused, it may be necessary to discard entries from a different instantiation of process 9313. It would be easier to act on the logs if the last line included the identity tag from the previous entry, from which it could be separated by quite some distance (notice the timestamps).

To be sure, there is a countervailing force, which is why our log files don't read that way. In any heavily used system, the size of the log files is a serious concern. A log file that can be searched by standard UNIX tools (awk, grep, and so on) is much more valuable than one containing randomly formatted lines. It's always easier to produce fancy reports from fixed-format log files than vice versa; systems should always generate the latter and use back-end programs to produce the former if desired.

By far, the easiest way to produce consistent log files is to use a common set of routines to generate all entries. A small amount of code in one spot can be kept consistent; random print statements scattered throughout a large system cannot.

Note that we are not talking here about a log file output mechanism, such as syslog(). A simple mechanism for physically writing the messages is useful; however, we are focusing here on the *content* of the messages.

Two related issues concern selective auditing and *denial of service* attacks. It is often useful to be able to log material selectively. Information that is too voluminous to be kept in general, such as traces of all `open()` requests, may be useful when focused on a particular user. The logging subroutines need the ability to alter the scope of such messages dynamically.

In the other direction, attackers have been known to swamp log files with irrelevant entries before a real invasion. The idea is to fill up disk space, or to bury the people responsible for reading the logs with a mass of trivia so that they miss the important messages.

It is very hard to do much to defend against denial of service attacks. Some mechanisms are obvious, such as storing log files on a different disk than high-bandwidth input sources, such as mail. Other things that can help are semantic compression (log counts of repeated identical messages, rather than including each in its entirety) and attempts at rate-limiting message or input sources. But there is no general solution as long as it is cheaper for the attacker to generate a message than it is for the target to process it.

7.6   Evaluating Security

No discussion of security and software engineering is complete without some mention of the famous "Orange Book" [DoD85a]. The Orange Book—more formally, the *Department of Defense Trusted Computer System Evaluation Criteria*—contains the standard the U.S. military uses to evaluate secure computer systems. Ratings range from D–a system that doesn't meet the minimum criteria for any other class–through C1, C2, B1, B2, B3, and A1.

Most people cite lists of features as the major difference between the different levels. Thus, B1 adds mandatory access controls, wherein an administrator can control who has access to various files. But, such lists miss an important point: the increasing assurance requirements at different levels.

This can be seen clearly by contrasting B2 to B3. Few new features are required; what is different is the degree of confidence demanded; much of which is to be achieved by proper structuring of the *TCB* (Trusted Computing Base).

Much of the required structure mirrors what we have said here. Consider this requirement, from Section 3.3.3.1.1:

> The TCB shall be designed and structured to use a complete, conceptually simple protection mechanism with precisely defined semantics. This mechanism shall play a central role in enforcing the internal structuring of the TCB and the system. The TCB shall incorporate significant use of layering, abstraction and data hiding. Significant system engineering shall be directed toward minimizing the complexity of the TCB and excluding from the TCB modules that are not protection-critical.

In other words, sound software engineering principles should be followed. Note, also, that it is difficult to retrofit B3 security to an existing insecure system without a major rewrite; the TCB must be highly structured with clean interfaces to security services *enforced*.

Other requirements have a similar flavor. For example, the log files must contain sufficient information to show which authorized user has performed any sort of privileged operations.

Assurance is important for two reasons. First, of course, one needs to *know* that a system is secure, with a fair degree of confidence. Only then can one make a rational decision about how much trust should be placed in it. A less secure (and probably less expensive) system might suffice for noncritical applications; on the other hand, a highly rated system would be more appropriate for such things as nuclear weapons command and control.

In the military world, this, too, is formalized. A sister publication to the Orange Book–the Yellow Book [DoD85b]–derives how secure a system need be based on the sensitivity of the information stored on it and the security clearances of the users of it. An unrated system can hold Top Secret data–but only if all users of it are cleared for that data. If uncleared users will be present, a highly rated system must be used instead.

The second reason for demanding assurance of security is less obvious. A complex system is extremely unlikely to be secure; making a system simple enough to understand and evaluate will, in and of itself, make it more secure. In other words, the process itself helps to produce the desired effect. Again, this is apparent in the process by which Orange Book evaluations are performed. One does not hand a completed system to the evaluators; instead, the system is developed in cooperation with them to assure that the structuring is adequate. (It is also necessary to use systems of a certain minimum security level when developing more secure systems, to avoid attacks on the development machines.)

As useful as the Orange Book is as a model, the precise security criteria it outlines are not universally applicable. Specifically, it concentrates on access control: ensuring that unauthorized individuals cannot get at classified data. While the civilian world has that concern as well, data integrity is generally far more important. Put another way, while a bank may not want an outsider to read customer account data, it would much prefer that to the chance of an outsider *modifying* account data. Accordingly, new sets of evaluation criteria are being developed. This is not just a U.S. effort [FCI92]; the Canadian government [NIT93] and the European Community [ITS91] are developing their own standards, and there is an effort underway to harmonize the different standards.

Apart from differences in the desired functionality, assurance is now orthogonal to the feature list. To quote the Canadian document:

> The Assurance criteria, on the other hand, reflect the degree of confidence that a product correctly implements its security policy. Assurance applies across the entire product under evaluation. For example, a product given a T-4 assurance rating has had this level of assurance applied across all the security services within the product.

The minimum assurance level (T-1) requires such things as use of an approved configuration management system and an informal description of the system architecture; the highest level (T-7) requires formal design descriptions, physical security during the development process, personnel security practices, and so on. All of these things are related. A determined adversary may find it easier to bribe an employee than to find a flaw in the code–but the end result is the same.

7.7 Conclusions

No development techniques can guarantee that a given system will be secure. That is simply beyond the state of the art. Even the best formal methods will not suffice here; no formal system we have seen can prove that an employee is incorruptible but it is possible to shift the odds.

More than in most other areas, sound software engineering principles help. Modularity, simple designs, and explicit preconditions are always a good idea. This is especially true for security modules, even though the actual code is likely to be quite small. The key, though, is design that incorporates security from the beginning.

8

A Software Fault Tolerance Platform

Yennun Huang and Chandra Kintala

8.1 Introduction

The previous chapter dealt with one of the important properties of computer programs, namely, security. This chapter deals with another such property: fault tolerance and high availability . Often the high-availability property effectively determines the usefulness of a piece of software. Just like a partially insecure program, software that is not fault tolerant may render it useless. This chapter discusses techniques and software components for providing fault tolerance for a wide range of software.

In a telecommunications network, switching systems are known to have the highest degree of reliability, that is, availability and data consistency. There are, however, hundreds of other systems to provision, process, operate, administer, and maintain a large reliable telecommunications network and its services.

It would be desirable to have all those systems be also highly available, like switching systems, if the costs and technologies permit them to be so [Ber93]. Traditionally, high availability is provided through fault tolerance technology in the hardware, operating system, and database layers of a computer system executing the application software (see Figure 8.1).

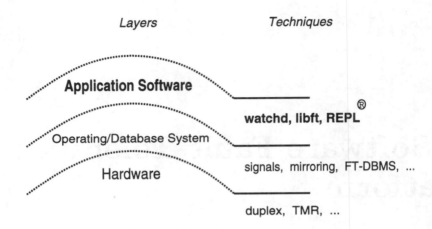

Figure 8.1 Layers for fault tolerance.

Two trends are emerging in the marketplace and are changing this tradition for providing fault tolerance:

1. Standard commercial hardware and operating systems (for example, Sun and Silicon Graphics workstations and desktop PCs) are becoming highly reliable, distributed, and inexpensive to the extent that they are now off-the-shelf commodity items. We refer to those systems as *standard computers* to contrast them with *fault-tolerant computers* (for example, Tandem's FT Systems) which have special architectures to handle hardware and operating system faults.

2. The proportion of failures due to faults in the *application software* is increasing due to increased size and complexity of software being deployed [GS91, SS92], and to increased hardware reliability.

Taking advantage of the first trend, we propose a network of standard computers to provide fault tolerance service and increase the availability of an application inexpensively. The application will be running actively on one computer (host or node), and another node on the network will be a backup node for that application. The application would need mechanisms to checkpoint its data, log its messages, watch, detect, restart, and recover from failures. Implementing these fault tolerance tasks individually requires expertise in fault tolerance, and should not be done ad hoc in each application.

We developed a set of reusable software components (*watchd*, *libft*, and REPL [HK93]) to perform those fault tolerance tasks in any application executing on that generic platform. *watchd* is used to detect failures of processes and processors. *libft* is a collection of C and C++ routines for checkpointing and recovering internal data, and for fault-tolerant interprocess communication. REPL provides services for replicating critical files onto a backup computer. These three components are reusable, that is, they can be embedded in any application with minimal software development effort and no additional hardware. They have been ported to a number of UNIX platforms, including Sun, SGI, Motorola, and HP. The generic platform and these three components are described in Section 8.2.

The second trend listed earlier forces us to focus more on failures (also called *software errors*) due to software faults (also called *software bugs*). We assume that most responsible software products, especially distributed telecommunications software systems, are thoroughly tested before they are deployed in the field. However, the size and complexity of software in those systems is such that even the most advanced software validation and verification methods and tools do not remove *all possible* faults in that software. So, there are residual faults in most software systems deployed in the field.

But, unlike in hardware, all those faults in software are design and coding faults and are permanent. However, the failures exhibited by those software faults can be *transient*, that is, the failure may not recur if the software is reexecuted on the same input. This is because the behavior of a program, especially a client-server application running on a distributed system, depends not only on the input data and message contents, but also on the timing and interleaving of messages, shared variables, and other *state* values in the operating environment of the application [HJK94]. Thus, the residual faults get triggered occasionally, leading to erroneous behavior or failures. This observation leads us to employ the following methods for transient software error recovery, using the reusable software components, *watchd*, *libft*, and REPL mentioned earlier.

One method is to simply *rollback* and *restart* the failed process and *replay* the logged messages. It is hoped that some part of the environment will change during replay so that the process will not fail upon reexecution. Another method is to *reorder* the messages during replay [WHF93] so that errors due to unexpected event sequences can be masked. These methods are *reactive* in nature, that is, they attempt to recover the application *after* a failure has occurred.

There is also a complementary approach, called *software rejuvenation*, to handle transient software failures. Software rejuvenation *prevents* failures from occurring by periodically and gracefully terminating an application and immediately restarting it at a clean internal state. Restarting an application involves queuing the incoming signals and messages temporarily, respawning the process or processes corresponding to the application at an initial state, reinitializing the in-memory volatile data structures, logging administrative records, and so on. The interval for periodic rejuvenation, if used, can be determined through analysis [HKKF94] and experience with the application.

Even though the above methods (rollback, restart, and rejuvenation) are widely used in hardware, and sometimes manually in some applications, they have not been previously available as reusable components to provision the techniques automatically in an application. Our components and libraries, *watchd*, *libft*, and REPL, facilitate embedding of those methods for high availability in any application easily. As mentioned in Section 1.6.2, those components form the infrastructure for fault tolerance as an architecture service in an application. The application developers get large-scale reuse of the software inside those components for performing the basic but complex tasks for fault tolerance. Also, the components provide enough flexibility for configuring the frequency and amount of checkpointing, frequency for polling the liveness of the application processes, frequency for rejuvenation, files for replication, and various other application-dependent aspects of fault tolerance. The three components have been found to be useful in a wide spectrum of applications on AT&T's worldwide telecommunications network, including Transmission, Communication Services, Operations Systems, and Switching Systems. We discuss some examples of how they have been used in Section 8.3.

8.2   Platform and Components

For simplicity in the following discussions, we consider only client-server based applications running in a local or wide-area network of computers in a distributed system. Each application has a server process executing in the application layer on top of a vendor-supplied hardware and operating system. To get services, clients send messages to the server; the server process acts on those messages one by one and, in each of those message processing steps, updates its data. We sometimes call the server process the *application*. Each executing application has *process text* (the compiled code), *volatile data* (variables, structures, pointers, and all the bytes in the static and dynamic memory segments of the process image), and *persistent data* (the application files being referred to and updated by the executing process).

For fault tolerance purposes, the nodes in a distributed system are viewed as being in a circular configuration so that each node can become a backup node for its left neighbor in that circular list. We use a modified primary-site approach to software fault tolerance [HJ92b]. In the primary site approach, the service to be made fault tolerant is replicated at many nodes, one of which is designated as primary and the others as backups. All requests for the service are sent to the primary site. The primary site periodically checkpoints its state on the backups. If the primary fails, one of the backups takes over as primary. Huang and Jalote [HJ92b] have analyzed this model for frequency of checkpointing, degree of service replication, and the effect on response time. This model was slightly modified to build the three components described in this chapter.

The tasks in our modification of the primary site approach are illustrated in Figure 8.2 and described here:

- A watchdog process (*watchd* in our platform) runs on the primary node watching for application failures, that is, crashed or hung processes.
- A watchdog process running on the backup node watches for primary node crashes.
- The application periodically checkpoints its critical volatile data (using *libft* in our platform).

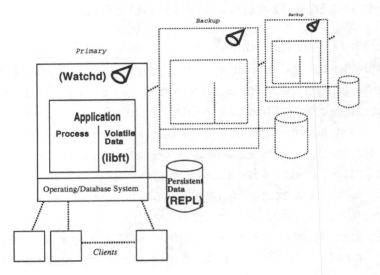

Figure 8.2 Platform and components of software-implemented fault tolerance.

- Client messages to the application are logged between checkpoints (using *libft*).
- Application replicates its persistent data and makes them available on the backup node (using REPL in our platform).
- When the application on the primary node crashes or hangs, it restarts, if possible, on the primary node; otherwise, on the backup node.
- The application is recovered to the last checkpointed state and the logged messages are reexecuted.
- If the application restarts on the backup, the replicated files on the backup node are connected to the application.

Observe that the application process on the backup node is not running until it is started by the watchdog process; this is unlike the process-pair model [GS91], where a backup process will be passively running even during normal operations.

The degree to which the above software fault tolerance tasks are used in an application determines the availability and data consistency of that application. They are adjusted by tuning the number of nodes in the distributed computing network supporting the application and the amount and frequency of checkpointing and logging of application data that is to be recovered after a failure. Each application determines its degree of availability by doing an engineering trade-off between the need and costs for providing the required level of fault tolerance.

Many applications perform some of these software fault tolerance features by coding them directly in their programs. We developed three reusable components—*watchd*, *libft*, and REPL—to embed those features in any application with minimal programming effort. These are described shortly.

8.2.1   *watchd*

watchd is a watchdog daemon process that runs on a single machine or on a network of machines to detect application process failures and machine crashes. It continually watches the life of a local application process by periodically sending a null signal to the process and checking the return value to detect whether that process is alive, hung, or dead. *watchd* runs on each machine, and a machine crash is detected if the *watchd* that was running on that machine fails to respond to a polling request. Once a machine crash is detected, the *watchd* that discovered the failure can take a predefined action to recover applications on the failed machine.

To make fault detection and the recovery mechanism reliable and efficient, the design of *watchd* is based on the following principles:

- *Simplicity*: There are no complicated diagnostic and recovery messages between nodes and between processes.
- *Fairness*: The responsibilities for fault diagnosis and recovery are shared among all participating nodes.
- *No central control*: Information, decision, and control of the fault recovery protocol are fully distributed.
- *Flexibility*: Removing or adding machines and processes is easy to do.

watchd detects a process crash by either polling the process (using `kill(0,pid)`) or receiving a `SIGCHLD` signal. *watchd* detects whether that process is hung by using one of the following two methods. The first method sends a `ping`-like command to the local application process using IPC (Inter Process Communication) facilities on the local node and checks the return value. If it cannot make the connection, it waits for some time (specified by the application) and tries again. If it fails after the second attempt, *watchd* interprets the failure to mean that the process is hung. The second method allows the application process to send a heartbeat message to *watchd* periodically, and *watchd* periodically checks the heartbeat. If the heartbeat message from the application is not received by a specified time, *watchd* assumes that the application is hung. *libft* provides the function `hbeat()` for applications sending heartbeats to *watchd*. The `hbeat()` function takes an argument that specifies the maximum duration between heartbeats.

When it detects that the application process crashed or hung, *watchd* recovers that application at an initial internal state or at the last checkpointed state. The application is recovered on the primary node if that node has not crashed; otherwise, on the backup node for the primary, as specified in a configuration file. If *libft* is also used, *watchd* sets the restarted application to process all the logged messages from the log file generated by *libft*. Since the messages received at the server site are logged and only the server process is recovered in this scheme, the consistency problems that occur in recovering multiple processes [Jal89] are not issues in this implementation.

Each *watchd* watches one neighboring *watchd* (left or right) in a circular fashion to detect node failures; this method is similar to the adaptive distributed diagnosis algorithm [BB91]. When a node failure is detected, the neighboring *watchd* can execute user-defined recovery commands and reconfigure the network. When a node is repaired, it can rejoin the network simply by starting the *watchd* daemon. To distinguish node failures from link failures, although not definitively, *watchd* can use two communication links for polling a neighboring node. It reports a node failure only when it fails to contact a neighboring node through both links.

To make *watchd* itself very reliable, we implemented a self-recovery mechanism into *watchd* in such a way that it can recover itself from an unexpected software failure. When *watchd* finishes initialization, it forks a backup *watchd*, which executes a loop and keeps polling the primary *watchd*. If the primary *watchd* fails, the backup *watchd* breaks the polling loop and resumes the primary *watchd* responsibility. At the same time, it spawns another backup *watchd* for watching itself (the new primary *watchd*). If the backup *watchd* fails, the primary *watchd* gets a signal from the operating system, since the backup *watchd* is a child process of the primary *watchd*.

watchd also facilitates restarting a failed process, restoring the saved values, and reexecuting the logged events, and provides facilities for rejuvenation, remote execution, error reporting, remote copy, distributed election, and status-report production. Several commands are also provided for operating, administrating, and maintaining a network using *watchd* daemons. For example:

addnode Adds a machine into the *watchd* ring

delnode Removes a machine from the *watchd* ring

addwatch Informs *watchd* to watch a process

delwatch Removes a process from the watch-list of the *watchd*

addrejuv Registers a process to *watchd* to be rejuvenated at a scheduled time

moveproc Moves a process from a node to another node

8.2.2   *libft*

libft is a user-level library of C functions that can be used in application programs to specify and checkpoint critical data, recover the checkpointed data, log events, and locate and reconnect a server.

libft provides a set of functions (such as `critical()`) to specify critical volatile data in an application. These critical data items are allocated in a reserved region of the virtual memory and are periodically checkpointed. Values in critical data structures are saved using memory copy functions, and thus avoid traversing application-dependent data structures. When an application does a checkpoint, its critical data are saved on the primary and backup nodes. Unlike other checkpointing methods [LFA92], the overhead in our checkpointing mechanism is minimized by saving only critical data and avoiding data-structure traversals. This idea of saving only critical data in an application is analogous to the Recovery Box concept in Sprite [BS92].

The following functions in *libft* perform the necessary critical memory allocation, checkpointing and recovery:

- `ft_start()` reserves a block of critical memory. The function takes two arguments–the size of the critical memory and the filename for checkpoint data. When in recovery, `ft_start()` restores the data structures from the critical memory in reserved address space.
- `t_critical()` declares critical global variables, along with an `id` to identify the thread that made the call; function `critical()` is similar to `t_critical()` without the identifier. Both functions take a list of variables and their sizes as input arguments.
- `t_checkpoint()` and `checkpoint()` save the values of critical variables and the critical memory onto a file.
- `t_recover()` and `recover()` restore the values of critical variables and critical memory.
- `ftmalloc()`, `ftcalloc()`, and `ftrealloc()` are used to allocate space from the critical memory, and function `ftfree()` is used to free space to critical memory.

libft also provides `ftread()`, and `ftwrite()` functions to automatically log messages. When the `ftread()` function is called by a process in a normal condition, data is read from a channel and automatically logged on a file. The logged data is then duplicated and logged by the *watchd* daemon on a backup machine. The replication of logged data is necessary for a process to recover from a primary machine failure. When the `ftread()` function is called by a process that is recovering from a failure in a recovery mode, the input data is read from the logged file before any data is read from a regular input channel. Similarly, the `ftwrite()` function logs output data before it is sent out. The output data is also duplicated and logged by the *watchd* daemon on a backup machine. The log files created by the `ftread()`, and `ftwrite()` functions are truncated after a `checkpoint()` function is successfully executed. Using functions `checkpoint()`, `ftread()`, and `ftwrite()`, one can implement either a sender-based or a receiver-based logging and recovery scheme [Jal89]. There is a slight possibility that some messages during the automatic restart procedure may get lost. If this is a concern to an application, an additional message synchronization mechanism can be built into the application to check and retransmit lost messages.

The following functions in *libft* perform fault-tolerant versions of the network and file system calls:

- `getsvrloc()`, `getsvrport()`, `ftconnect()`, and `ftbind()` facilitate clients to locate servers and reconnect to them in a network environment. They intercept standard socket function calls for transparent client-server reconnection once a network failure is detected.
- `ftfopen()`, `ftfclose()`, `ftcommit()`, and `ftabort()` help in committing and aborting file updates. Files updated using `ftfopen()` can be committed only by calling `ftfclose()` or `ftcommit()`. Therefore, in the case of process rollback recovery, file updates can be rolled back to the last commit point.

The program fragment in Figure 8.3 is an example of a server program using *libft* library for checkpointing. In this example, the server reads a number from a client program and pushes the number onto the top of a stack. The stack is implemented as a linked list. Critical data for the server program are the stack itself and the pointer to the head of the stack.

The critical data in the program shown are the stack and the pointer to the head, `pHead`. To save the head pointer, we declare variable `pHead` critical. To save the contents of the stack, we have to store the stack in critical memory, which is created by the `ft_start()` function. To allocate critical memory, we use function `ftmalloc()`. The size of the critical memory is declared to be 16 kilobytes. The size of the critical memory can be dynamically increased as needed. The checkpoint filename is `/tmp/examp1.ckp`, specified by the `ft_start()` call, and the log filename is `/tmp/examp1.log`, specified by the `setlogfile()` call. The flag `INFILE` indicates that the checkpoint data is to be saved on and recovered from a stable file system. Normally, each message is read and logged by function `ftread()`. When in recovery, function `ftread()` reads data from the log file instead of the regular socket channel, `so`. Note that the file descriptor `so` is not used in recovery. A checkpoint is taken after every 200 messages

```
#include <ft.h>
...
struct llist {
        struct llist *link;
        int data;
        ...
}
...
main(){
        struct llist *pHead=NULL, *ptmp;
        int s, indata;
        ...
        ft_start("/tmp/examp1.ckp",16384);
        setlogfile("/tmp/examp1.log");
        critical(&pHead, sizeof(pHead),0);
        ...
        if (in_recovery()) recover(INFILE);
        for (;;) {
                ...
                if (!in_recovery()){
                    cnt++;
                    if (cnt>200)
                        checkpoint(INFILE);
                    so=accept(..);
                }
                ...
                ftread(so,indata,MaxLen);
                ptmp=(struct llist *) ftmalloc(sizeof(struct llist));
                ptmp->link=pHead;
                ptmp->data=indata;
                pHead=ptmp;
                ...

        }
}
```

Figure 8.3   Use of *libft* for checkpointing.

received by the server. Every checkpoint saves the data in variable pHead and data in the critical memory. When a checkpoint is performed, the log file is truncated to zero length. In recovery, function ft_start() preallocates critical memory and, when function recover() is called, critical data is restored from the checkpoint file to the critical memory.

Speed and portability are primary concerns in implementing *libft*. The *libft* checkpoint mechanism, as it is currently implemented, is not fully transparent to programmers. However, it checkpoints only the critical data and reduces the checkpointing overhead. In addition, *libft* does not require a new language, a new preprocessor, or complex declarations and computations to save the data structures [GS91]. The sacrifice of transparency for speed has been proven to be useful in many projects using *libft*. Installation of *libft* doesn't require changes to UNIX-based operating systems; it has been ported to several platforms.

8.2.3   REPL

REPL * is a file replication mechanism running on a pair of machines[†] for online replication of critical files, which are specified by users using an environment variable. It is often used in conjunction with the *n-DFS* shared library (Section 2.5), but is not always necessary. The mechanism uses dynamic-shared libraries (such as *n-DFS*) to intercept file system calls. When a user program issues a file update, the shared library intercepts the request, performs the update locally, and passes the update message to the remote REPL servers. Upon receiving the message, the remote REPL servers then replay the message and perform the file update. REPL is built on top of standard UNIX file systems, so its use requires no change to the underlying file system. Speed, robustness, and replication transparency are the primary design goals of the REPL replication mechanism.

REPL consists of four main components (see Figure 8.4):

---

*The authors would like to thank D. Korn, G. Fowler, and H. Rao for their help in the design and development of REPL.

[†]It can be used on any number of machines; but, for simplicity, we discuss only the duplex architecture here.

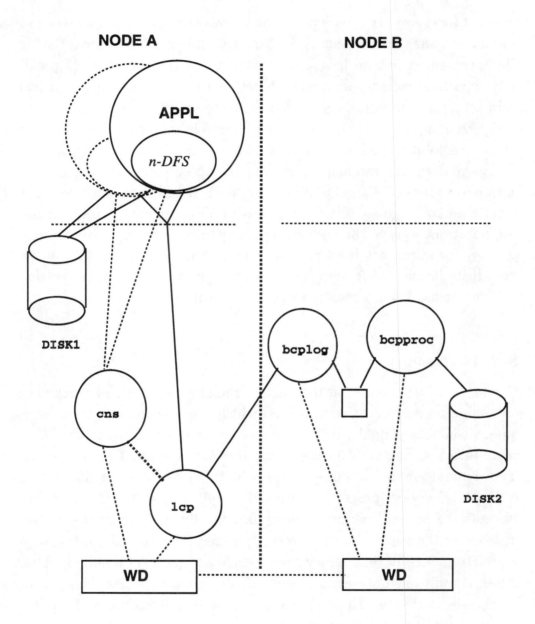

Figure 8.4   Software architecture of the REPL mechanism.

- Relay server (lcp): Its tasks, when the remote is up, are to establish a connection to bcplog (a REPL logging process on the remote backup node described shortly), read messages from applications (linked with the *n-DFS* library), and pass those messages to the remote bcplog; when the remote is down, its tasks are to create a log file and save data to the log file.
- Connection server (cns): It is used to establish a connection to the lcp, maintain a file descriptor for the connection, and send the file descriptor to applications.
- Log server (bcplog): It receives update messages from the lcp on the other node and logs the messages onto a log file.
- Process server (bcpproc): Normally, it reads the log file generated by bcplog and replays the update messages; in recovery, it copies files from the other node for files resynchronization.

Note that all four components are active on both machines. Therefore, updates of critical files can originate from either machine. However, to avoid update contention, it is recommended that all the processes belonging to one application designate one machine as the primary and use the other as the backup. Load can be distributed when applications are allocated on different machines.

When an application opens a critical file for the first time, the REPL shared library intercepts the open system call and sends a request to cns. Upon receiving the request, cns returns a file descriptor to the application (normally, it is the connection between cns and lcp). The REPL library then uses the file descriptor to pass messages to the backup.

There are two other processes which are used to ensure data consistency between the machines: file-check process (bcpchk) and name-mapping process (fnmapper). In case of an update failure on the backup machine, two recovery actions could be taken, depending on the severity of the failure. If the failure is recoverable (such as lost or corrupted messages), the information for the update operation (device number and i-node number) is passed by the backup bcpproc to the backup bcpchk. Then, the bcpchk process sends a request to the primary fnmapper to locate the filename using the device number and i-node number. Once the filename is located, the file is copied by the bcpchk process to the backup machine to ensure data consistency. On the other hand, if the failure is nonrecoverable (such as a file system being full or an I/O error), after a few retries, the backup **bcpchk** shuts down the backup machine to prevent any out-of-date data from being read.

The implementation of REPL uses the following technologies:

- *sfio library*: for reliable and fast file input and output
- *libcs library*: for file descriptors passing between processes
- *watchd daemon*: for fast recovery and failure detection remote file copy, remote command execution, and file descriptor checkpoint
- *libft library*: for checkpoint and recovery of critical data in REPL processes

REPL itself is a good reuse example; it uses *watchd* and *libft* to achieve high availability. Details of this reuse are described in Example 4 in the next section.

8.3   Experience

Fault tolerance in some of the newer telecommunications network management products in AT&T has been enhanced using *watchd*, *libft*, and REPL. Experience with those products to date indicates that these technologies are indeed economical and effective means to increase the level of fault tolerance in application software. All three components are highly portable: They have been ported and used on many hardware platforms running UNIX operating systems. The performance overhead due to these components depends on the desired level of fault tolerance, the amount of critical volatile data being checkpointed, frequency of checkpointing, and the amount of persistent data being replicated. Experience shows that the overhead ranges from 0.1 percent to 14 percent depending on the application and the above factors. We describe some of these products to illustrate the availability, flexibility, and efficiency in embedding software fault tolerance using these three components. To protect the proprietary information in these products, we use generic terms and titles in the descriptions.

8.3.1 A Network Service Application

Application C monitors and analyzes data in a special-purpose, online billing system on AT&T's network. It uses *watchd* to check "liveness" of some service daemon processes in C at 10-second intervals. When a process fails, that is, crashes or hangs, *watchd* restarts that process at its initial state. The application C is started by a shell script that also brings up *watchd*. Then, 30 seconds later, the command `addwatch` is issued to register all critical processes. In this product, the use of *watchd* required no change to the application and a small change to the startup script. Other potential uses of this kind of fault tolerance would be in general-purpose computing environments for stateless network services, such as those provided by `lpr`, `finger`, or `inet` daemons. Using checkpointing in those daemons would be unnecessary.

8.3.2 An Event-Action Tool Application

watchd and *libft* are used to make YEAST (see Chapter 9) tolerant to machine crashes. YEAST triggers actions when specified event patterns are matched in a computing environment. The critical data in YEAST are the event tables and all the global variables that reference those tables. *cia* (see Chapter 6) was used to generate and identify the list of global critical data in YEAST and the function `checkpoint()` is inserted into the YEAST server code to save critical data on a backup machine. To save the critical data in critical memory, the function `ftmalloc()`, instead of regular `malloc()`, is used for dynamic memory allocation. In the event of a primary machine crash, *watchd* on the backup machine detects the failure and migrates the YEAST server to the backup machine with its last checkpoint state. The number of lines added or changed in the original YEAST source code of 10K lines is only 40. The checkpointing overhead, in terms of increase in response time from the service, is measured to be about 10 percent. (Also see Section 9.6.2.1.)

8.3.3 A Call-Routing Application

Application N maintains a certain segment of the telephone call routing information on a Sun server; maintenance operators use workstations running N's client processes communicating with N's server process using sockets. The server process in N was crashing or hanging for unknown reasons. During such failures, the system administrators had to manually bring back the server process, but they could not do so immediately because of the UNIX delay in cleaning up the socket table. Moreover, the maintenance operators had to restart client interactions from an initial state. Replacing the server node with fault tolerant hardware would have increased their capital and development costs by a factor of four. Even then, all their problems would not have been solved; for example, since the client processes run on standard workstations, their states of interactions would not have been saved. Using *watchd* and *libft*, system N is now able to tolerate such failures. *watchd* also detects primary server failures and restarts it on the backup server. Location transparency is obtained using `getsvrloc()` and `getsvrport()` calls in client programs, and `ftbind()` in server program. The critical data in the server process are the call routing information, the client information, and the client-server connection information. These data are needed in recovery to locate the clients, reconnect the clients, and regain the call data. *libft*'s checkpoint and recovery mechanisms are used to save and recover all critical data. Checkpointing and recovery overheads are below 2 percent. The use of the *watchd* and *libft* in application N required a small change to the server code. Installing and integrating the two components into the application took six person-days.

8.3.4 REPL Application

REPL relies on *watchd* for crash detection and fast recovery, and uses *libft* functions for checkpoint and recovery (including communication and data). As mentioned earlier, REPL consists of four main processes—`bcplog`, `bcpproc`, `lcp`, and `cns`; (see Figure 8.4). If one of the components fails, *watchd* daemon detects the failure and recovers the failed component. For example, if `bcpproc` fails, *watchd* daemon restarts the `bcpproc` process immediately. Using the *libft* checkpoint and logging mechanism, `bcpproc` is restored to the state just before the failure. The critical data in `bcpproc` is a table that maps device numbers and i-node numbers to filenames on the other machine. An entry is inserted into that table in bcpproc when a new file is opened for update. Later, when a write operation on the file is performed, a message is sent to the backup with only the device number and the i-node number of the file, but not the filename. The remote bcpproc has to locate the file using the device number and i-node number to perform an update. Therefore, the table is essential for the bcpproc to process file replication requests. Without checkpoint and message logging, the crash of the bcpproc process could result in a loss of the table and make the recovery of the bcpproc process very difficult. To improve the search efficiency, a hash table based on i-node numbers is used. To recover the state of bcpproc, both tables have to be checkpointed. To save space and time in checkpointing, we use the *libft* dynamic memory allocation routines, ftmalloc() and ftfree(), for allocating entries in both tables. When function checkpoint() is called, both tables are saved onto a checkpointed file.

If bcplog on the backup machine fails, the connection between lcp and bcplog is broken. In this case, the recovery procedure is more complex. It takes the following steps to recover a failed bcplog:

1. The *watchd* on the backup node brings up bcplog immediately. Once restarted, bcplog creates a new communication channel; the information for this new channel is recorded by the *watchd*.
2. bcplog sends a signal to the lcp on the primary node to inform lcp that a new bcplog is up.
3. Upon receiving the signal, lcp on the primary node asks the *watchd* for information for the new channel; with the information, lcp re-establishes the connection.
4. Finally, lcp forwards all file updates to the new bcplog.

Bcplog reads messages from the lcp process and writes them to a log file. Since the size of a log file is limited, bcplog has to switch to a new log file once the size of the current log file is over a predefined threshold. Thus, the critical data for process bcplog is the name of the current log file. During recovery, bcplog restores the filename, reopens the file, puts an end message, closes the file, and switches to a new log file.

If lcp fails, the following recovery procedure is taken:

1. cns receives a SIGCHLD signal when lcp dies.

2. `cns` restarts the `lcp`.
3. After restart, `lcp` sends a signal (SIGTERM) to the remote `bcplog` through *watchd* to kill the remote `bcplog`.
4. The remote *watchd* detects the failure of the `bcplog` and restarts the `bcplog`.
5. `lcp` reconnects itself with the restarted `bcplog` and the recovery is complete.

When `lcp` is restarted, the communication channel between applications and the old `lcp` fails. In this case, all applications that use the REPL shared library get an I/O error (for example, SIGPIPE). As a result, all applications talk to `cns` to receive a new connection to the newly started `lcp`. With the new channel, the applications can again pass the file update information through `lcp` to the remote `bcplog`.

If `cns` fails, *watchd* restarts `cns` immediately. When `cns` is restarted, it retrieves the communication channel information (connection between `cns` and `lcp`) from *watchd* and reuses the communication channel. In this case, no other process needs to be restarted. The critical data for `cns` is the communication channel information. It is checkpointed when `cns` is started.

If the remote machine fails, the primary *watchd* detects that failure within 20 seconds (tunable parameter) and sends a signal (SIGPIPE) to the local `lcp`. Then, `lcp` opens a local log file and writes all incoming update messages to that file (see Figure 8.5).

After the remote (backup) machine is repaired and rebooted, the remote `bcplog` is restarted and the the local `lcp` receives a signal (SIGTERM) from *watchd*. Upon receiving that signal, `lcp` establishes communication with the remote `bcplog` and forwards file update requests to the remote `bcplog`. At the same time, `bcpproc` on the backup machine is also restarted. It first copies the down-time log file (created by `lcp` when the backup machine is down) from the primary machine. Then, it processes the log data to catch up with the state of the primary file system (see Figure 8.6).

There are two modes that `bcpproc` may use to catch up with the primary file systems: replay mode and copy mode. The replay mode replays

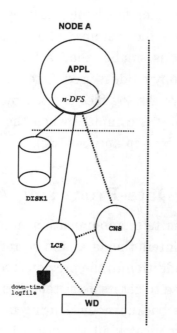

Figure 8.5 Failure of the backup node in REPL.

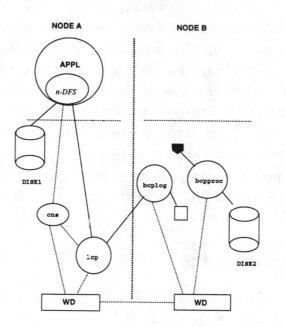

Figure 8.6 Rejoin of the backup node in REPL.

each message in the down-time log file, while the copy mode copies all the critical files from the primary file systems. The replay mode is invoked when the down-time log file is smaller than a limit determined by the application; otherwise, the copy mode is used. Once the down-time log file is processed, `bcpproc` replays the log files created by the `bcplog` during recovery. The backup recovery is complete when the `bcpproc` consumes all the logged data (created by `lcp` and `bcplog`).

8.3.5   A Switching Data-Processing Application

Application U is a real-time telecommunication network system which fetches data from a switch, filters the data, and stores them for some off-line operations systems. In addition to the previous requirements for fault tolerance, this product needed to get its persistent files online immediately after a failure recovery on a backup node. During normal operations on the primary server, REPL replicates all the critical persistent files on a backup server with an overhead of less than 14 percent. When the primary server fails, *watchd* starts the application U on the backup node and automatically connects it to the backup disk on which the persistent files were replicated. To distinguish a node failure from a link failure, *watchd* was configured to use an Ethernet and a Datakit (an AT&T Virtual Circuit Switch (VCS) based networking product) for polling. A fail-over takes place only when the *watchd* on the backup site cannot poll the primary site using both Ethernet and Datakit. The fail-over takes about 30 seconds to finish. Most of the processes in application U are stateless and, hence, require no checkpointing. However, to prevent message loss in the event of a machine crash, messages are logged before processing. To make file update atomic, functions `ftfopen()` and `ftfclose()` are used.

8.4   Conclusions

The three components, *watchd*, *libft*, and REPL, form the core technology to provide fault tolerance as an architecture service. They allow fault tolerance to be embedded when applications are being newly designed or reengineered. They also give flexibility in the level and amount of fault tolerance to be implemented. This flexibility, of course, comes at certain cost in transparent use of these components. For example, *libft* requires users to insert some code in the application programs to declare critical data structures and REPL requires users to specify critical files. This form of architecture service provided by these components forces users to carefully think about the recovery techniques and apply them only when and where they are appropriate. In our experience, it is difficult to achieve an efficient and robust fault tolerant mechanism in software systems without users' participation. We made the platform and its components simple, portable, and reusable to reduce that effort.

The three components reuse each other, as well as use other components described in this book. In summary, REPL uses *watchd* and *libft* for its own fault tolerance, *watchd* watches itself for self-recovery, all the three components use *sfio* and *vmalloc*, and REPL uses the *n-DFS* shared library for intercepting file system calls to perform file replication; it also provides a lighter version of shared library (*librepl.a*) for replicating files and transactions on files.

As mentioned in Chapter 1, research, development, and deployment of these software fault tolerance components in the first few projects took a remarkably short time compared to any of our previous experiences with new technologies. We attribute this success largely to our customers: If the value of goods we supply to them is not higher than what they can find in the market, they simply will not use our products. It may not sound profound to the general business community, but software researchers are still learning this fact. Also, interacting with the customers in the early stages gave us positive feedback to the research and technology in those components.

The three components described in this chapter have been used within AT&T and are also available from Tandem Computers Incorporated as a product named HATS (High-Availability Transforming Software). Interested readers should contact the authors ([cmk,yen]@research.att.com) or Tandem Computers for further information.

9

Generalized Event-Action Handling

David Rosenblum and Balachander Krishnamurthy

9.1 Introduction

An *event-action system* is a software system in which events occurring in the environment of the system trigger actions in response to the events. The triggered actions may generate other events, which trigger other actions, and so on. A wide variety of software applications can be naturally characterized as event-action systems.

Most existing event-action systems are special-purpose systems that support a particular application domain. For example, Field [Rei90] is a tool integration service for software development environments, supporting tool integration with a broadcast message server (BMS) that allows tools to register interest in events that are generated by other tools. *Active databases* are database systems containing an event-action subsystem in which the events typically correspond to violation of an integrity constraint on the database, and the actions are operations that restore database integrity.

Given the prevalence of event-action processing within a multitude of applications, it would be desirable to provide a general event-action capability that can be easily and reliably integrated with applications

that need its services. In this chapter, we describe a general-purpose
event-action system called YEAST (Yet another Event-Action Specification Tool). YEAST is a platform for constructing distributed event-action
applications using high-level event-action specifications. YEAST can support a wide variety of event-action applications, including calendar and
notification systems, computer network management, software configuration management, software process automation, software process measurement, and coordination of wide-area software development. YEAST
enhances and generalizes the capabilities of the systems just discussed in
several ways–by supporting automatic recognition of a rich collection of
predefined event classes, by providing extensibility as user-defined events,
and by providing a general, application-independent encapsulation of the
event-action model.

9.2   Architecture and Operation of YEAST

Figure 9.1 depicts the architecture of YEAST. The figure depicts processes
in ovals and data objects in rectangles, with interactions between components being either synchronous (solid arrows) or asynchronous (dashed
arrows). As shown in Figure 9.1, the architectural style of YEAST is that
of a client/server system, in which the server is a central entity accepting
client commands from many (possibly remote) users. The user invokes
client commands through the computer system's command interpreter
(such as the KornShell—see Section 4.1); the interaction between user
and server during client command invocation is synchronous and interactive. Client commands are used to register specifications with the server
and to perform various definition, query, and specification management
chores. Client commands can originate from any machine, including machines outside the local network in which the server is running. The client
commands are described in further detail in Section 9.3.2.

Each YEAST specification comprises an event pattern and an action.
The event pattern is a pattern of *primitive event descriptors*. The action
is any valid sequence of commands that can be executed by the computer
system's command interpreter, including YEAST client commands.

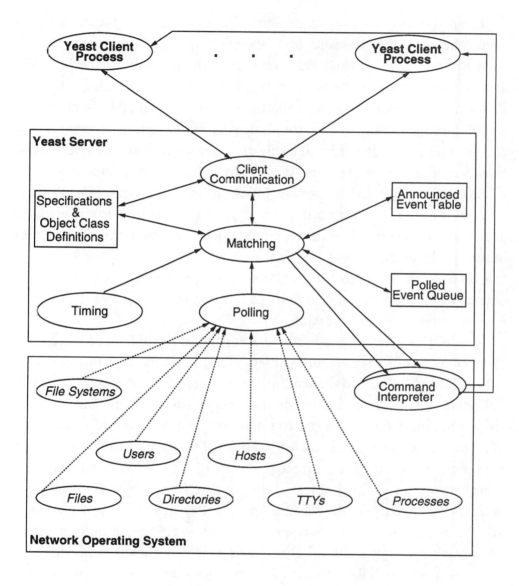

Figure 9.1 Architecture of the YEAST system.

The server invokes the computer system's command interpreter to execute the action component of a specification at the earliest possible time after it has matched the event pattern of the specification. The action is executed on the host on which the server is running; however, the action can explicitly call remote execution commands, such as the UNIX command rsh, to execute all or part of the action on remote machines. The action is executed using the user's environment information that was in effect at the time the user registered the specification; in a UNIX system, this environment includes the user's command search path, current working directory, alias list, and so on. Because the user interacts with the server solely through brief client command invocations, any other specification-related information the server must communicate to the user—such as problems that arise during specification matching, or output from a specification action—is sent via electronic mail to the user who registered the specification.

A primitive event corresponds to a change in the value of an attribute of an object belonging to some object class. *Predefined* primitive events can be automatically detected by the server; in particular, the server polls the system environment for their occurrences. *User-defined* primitive events must be announced to the server by a user, because the server does not have sufficient knowledge about the semantics of user-defined events to detect their occurrences automatically. Predefined primitive events involve predefined object classes and attributes that the server can poll. User-defined primitive events involve user-defined object classes or attributes. The server stores a specification's event descriptors for predefined primitive events in the Polled Event Queue in the order in which the server will next poll for a match. The server stores a specification's event descriptors for user-defined primitive events in the Announced Event Table, where they are consulted as the server receives announced events.

The server stores specifications and their associated information (such as the login ID of the owner of the specification) in the Specification Database while the specifications are active. The Specification Database includes a persistent copy of the specification stored in the file system. Whenever the server is restarted after a machine crash, the server reregisters the file-system copies of specifications that were active at the time of the crash. The server stores the definitions of object classes and attributes in the Object Definition Database. This latter database contains the definitions of object classes and attributes that are predefined at the time of starting the server, and of object class and attribute definitions that are defined by users. The set of predefined object classes can vary from machine to machine and is dependent on the resources that are available in the computer system on which the server executes.

9.3 Features of YEAST

In this section, we first describe the language of YEAST specifications, including a description of the predefined object classes and attributes. We then describe the client commands that are used to interact with the YEAST server.

9.3.1 The YEAST Specification Language

A YEAST specification consists of an event pattern along with an action, written with the following syntax:

> *event_pattern* **do** *action*

The event pattern contains two kinds of primitive event descriptors: (1) *time-event descriptors*, which match predefined temporal events, and (2) *object-event descriptors*, which match either predefined or user-defined nontemporal events. Compound patterns of primitive event descriptors are formed using the connectives **then** (*sequence-of*), **and** (*all-of*), and **or** (*one-of*).

9.3.1.1 Time-Event Descriptors

A time-event descriptor matches the passage of a *relative* amount of time (for example, 20 minutes) or the occurrence of an *absolute* time (for example, 7 A.M. Monday).

Relative time-event descriptors are specified by the keywords **in** and **within**, and the relative times can be specified in days, hours, minutes, and seconds. An **in** event descriptor matches forever *after* the specified time has elapsed, while a **within** event descriptor matches *until* the specified time has elapsed. The following are some examples of relative time-event descriptors:

- **in** 2 hours 10 minutes–matches forever after 2 hours and 10 minutes have elapsed from now.*
- **within** 6 days 10 hours–matches from now until 6 days and 10 hours have elapsed.

Absolute time-event descriptors are specified by the keywords **at** and **by**. An **at** event descriptor matches forever *after* the specified time has been reached, while a **by** event descriptor matches *until* the specified time has been reached. Absolute times must at least specify a time of day, with an optional day of week or date; the optional date can specify either a day, a month and a day, or a month, day, and year. Absolute time specifications implicitly specify the next occurrence of the specified time. The following are some examples of absolute time-event descriptors:

- **at** 8am–matches forever after the next occurrence of 8 A.M.
- **by** 8am–matches from now until the next occurrence of 8 A.M.
- **at** 8am saturday–matches forever after the next occurrence of 8 A.M. on a Saturday.
- **at** 8am 31–matches forever after 8 A.M. on the last day of the current month.
- **by** 8am august 31–matches from now until 8 A.M. on the next occurrence of August 31.
- **at** 8am august 31 1960–matches forever from now, since the specified time and date have already passed.
- **by** 8am august 31 1995–matches from now until 8 A.M. on August 31, 1995.

Absolute time-event descriptors can be modified by one of the following modifiers, which constrain matching to individual days:

- **daily**, **today** and **tomorrow**–used only with a time of day.
- **weekly**–used with a day of week.
- **monthly**–used with a day of month.

---

*In Section 9.3.1.3, we describe in more detail what "now" and "next" mean to the YEAST server.

- **yearly**–used with a month and day of the month.

The modifiers have their obvious meaning, with the further constraint that **at** event descriptors match between the specified time and the end of the day on matching days, while **by** event descriptors match between the beginning of the day and the specified time on matching days. The following are some examples of modified absolute time-event descriptors:

- **by** 10pm **today**–matches between now and 10 P.M. today, or never if it is after 10 P.M. today.
- **at** 8am **daily**–matches between 8 A.M. and the end of the day every day.
- **by** 8am saturday **weekly**–matches between the beginning of the day and 8am every Saturday.
- **at** 8am 31 **monthly**–matches between 8 A.M. and the end of the day on the last day of every month (including months with less than 31 days).
- **by** 8am dec 31 **yearly**–matches between the beginning of the day and 8 A.M. every December 31st.

9.3.1.2   Object-Event Descriptors, Object Classes, and Attributes

Object-event descriptors use a relational test to specify a change in the value of an attribute of an object. They have the following syntax:

object_class   object_name   object_attribute   relational_test

The *object_class* and *object_attribute* must either be predefined or must have been defined to YEAST using the client commands **defobj** and **defattr** (described shortly). The *relational_test* of an object-event descriptor is a test against the value of the specified *object_attribute* of the specified *object_name* at the time a match of the descriptor is attempted. The special relational tests **changed** and **unchanged** are available for some predefined attributes. The *object_attribute* has a type, which is one of the predefined types **boolean**, **integer**, **procstatus** (status values of operating system processes), **real**, **reltime** (relative times), **string**, and **systime** (unmodified absolute times).

Table 9.1 lists the predefined object classes and their predefined attributes. The following examples illustrate event descriptors involving some of the predefined object classes and attributes:

Table 9.1 Predefined Object Classes and Attributes of YEAST

Object Class	Attribute	Description
dir	atime	Last access time
(directories	count	Number of files in the directory
in the file	mode	Access permissions
system)	mtime	Last modification time
	owner	Login ID of owner
file	atime	Last access time
(files in the	mode	Access permissions
file system)	mtime	Last modification time
	owner	Login ID of owner
	size	Number of bytes in the file
filesys	capacity	Percentage of total capacity in use
(mounted file systems)	size	Total capacity in kilobytes
host	load	Load average
(named computer	up	Whether or not the host is operational
hosts)	users	Number of users logged on
process	etime	Elapsed clock time
(operating	size	Kilobytes of memory used
system	status	Execution status
processes)	stime	CPU time in privileged mode
	utime	CPU time in user mode
tty	mode	Access permissions
(terminal devices)	mtime	Last modification time
user	location	Tty of login session
(user login IDs)	loggedin	Whether or not the user is logged in

- **file** foo mtime > 8am Jan 1 1994–matches forever once file **foo** has been modified after 8 A.M. on January 1, 1994.
- **file** foo mtime **changed**–matches forever after the next time file **foo** has been modified.
- **user** dsr@research loggedin == true–matches whenever user **dsr** is logged in on host **research**.
- **host** research load < 2.0–matches whenever the load on host **research** is less than 2.0.

All **file**, **dir**, and **tty** objects named without full pathnames are implicitly prefixed by the current working directory that was in effect at the time the enclosing specification was registered. Event descriptors involving predefined attributes of the object class **file** have special semantics when the specified file is a directory. In particular, the event descriptor is matched if it matches either for the specified directory itself or for any of the files contained in the directory. This semantics applies only to the top level directory, not recursively to the complete subdirectory structure.

9.3.1.3   Compound-Event Descriptors

As mentioned at the beginning of this section, compound-event patterns are formed using three connectives, which, in order of decreasing priority, are **then**, **and**, and **or**. Parentheses can be used to enforce any desired grouping. A compound-event descriptor combined with **and** is matched whenever the constituent event descriptors match at the same time. A compound-event pattern combined with **or** is matched whenever any of the constituent events match. For a **then** connective, the server matches the event pattern on the left side of the operator **then** before it attempts to match the event pattern on the right side of the operator **then**; only after the right side is matched is the complete pattern combined with **then** considered to be matched.

Note that, in general, it is possible to write specifications whose event patterns will never match once certain time-event descriptors stop matching. If the server detects that a specification is unmatchable, the server removes the specification, and the user who registered the specification is notified of the failed match by electronic mail.

9.3.2   Client Commands

Users interact with the YEAST server through a collection of client commands that are invoked through the computer system's command interpreter. The YEAST client commands can be categorized as follows:

1. **addspec** and **readspec**–Commands for registering new specifications
2. **defobj** and **defattr**–Commands for defining new object classes and attributes
3. **announce**–A command for generating events involving user-defined object classes or attributes
4. **lsspec**, **rmspec**, **fgspec**, **suspspec**, and **modgrp**–Commands for manipulating registered specifications
5. **lsobj**, **rmobj**, **lsattr**, and **rmattr**–Commands for manipulating object classes and their attributes
6. **authobj**, **authattr**, and **lsauth**–Commands for controlling and determining access to object classes and attributes

7. **regyeast** and **unregyeast**–Commands for registering and unregistering users with YEAST

Users must register themselves with the YEAST server via the client command **regyeast** before they can carry out other client interactions.

9.3.2.1 Registering Specifications

Users register specifications with the YEAST server via the client command **addspec**, which has the following syntax:*

> **addspec** [repeat] {+group_name} Yeast_specification

The syntax of the *Yeast_specification* was described in Section 9.3.1. The optional specifier **repeat** indicates that the specification is to be immediately reregistered with the YEAST server whenever the server matches the event pattern and triggers the action, or whenever the server removes the specification because it is unmatchable. A specification can optionally be given one or more *group_name*s. Group names are used in client commands that manipulate specifications (such as those commands in category 4 listed in the previous section) to refer to a group of specifications with a single name, and to refer to specifications from within the action component of other specifications.

The client command **readspec** can be used to register a collection of specifications stored in a file.

9.3.2.2 Defining Object Classes and Attributes, and Announcing Events

New object classes and attributes are defined to YEAST with the client commands **defobj** and **defattr**, respectively. Events involving user-defined object classes and attributes must be announced to YEAST with the **announce** command, which has the following syntax:

> **announce** object_class object_name object_attribute = attribute_value

Given the importance of announcements as the fundamental mechanism for generating user-defined events, a version of the client command **an-**

---

*In describing the syntax, we use the convention that square brackets denote optional tokens, while curly braces denote tokens that can appear zero or more times.

nounce is available as a library routine that can be linked with application programs that need to generate YEAST announcements. Applications can invoke the **announce** routine at appropriate points from within their application.

9.3.2.3 Manipulating Specifications, Object Classes, and Attributes

Several client commands are available for manipulating existing specifications, object classes, and attributes.

The command **lsspec** lists a user's active specifications and shows the internal number that the YEAST server has assigned to each specification. **Rmspec** is used to remove specifications. **Suspspec** is used to suspend matching on the event patterns of specifications, while **fgspec** is used to resume matching on the event patterns of specifications. **Modgrp** is used to add specifications to and remove specifications from specification groups. All of these commands operate on both specification numbers and specification groups. Users can execute these specification-related commands only for the specifications they have registered via **addspec**.

The command **lsobj** lists all the predefined and user-defined object classes, and the command **lsattr** lists the attributes of an object class along with their types. **Rmobj** is used to remove a user-defined object class, while **rmattr** is used to remove a user-defined attribute.

9.3.2.4 Controlling and Determining Access

All client interactions with the YEAST server undergo authentication to ensure that YEAST users do not interfere with one another (accidentally or otherwise). When a user defines a new object class via **defobj**, the new object class is owned by that user; ownership is determined likewise for attributes defined via **defattr**.

An owner can use the client commands **authobj** and **authattr** to give another user one of four levels of access to an object class or attribute, respectively:

- *Read access*–The user can make specifications whose event patterns involve the object class or attribute.

- *Announce access*–The user can announce events involving the object class or attribute; announce access includes read access.
- *Write access*–The user can define and remove attributes of the object class; write access includes announce access.
- *Owner access*–The user can delete and remove the object class or attribute; owner access includes write access.

For example, the owner of an object class might give other users announce access for a particular attribute and read access for all other attributes. The commands **authobj** and **authattr** can also be used to remove a user's access privileges. The predefined object classes and attributes are owned by YEAST, and all users are given read access to them. The client command **lsauth** lists the authentication information of an object class and its attributes.

9.4   Elimination of Polling in YEAST

In this section, we describe some details of the implementation of YEAST, including a discussion of how we avoid polling in one version of YEAST for file-related events.

The YEAST server is a single process that must handle both client connections and checking the queue of polled-event descriptors for potential matches. If the server is busy checking event descriptors in this queue, client connections may be blocked. Likewise, if several client communications occur in a row, the server may not be able to check the Polled Event Queue, thus delaying the triggering of actions. Fairness is guaranteed by ensuring that every so often client connections are checked. There is a slight bias in favor of checking the Polled Event Queue to ensure that specifications already registered with YEAST are promptly matched.

File-related events are frequently of interest to YEAST applications, and we therefore took a close look at improving the efficiency of matching these events. Users are typically interested in file creation, change, and deletion events. With the 3D File System [KK90], YEAST is able to automatically detect occurrences of such events without having to poll.

Since the 3D File System implementation traps all operating system calls that correspond to YEAST file events, we enhanced the 3D File

System to announce occurrences of YEAST file events to the Yeast server. These enhancements required a small change to 3D File System, which was then generalized and implemented in a system called COLA [KK92]. Generating announcements to user-level processes was further generalized and built into the new version of 3D File System–n-Dimensional File System (described in Chapter 2).

The advantage of this scheme is that it eliminates wasteful polling for events that may happen infrequently, and it never misses events that may be missed because of long polling intervals. Being able to trap specific file events efficiently is a useful ability. We made significant use of this when we reused YEAST as a component of PROVENCE (Chapter 10).

9.5   An Example Application of YEAST

As described briefly in Section 1.3.1, we developed a collection of YEAST specifications that automate portions of a software distribution process. We describe the process in more detail here and illustrate some of the YEAST specifications.

As should be clear by now, many of the tools in our department are dependent on one another. Thus, each tool owner must keep track of the activities of several other tool owners. The management of this collection of tools has been centralized under the control of a meta-user called ADVSOFT, who gathers and distributes the official versions of the tools.

Figure 9.2 depicts the process that ADVSOFT manages. In the figure, the circles represent subprocesses, and the arrows represent data flow between subprocesses. As shown in Figure 9.2, tool owners submit the newest versions of their tools to ADVSOFT in cycles that currently occur two times a year. The figure depicts in detail how the process is carried out for the tool *libx* (solid lines), while showing that an identical process is carried out for all other tools T in parallel (dashed lines). The rest of the diagram should be self-explanatory.

We describe a collection of YEAST specifications that automate the primarily bookkeeping activities of ADVSOFT. The specifications automate the portions of the diagram of Figure 9.2 that appear in boldface.

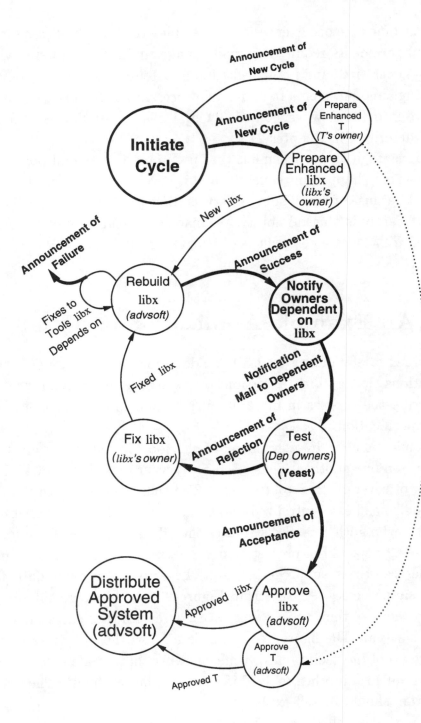

Figure 9.2 The ADVSOFT software tool distribution process.

9.5.1 Object Classes

To model the ADVSOFT process in YEAST and develop the specifications, it was first necessary to identify the kinds of objects that ADVSOFT manages, along with their attributes. The object classes we identified include *tools* and tool *owners*, which have the following attributes:

- Tools:

  Rebuilt–A boolean-valued attribute that becomes true for a tool T whenever a new version of T has been built successfully.

  Accepted–A boolean-valued attribute that becomes true for a tool T whenever T has been accepted by *all* owners of tools that are dependent on T.

- Owners:

  Accepts–A string-valued attribute specifying a tool T that has been accepted by an owner U.

  Rejects–A string-valued attribute specifying a tool T that has been rejected by an owner U.

The owner of a tool is simply the person or persons who built the tool and who are responsible for making fixes and enhancements to the tool. The following commands register these object classes and attributes with YEAST:

> **defobj** tool
> **defattr** tool accepted boolean
> **defattr** tool rebuilt boolean
>
> **defobj** owner
> **defattr** owner accepts string
> **defattr** owner rejects string

Because these object classes are user-defined, their events must be announced to YEAST. As will be seen, all of the necessary announcements are generated automatically by YEAST specifications and by other programs.

9.5.2   Specifications

To initialize the ADVSOFT process, we run a command script called
genspecs that generates all the specifications that are used to automate
the process. The specifications are generated for all tools and owners that
are known to ADVSOFT, using dependency information maintained in the
ADVSOFT tool database. As an example of the specifications generated
by **genspecs**, the following specifications automate the "Notify Owners"
subprocess of Figure 9.2 for the tool *libx*:

addspec repeat +advsoft +libx file /home/advsoft/src/libx/BUILT mtime
changed **do announce** tool libx rebuilt = true

addspec repeat +advsoft +libx file /home/advsoft/src/libx/ERROR mtime
changed **do announce** tool libx rebuilt = false

addspec repeat +advsoft +libx tool libx rebuilt == true
do Mail -s "libx was rebuilt" uid_1 uid_2 ...

   The first two specifications define the low-level, predefined YEAST
events that determine when a new version of a tool has been built. Each
tool (such as *libx*) exists in its own subdirectory of **/home/advsoft/src**.
Whenever a tool is rebuilt, the file **BUILT** is created in the tool directory
if the build succeeded, while the file **ERROR** is created if the build failed.
The first specification says that whenever the file **BUILT** is modified, then
the high-level event "tool *libx* was successfully rebuilt" is automatically
announced. The second specification says that whenever the file **ERROR** is
modified, then the high-level event "tool *libx* was unsuccessfully rebuilt"
is automatically announced. Thus, the first two specifications serve to
translate the low-level file system events into process-level tool-change
events. The third specification illustrates one of the actions that is performed as a result of a successful rebuild; it says that whenever *libx* has
been rebuilt, electronic mail is sent to uid_1, uid_2, ..., who are the owners
of tools that depend on *libx* (as determined by **genspecs**).

   Once tool owner uid_i receives a "*libx* rebuilt" message, that owner
runs regression tests on his or her dependent tools, and then makes one
of the following two announcements, corresponding to the "Acceptance"

and "Rejection" announcements of Figure 9.2:

$$\textbf{announce} \text{ owner uid}_i \text{ accepts} = \text{libx}$$
$$\textbf{announce} \text{ owner uid}_i \text{ rejects} = \text{libx}$$

In practice, these announcements can be generated automatically by the regression test scripts themselves. These announcements trigger other actions that are defined by the following specifications, which partially automate the "Test" subprocess of Figure 9.2; in these specifications, uid_{libx} is the owner of *libx*:

$$\textbf{addspec} \text{ repeat } +\text{advsoft} -\text{libx owner uid}_1 \text{ accepts} == \text{libx}$$
$$\textbf{and} \text{ owner uid}_2 \text{ accepts} == \text{libx}$$
$$\textbf{and} \ldots$$
$$\textbf{do} \text{ Mail -s "libx accepted" advsoft uid}_{libx}$$
$$\textbf{announce} \text{ tool libx accepted} = \text{true}$$

$$\textbf{addspec} \text{ repeat } +\text{advsoft} +\text{libx owner uid}_1 \text{ rejects} == \text{libx}$$
$$\textbf{or} \text{ owner uid}_2 \text{ rejects} == \text{libx}$$
$$\textbf{or} \ldots$$
$$\textbf{do} \text{ Mail -s "libx rejected" advsoft uid}_{libx}$$
$$\textbf{announce} \text{ tool libx accepted} = \text{false}$$

The first specification automatically announces acceptance of *libx* once *all* dependent tool owners have announced his or her individual acceptance of *libx*. The second specification automatically announces rejection of *libx* once *any* dependent tool owner announces his or her individual rejection of *libx*.

In testing some dependent tool against a new version of *libx*, the owner of the dependent tool may find it necessary to submit a new version of the dependent tool in order to account for interface changes and/or new features in the new version of *libx*. In such a situation, the dependent owner might withhold acceptance or rejection of *libx* until the new version of the dependent tool has itself been developed and made ready for submission to the ADVSOFT process.

9.5.3   Changes to Tools and Owners

The tool dependency specifications shown in the previous section can become obsolete as the owners of and dependencies among existing tools change, and as new tools come into existence. Other specifications are used to automatically delete obsolete tool dependency specifications and add new ones whenever such events occur. This is accomplished by combining the specifications in the previous section into several specification groups, each of which can be removed by name and reconstructed as changes in dependencies occur. For instance, the acceptance and rejection specifications shown in the previous section are in the specification group *libx*. The following specification regenerates the *libx* specifications whenever changes are made to the *libx* tool area:

```
addspec repeat +advsoft dir /home/advsoft/src/libx mtime changed
do rmspec libx
   genspecs libx
```

That is, if the *libx* tool directory is modified, then the *libx* specification group is removed using the YEAST client command **rmspec**, and **genspecs** is invoked to regenerate the *libx* specifications.

Similarly, if a brand new tool is submitted to ADVSOFT, then all of the existing ADVSOFT specifications are assumed to be obsolete because of the potential introduction of new or altered dependencies between tools. Therefore, the following specification is used to delete and regenerate the complete set of specifications (such as the specification group **advsoft**) whenever a new tool is introduced (as indicated by a change in `/home/advsoft/src`):

```
addspec repeat dir /home/advsoft/src mtime changed
do rmspec advsoft
   genspecs
```

9.5.4   Discussion of ADVSOFT

ADVSOFT provides a real-world application for gaining experience with YEAST and identifying shortcomings in YEAST. Indeed, the specification group feature was added in response to the need for the action of one specification to manipulate other specifications.

We have illustrated just a few of the specifications we have developed to automate the ADVSOFT process. In total, ADVSOFT controls 64 tools, which require 291 YEAST specifications to automate the portions of the process we have automated. The regularity of the specifications allows the use of the simple command script **genspecs** to generate the entire set of specifications.

Note that because many events in this process are represented by YEAST announcements, individual tool owners can register additional specifications that provide other kinds of automated support customized to their particular needs (such as daily reminders to test their dependent tools). Note also that the process as currently defined contains several "holes", such as a lack of enforced deadlines. Such refinements to the process can be easily incorporated with additional specifications.

The ADVSOFT process, of course, involves another set of activities; namely, those associated with the management of distribution requests and problem reports from external tool customers. We have just begun to model and automate these activities.

9.6   Reuse

9.6.1   Architectural Style of YEAST Applications

YEAST is a tool that naturally aids event/condition/action applications. An application that can be modeled as a set of conditions that are satisfied when a set of events occur, which, in turn, results in a set of actions being triggered, can use YEAST directly as an implementation vehicle. Unlike other tools, YEAST's extensibility (the ability to define new object classes and attributes as explained in Section 9.3.2.2) enables applications to map their conditions into the various event classes of YEAST. By default, YEAST tracks a variety of system events, but user-defined events are tracked through announcements. The open nature of YEAST, whereby any system action can be invoked, makes it possible for arbitrary applications to use it. By separating the action language portion of YEAST to be *ksh*, arbitrary scripts in the *ksh* language can be executed as a result of event patterns being matched.

The event/condition/action style (see Section 1.4) is general, and several YEAST applications can be cast naturally in this paradigm. With YEAST, arbitrary collections of users and application programs can interact in a loose manner via the event broadcast (and matching) mechanism [GN91]. A tool that embodies an architectural style may constrain the application, but the tool's implementation should be open so as not to interfere with the specific needs of the application. Keeping this in mind, YEAST was designed with a clear separation between the events being matched and the actions that could be triggered. There are no constraints on what actions can be triggered via YEAST including internal YEAST actions. However, there are constraints on the range of applications for which our implementation of YEAST could be reused. While the range of events matched by YEAST is wide, it is probably not suitable for applications with real-time constraints.

9.6.2   Architectural Services

The architectural services used by YEAST are fault tolerance and visualization. In Section 1.6.2, we used YEAST as an example for both these architectural services. We go into more detail here.

9.6.2.1   Fault Tolerance

As discussed in Sections 1.6.2.1 and 8.3.2, YEAST has been made fault-tolerant by grouping the critical data structures in a separate section of the code. When YEAST is linked with *libft*, the critical data structures are checkpointed and can be automatically recovered via recovery routines available also as part of *libft*. To detect machine failures and recover from them, YEAST is registered with a shadow process (*watchd*) along with a list of compatible hosts on which the YEAST server process can be restarted.

There were several requirements in making YEAST fault tolerant. Since YEAST runs as a continuously accessible server and accepts client commands from anywhere on the network, remote users should not be aware of the server machine failure. Additionally, events can occur at any time and specifications may be matchable at any time. Even if the server is restarted on a different machine upon machine failure, users on the network would have to be able to access it as before, that is, in a location-transparent manner. Additionally, since YEAST specifications can be complex (event descriptors linked with combinators), the partial match status of specifications has to be preserved to ensure that matching continues from the point where the last checkpoint was made.

9.6.2.2 Visualization

As with fault tolerance, visualization is another architectural service that is used by YEAST. However, use of visualization is not at a library level, but rather at a language level and at a process level. YEAST specifications can be visually represented as simple graphs with the event descriptors and combinators (**and/or/then**) as nodes, and the connection between the events represented as edges. Thus, the following specification

```
addspec at 8a and file foo mtime changed do action
```

is visualized, as shown in Figure 9.3. The specification label, the action string, and the connector (**and**) are shown along with the primitive-event descriptors. In the case of the temporal-event descriptor, the time at which it will be matched is displayed. For the object-event descriptor, the object class (**file**), the name of the object (**/home/bala/foo**), the attribute being matched (**mtime**), and the time at which the next attempt will be made to match this event descriptor are displayed.

Figure 9.4 shows a few more specifications; repeatable specifications are shown with an arrow pointing back to the specification.

Users wanted a dynamic, graphical front end showing the current partial match state of their YEAST specifications, that was updated as and when the specification matching state changed. In reusing an existing visualization tool, there were two design goals in mind: minimizing embedded knowledge of the visualization tool in YEAST (and vice versa), and ensuring that the dynamic front end did not impact the performance of YEAST.

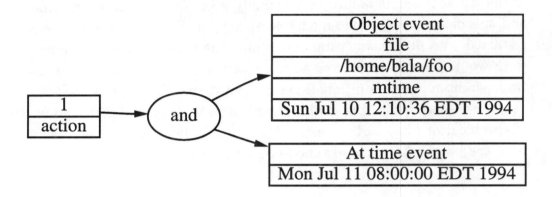

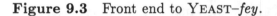

Figure 9.3   Front end to YEAST–*fey*.

The graphical front end for YEAST *fey* is a per-user front end; that is, each YEAST user invokes *fey* to visualize its collection of specifications. The displayed specifications include both active and suspended ones. *fey* shows the matching status and the time of the next matching attempt of each primitive-event descriptor in the specification.

When the *fey* front end is started, a YEAST client command *dumpspec* extracts a description of the user's set of specifications in the *dot* language format from the YEAST server. This *dot* description is sent to *dotty*, which generates the layout. The interesting aspect about *fey* is that it is a dynamic front end. Since the architectural service provided by *dotty* is via a running *dotty* process, we set up a dynamic link between YEAST and *dotty*. Thus, whenever there is a change in the status of any specification of a user, a notification is generated by YEAST and sent to the *dotty* process, which reinvokes *dumpspec* to get a new layout. The *dotty* process can stack the change notifications it receives from YEAST before requesting an update, lowering the burden on the YEAST daemon.

In keeping with the architectural-service notion, there is a clear separation of tasks between YEAST and *dotty*. YEAST continues to match events and only notifies *fey* about state changes. *fey* requests *raw* layout information at appropriate times, creates an aesthetic layout, and updates the display dynamically. There is *no* code dealing with layout handling, display, interaction with the front end, and so on, in YEAST. There is

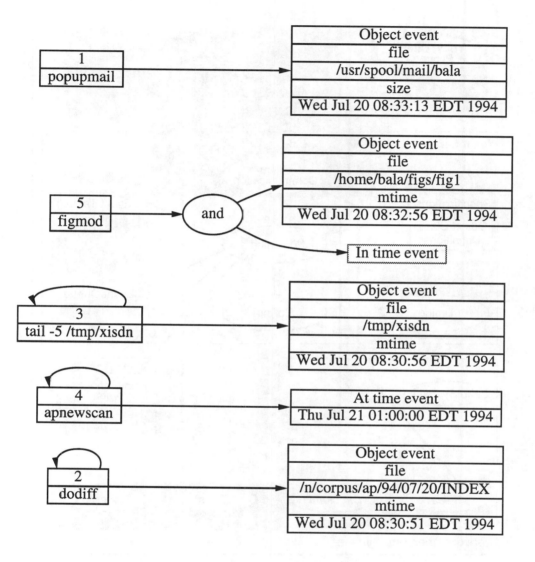

Figure 9.4 *fey* showing a collection of YEAST specifications.

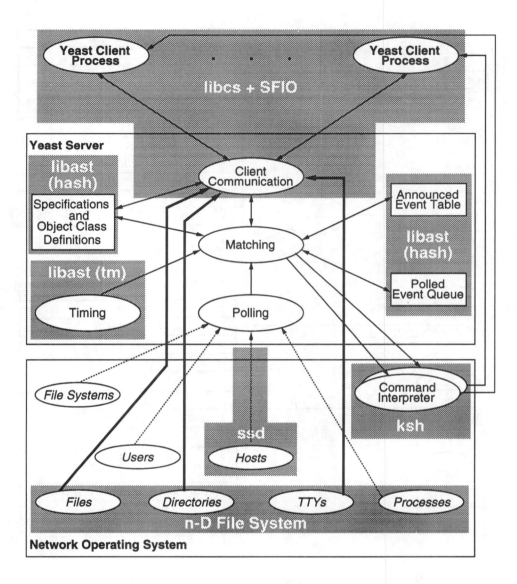

Figure 9.5 Enhanced architectural view of YEAST showing reused components.

no event matching code in *fey*. The architectural service of visualization provided by *dotty* makes this separation natural.

9.7 Reuse of Libraries and Components

Figure 9.5 shows the same architectural view of Figure 9.1, with the reused components highlighted. Figure 9.5 shows YEAST reusing libraries and components at all of the four levels discussed in Section 1.5. The following is a list of the stages at which we reuse existing components in our YEAST implementation:

- Linking with libraries
- Configuration and assembling
- Fault detection
- Reverse engineering
- KornShell as action language
- Auxiliary commands with running YEAST
- Distribution

9.7.1 Linking with Libraries

Significant use is made of *libast*'s hash table, time, and error-handling routines. The safe/fast I/O (*sfio*) library routines are used for a variety of buffers, from the commonly used error-message buffer to reading in incoming packets over the network. The *libcs* library is used for service naming. The numerous advantages of using *libcs* include the ability to run multiple instantiations of the same service using various restrictions (such as `user=uid` or `group=gid`) to restrict access, and client authentication (without requiring a privileged service). Details on *libcs* can be found in Section 2.2.7.

9.7.2 Configuration and Assembling

YEAST was jointly developed by the authors of this chapter and we worked off the same code base. One author used *n-DFS* (see Chapter 3) exclusively for viewpathing to ensure that changes made during development did not affect the other author. The other author used the view-pathing mechanism of *nmake* at build time to share the sources. The maintenance of multiple parallel versions–a requirement because there were several simultaneous extensions being made to YEAST (visualization, semantic analysis, and so on)–was thus made easier.

For portability, we relied on *iffe* (Section 3.2). Since kernel data structures vary across machine architecture, code relating to the predefined object-class *process* required different features. The choice of the mail program (used to send the result of any YEAST-triggered action), the absence or presence of system files (and, if present, their location such as /usr/spool/rwho files), and so on, were all determined via use of *iffe*. We also used *proto* to convert our code to be ANSI-C compliant.

9.7.3   Fault Detection

Yeast provided the first opportunity to apply APP, the Annotation Pre-Processor for C (see Chapter 5), to the development of a serious application. One of the authors used APP assertions–116 assertions were made in 95 assertion regions. Of these 95 assertion regions, 39 are function interface specifications, which contain a total of 61 assertions.

In the course of applying APP to the development of Yeast, faults were found in the APP implementation, and APP's capabilities were adjusted in minor ways to make the tool and assertion language easier to use. More significant, however, was the benefit APP brought to the development of Yeast, proving APP's utility as a high-level, systematic aid to fault detection and isolation. In particular, since first releasing YEAST to other people within AT&T, we have discovered and removed 19 faults. Of these 19 faults, eight were discovered by one or more assertion violations. Of the 11 faults that were not detected by assertions, six could have been caught by assertions that were not written; two were detected by a heap storage certification routine; and the remaining three could have been detected only with an assertion language more powerful than APP's. The experience of applying APP to the development of YEAST has been described in detail separately [Ros92].

9.7.4   Reverse Engineering

Both during development and debugging, we used *cia* and the collection
of tools built on top of *cia* (see Chapter 6). Specifically, while adding a
new feature to YEAST, we were able to quickly locate the parts of the code
that would be affected by the proposed enhancement. After the feature
addition, we were able to go back and generate the collection of files and
functions that were affected by the enhancement; this enabled isolation
of files and functions that needed to be looked at while debugging the
feature.

After a few early versions of YEAST, we went back and used *incl* to
weed out unnecessary include files that had agglomerated. Function call
graphs generated via *dagger* (Section 6.4) were handy as the code increased in size and complexity. While making YEAST fault tolerant, *cia*
was used to generate a list of global data structures. This resulted in the
creation of a routine (`gblgen`) that has since been reused in many other
projects that required fault tolerance. This is a good example of how work
on top of a tool for use within another tool in the department led to a
generic routine that has since been reused many times for tools outside
the department.

9.7.5   KornShell As Action Language

YEAST specifications consist of event patterns and KornShell actions to
be triggered when the pattern has been matched. The advantages of using
KornShell as the action language of YEAST include:

- Command interpretation is outside of YEAST, enabling separation of
  tasks as well as reducing the size of YEAST.
- Numerous language features and existing command scripts of KornShell
  can be used in YEAST.
- Since KornShell is the command interpreter of choice for a very high
  percentage of users, *anything* that can be done via *ksh* can be triggered
  as a result of matching a YEAST specification. This factor has led to
  easier comprehension, quicker appreciation, and widespread usage of
  YEAST.

9.7.6 Auxiliary Commands

Two processes that we use in conjunction with YEAST are *cs* (the connection service) and *ssd* (the system status daemon). The *cs* command can be used to inquire about the status of a collection of YEAST specifications. The *ssd* process reports network status that the *cs* server uses for matching event descriptors using attributes of `host` object class.

9.7.7 Distribution

YEAST was distributed like other tools in our department to many sites within the company. During this process, we came up with the notion of modeling the distribution process itself, as well as to use YEAST to automate parts of the process. In Sections 1.3.1 and 9.5 we discussed the ADVSOFT process. YEAST's modeling led to better understanding of the process.

9.8 Conclusion

We have described the event-action system YEAST. Several projects within AT&T are using it for a variety of applications. Some of these applications include wide-area software development, requirements tracing, software tracking, security monitoring, and process measurement. The generality and extensibility of YEAST have made it highly amenable to the differing needs of these applications. The availability of several lower-level libraries have enabled a significant amount of software reuse within YEAST. Additionally, YEAST has shown the viability of reuse of architectural services (such as fault tolerance and visualization).

10

Monitoring, Modeling, and Enacting Processes

Naser Barghouti and Balachander Krishnamurthy

10.1 Introduction

This chapter describes a process-centered software development environment called PROVENCE, built by connecting several of the tools described earlier in the book. The connection, unlike the tools described thus far, is at a component level. PROVENCE is an example of a tool in the connected tools layer, as described in Section 1.5. We begin with a description of a software development process, followed by a description of the architecture of a process-centered environment. We then explain the details of PROVENCE, an instance of this architecture, with an eye toward reuse and componentization.

10.2 Software Development Process

A software development process is a partially ordered set of steps that are followed in developing a target system. Processes vary across organizations and involve both humans and tools. A process-centered environment (PCE) is a software tool that assists in modeling and enacting software processes. The thrust of research in the area of process-centered environments has focused on two objectives: (1) to devise useful notations, called *process modeling languages*, by which the environment is tailored to the desired process; and (2) to investigate mechanisms, called *process enactment engines*, by which PCEs assist users in analyzing, simulating, carrying out, and automating the specified processes.

By providing a powerful process modeling language, the PCE enables a systems/process engineer to write a specification that models the structural attributes of a system (often called the data model or the information model) as well as the behavioral attributes (the processes). The enactment engine of the PCE uses the specification to tailor its runtime assistance. In particular, existing PCEs provide the following forms of assistance

- Monitoring the actual process execution to verify that developers are following a particular process
- Planning future development activities
- Automating parts of the process
- Enforcing a specific process

These forms of assistance, if provided in a nonintrusive manner, are particularly useful in software engineering environments. For example, they would allow a systems engineer to model a reengineered process, simulate the execution of this new process in a test environment, and analyze the performance of the process before actually employing the new process. PCEs also enable process engineers to collect data about the performance of various processes and measure the effectiveness of these processes.

Several PCEs have been proposed and some have been built in the past few years [Tho91, Wil93]. Most existing PCEs, however, have been built as monolithic systems with a closed interface in which users (software developers, process engineers, managers, and so on) work entirely within the PCE; that is, all interaction between the users and the project's components is done via the PCE. This approach, called the *monolithic environment approach*, assumes that organizations adopting process technology will alter their working environment significantly.

Message-passing environments, such as Forest [GI90] and Field [Rei90], remove the restriction that all development has to be done from within the environment. However, this approach, called the *tool integration approach*, requires that all tools used during the execution of a process be enveloped to permit interaction via the message server in the environment; that is, the developers cannot use a new tool without enveloping it. Tool envelopes range from simple wrappers to complicated encapsulations of tool functions, depending on the function of the tool and the level of desired integration.

Both of these approaches suffer from major drawbacks. First, it is difficult to convince software developers to move to a completely new family of software development environments (SDEs), especially when the advantages of PCEs over more traditional SDEs have not yet been demonstrated. Second, the two approaches cannot readily integrate existing technology or use new technology, such as software tools, but must instead provide alternatives.

In this chapter, we present a PCE architecture, called PROVENCE, that overcomes both of these shortcomings. With respect to the first shortcoming, the architecture makes it possible to introduce features of process-centered environments incrementally to convince developers that there is an added value to using them. Second, the architecture is component-based, where software tools that are already being used by developers fill in as most of the components; new tools can be integrated through a well-defined interface among the components.

10.3   The PROVENCE Architecture

The main principle behind the PROVENCE architecture is to distinguish between the enactment of a software process *model* and the actual execution (or performance) of the process itself. The conceptual distinction between the two has been pointed out by Fernström and Dowson [Fer93, DF93]. Separating the two domains is the means through which PROVENCE is able to provide nonobtrusive process-centered assistance, that is, without changing the project's working environment (the set of tools and the file system utilities used by project personnel, the way the project's information is organized, and so on). Figure 10.1 illustrates

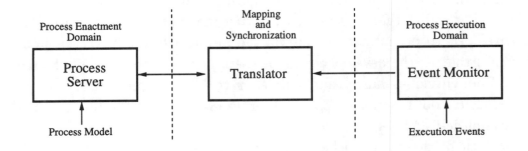

Figure 10.1 Separating model enactment from process execution.

the separation between process model enactment and process execution in PROVENCE.

We have analyzed the requirements for achieving this separation and have identified six necessary components:

1. A *process server* that stores and enacts a model of the processes
2. A *data management system* that stores process and product data in one or more databases and permits querying of the databases
3. An *operating system monitor* that detects and announces system-level events, such as tool invocations and events related to file accesses
4. An *event-action engine* that matches arbitrary event patterns and triggers corresponding actions
5. A *translator* that maps process steps onto system-level events
6. A *visualizer* to display an up-to-date view of the process state

Figure 10.2 depicts how these six components are integrated in PROVENCE.

The architecture achieves our main objective as follows. The structural and behavioral attributes of the system under purview is modeled in the process server, using the process modeling language provided by the process server. The model includes a description of the process steps, a portion of which corresponds to actions performed on entities that reside on the native Operating System, such as modifying a file, invoking a tool, and using a device. This is the portion of the process steps that can be automatically monitored. A single process step may correspond to a sequence of primitive Operating System events. For example, the step

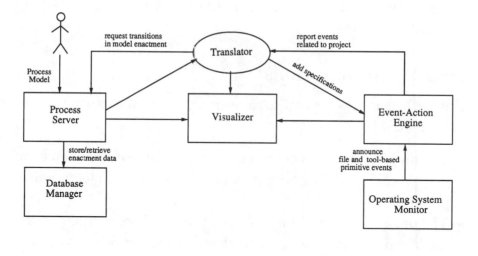

Figure 10.2   The PROVENCE architecture.

"review document" may correspond to four primitive events: Invoke the editor, open the document, read and perhaps modify the document, and close the document. A set of these monitorable steps is generated and conveyed to the translator.

Given the set of process steps, the translator generates a set of event-action specifications. Each specification is of the form "if the event pattern x occurs, send a notification to the translator and provide relevant information about the events." These specifications are registered with the event-action engine, which activates them.

The operating system monitor traps primitive operating system calls (for example, open a file) via a library, and, when a system call occurs, a corresponding announcement is generated. The announcements are sent to the event-action engine, which matches the detected events against the event patterns in active specifications. When an event pattern of a specification is fully matched, the translator is notified.

The translator sends a process step notification to the Process Server to notify it that the particular step has occurred. The Process Server can then use this information to make a transition in its process model enactment, and, based on that, perform other forms of computer-aided process control, such as sending notifications or automatically invoking actions.

10.3.1   Assumptions

PROVENCE makes several assumptions about the projects that might benefit from it:

- The project either has clear, well-defined processes that can be modeled in a process modeling language, or is willing to develop a model of the processes.
- The project has a well-understood structure from which an information model can be developed, which identifies the components of the system, how they are related, and the organizational structure corresponding to the components.
- There are two kinds of activities involved in the project: online activities (such as software tool invocations and accessing files) and manual activities (such as attending meetings and making decisions). Online activities can be detected automatically, whereas the occurrence of manual activities must be announced.
- There is a mechanism to announce the occurrence of manual activities to a software tool through a simple interface (for example, command-line oriented).

Given a project that meets these expectations, PROVENCE:

1. Monitors the development process of a project without forcing developers to change their working environment.
2. Maintains data about the process and the end product of a project.
3. Answers queries about the status of the software process and the various components of the project, based on the information it collected during the life cycle.
4. Dynamically visualizes transitions in the process.

A further step would be to let PROVENCE automate certain parts of the process in as nonintrusive a manner as possible. Eventually, PROVENCE will have the capability to enforce a specific process. The level of intrusion can be calibrated, depending upon the strictness of enforcement.

10.3.2   A High-Level Example

The functionality of PROVENCE is illustrated by a simple example. The development process of a software project typically consists of several phases. Considered here is the first phase, which involves business planning and requirements engineering. Business planning ensures that the end product makes business sense, and requirements engineering involves drafting a document that specifies the technical and functional requirements that the end product must meet. The business planning step is carried out by the business planning (BP) team headed by a manager. The requirements engineering step is done by the architecture team composed of two architects.

Assume the following process: The requirements engineering step cannot be started until the business planning team has created a draft of the business information. The architecture team uses the business information to draft a set of requirements for the project. Further steps, such as design, coding, and documentation, cannot start until a draft of the requirements document is created. Both the business planning document and the requirements document are stored as files; the two documents are modified in the *working* area of the project and moved to the *released* area upon finalization.

The following scenario illustrates the kind of assistance that PROVENCE would provide. Say that after the business planning team has worked on the business document for some time, the team's manager approves a draft of the document, which he or she moves to the *released area*. The operating system monitor component automatically detects that a draft has been created and notifies the process server via the event-action engine and the translator. The process server, through its automation, in turn notifies the architecture team that it can start working on the requirements document. In addition, the process server updates the project database to indicate that the business planning step has been completed and that the requirements engineering step can be started.

The two members of the architecture team create the requirements document and work on it for some time in the *working area*. Finally, they both agree on a draft of the document and move that draft to the *released area*. Again, this is automatically detected and the design team is notified that they can start working on the design document.

The project manager can inquire about the status of various project components or the state of the process. Since the developers' activities have been tracked, these queries can be answered accurately. In addition, PROVENCE can visualize all changes to the project components and the process.

10.4   A Realization of PROVENCE

To realize the PROVENCE architecture, we have mapped four existing software tools to five of the components of PROVENCE:

- MARVEL [BK91], which fills the roles of the process server and the database manager.
- The n-Dimensional File System (*n-DFS*, described in Chapter 3), which maps to the operating system monitor.
- YEAST (Chapter 9), which maps to the event-action engine.
- *dotty* (described in Section 11.2), which serves as the visualizer.

The different technologies of these four tools complement each other, and they can be combined to provide assistance in modeling and managing the development process.

Whereas MARVEL's rule language can be used to model the software process at a high level, YEAST can serve as a low-level monitor of process-related events. YEAST accepts notification of file-based events, which are automatically generated by *n-DFS*. *dotty* can visualize the information in the process and project database maintained by MARVEL and update the display whenever the database changes. Furthermore, the user can interact directly with *dotty*, providing another interface to the process server.

Figure 10.3 depicts how MARVEL, YEAST, *n-DFS*, and *dotty* are connected. This is one realization of the PROVENCE architecture; other realizations that use a different set of tools can be achieved with roughly the same amount of effort.

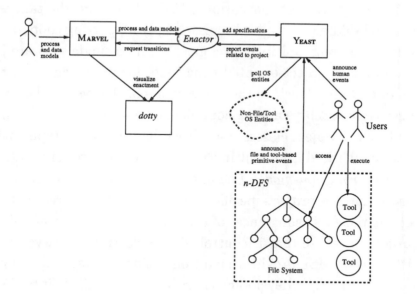

Figure 10.3 A realization of PROVENCE.

All four tools, which provide most of the functionality of the components, are fully implemented and currently available. *n-DFS*, YEAST, and *dotty* were designed to be open tools in the sense that they can interact with other tools at the operating system level (for example, via interprocess communication, files, and so on). We did not have to introduce any changes to *n-DFS* and *dotty*. The connection between *n-DFS* and YEAST and the connection between MARVEL and YEAST, which is done via another tool called the *Enactor*, required extending YEAST with the notion of event contexts and constraints (explained later).

In the rest of this section, we briefly describe Marvel, the *Enactor*, the extensions to YEAST, and how we connected the four tools.

10.4.1 MARVEL

MARVEL is based on four main ideas: (1) a powerful process modeling language called MSL that combines object-oriented data modeling with rule-based process modeling; (2) an enactment engine that supports rule inferencing and forward and backward chaining among rules; (3) facilitating the integration of conventional UNIX tools into the tailored PCE rather than building specialized tools; and (4) supporting cooperation and coordination among multiple developers within a single software process.

MSL provides object-oriented constructs for modeling the structural aspects of a system (such as the components of the system, how they are organized, relationships among components, and organizational information) in terms of object classes. Each class defines a set of typed *attributes* that can be inherited from multiple superclasses. The set of classes constitutes the *information model*. Loading the information model into MARVEL instantiates a project-specific environment. Users create the actual project components as instances of the classes; MARVEL stores all objects in a project database that is controlled by a centralized server.

With objects, MSL provides condition-action-effects rules that are used to model the project's development process. Each rule defines the condition for initiating a process step, the action (for example, invoking a tool) involved in the step, and the possible effects of the step on the objects in the database.

When a developer requests a command from the menu, MARVEL automatically fires a rule that implements the command by manipulating the attributes of the objects in the database. If the effect of a rule changes the values of objects' attributes in such a way that the conditions of other rules become satisfied, all of those other rules are fired automatically, in a forward chaining manner. Alternatively, if the condition of a rule is not satisfied, backward chaining is performed to attempt to make it satisfied. If that fails and the condition remains unsatisfied, then the rule cannot be executed at that time.

The interaction between MARVEL and its users is closed in the sense that developers must request all development activities via MARVEL. In the graphical interface, this is done by clicking on a command from either the built-in command menu or the project-specific command menu that corresponds to the loaded rules. All project components must be stored in the project database, which is controlled by MARVEL. Furthermore, all the tools used by a project must be enveloped to be integrated into the MARVEL environment.

In PROVENCE, we use MARVEL not as a closed environment, but as a process server. The role of MARVEL is to accept as input a process model that describes the actual processes that occur outside of Marvel, and an information (or data) model that describes the actual data involved in the project. We use MARVEL's database to store only an image of the project's data. The actual data (project artifacts, such as code, documentation, requirements and plans, information about personnel, resources, and so on) is expected to be stored on the file system and manipulated by the same set of tools that developers currently use.

MARVEL's role is to enact the process model on the image of the data. The enactment is driven by the actual process execution and not by user requests. By studying the information produced and maintained by MARVEL during process model enactment more carefully, one can distinguish between two kinds of information: *internal enactment information* and *external project information*. Enactment information is maintained by the enactment engine either to drive the rest of the enactment or to represent the state of the enactment. Project information, in contrast, represents external *real-world* objects, such as project artifacts, resources, personnel, and so on. Whereas transitions involving enactment information are triggered exclusively based on the state of the enactment, transitions involving project information could be triggered based on the occurrence of certain external events.

Consider a network maintenance process: When a sensor detects a failure, it logs the error in a special file called *alarm* and sends a visual notification to a human operator; the human operator retrieves the error log, creates a trouble ticket, and forwards it to the failure resolution team. An enactable process model might represent the file *alarm* as an object with an attribute called `modified` that indicates whether the actual file has been modified. The model might also represent each network failure as a separate object that has an attribute called `state`, which maintains the state of process enactment involving the failure.

The attribute `modified` is classified as project information because it represents the state of an external *real-world* object. The intention is to have the insertion of a failure log into the file *alarm* somehow trigger an enactment transition to change the value of the attribute `modified` of the corresponding object to reflect that. More specifically, this enactment

transition corresponds to a sequence of three external events: opening
the file *alarm*, writing an entry into it, and closing it. In contrast, the
attribute `state` of an object representing a network failure is classified
as internal enactment information because its value reflects part of the
internal enactment state; the transition to update this attribute is triggered by the occurrence of other enactment transitions and not directly
by the process execution state.

The two kinds of information can be distinguished in MARVEL via the
class definition and inheritance facilities provided by MSL. We created an
MSL specification that defines four classes corresponding to the *real-world*
entities that can be automatically monitored: *files*, *directories*, *tools*, and
user-announced events. For each of the four classes, the MSL specification
defines a set of rules whose triggering condition corresponds to a sequence
of external events. The process model of any project in PROVENCE must
import this MSL specification; all objects in the enactment domain that
correspond to *real-world* objects that should be monitored must be made
instances of one of these four classes (or one of their subclasses).

The following is the class definition of one of the four classes, a monitored file, and one of the rules pertaining to it:

```
MonitoredFile :: superclass ENTITY;
   path: string;              # pathname of external file
   modified: boolean;         # has the file been modified
   accessed: boolean;         # has the file been accessed
   host: string;              # host on which file accessed
   user: user;                # user who accessed it last
   timestamp: time;           # timestamp of last access
end

hide file_modified[?f:MonitoredFile]:
   :                          # triggered by external event
   { }                        # no action
   (and (?f.modified = true)
        (?f.timestamp = CurrentTime));

hide reset_file[?f:MonitoredFile]:
   :                          # triggered by file modification
   (or (?f.modified = true)
       (?f.accesses = true))
   { }                # no action
   (and (?f.modified = false)
        (?f.accesses = false));
```

In the model of the network trouble resolution process just described, the object representing file *alarm* would be an instance of `MonitoredFile`, where the attribute `path` would be set to the pathname of *alarm*.

Unlike in a closed MARVEL environment where all rules are triggered either directly by the user or indirectly during chaining, rules associated with monitored classes, like the rule `file_modified` just shown, are triggered by the occurrence of one or more external events. The event-monitoring components of PROVENCE can automatically detect the occurrence of such events. The execution of the rule `file_modified` would cause the firing of any other rule whose condition includes a predicate that checks if the attribute `modified` of an instance of `MonitoredFile` has the value *true*. This way, the actual modification of a file outside of MARVEL can trigger rules that enact the process model. The rule `reset_file` makes sure that the values of the attributes of monitored file object are reset. This is necessary for correct functioning of triggering in MARVEL.

To notify MARVEL about external events, there is a need for a liaison between MARVEL and the event-monitoring component. The *Enactor* plays this role.

10.4.2   The *Enactor*

The job of the *Enactor* is twofold: (1) to translate the *monitorable* steps in MARVEL's process model to system-level event patterns that can be monitored; and (2) to accept notifications about the occurrence of specific patterns of system-level events and translate these into process model enactment transitions. More concretely, the *Enactor* must generate a set of YEAST specifications based on MARVEL's high-level process and information models, and translate the matching of events in YEAST to actions that MARVEL can perform.

The *Enactor* is built as a client tool to both MARVEL and YEAST. It first establishes a connection to MARVEL, and then opens another channel for submitting YEAST specifications and accepting updates. The *Enactor* obtains from the MARVEL server the set of rule definitions and database objects belonging to the project and generates appropriate YEAST specifications. These specifications are registered with YEAST. The action portion of the specifications require a simple notification to be sent to the *Enactor* on matching of the specification. The *Enactor* maintains a translation table that map MARVEL rule names to YEAST specifications generated by the *Enactor*.

The *Enactor* assumes that MARVEL has complete information about all the *real-world* objects that are part of the project (such as the pathnames of files and executable tools). This is needed to be able to monitor these objects. For every object that is an instance of one of the four *monitorable* classes mentioned earlier, the *Enactor* generates YEAST specifications that monitor events on the corresponding *real-world* objects. Whenever specific sequences of events occur on these objects, YEAST (via *n-DFS*) supplies the *Enactor* with information about the contents and context of the events (explained in the next section). The *Enactor* maps these pieces of information to the name of a rule and the actual parameter of that rule. Finally, the *Enactor* instructs MARVEL to fire the rule, causing MARVEL to make all necessary transitions and updates in its database.

In the present model, MARVEL ensures that the events generated in the system are only the ones that can be mapped to the process model. This ensures that there can be no inconsistency between the events generated within MARVEL and those that are sent to MARVEL from the *Enactor*.

10.4.3   YEAST with Event Contexts and Constraints

As explained earlier, YEAST receives announcements about the occurrence of system-level events from *n-DFS*, and matches these announcements to event patterns in active specifications that are supplied by the *Enactor*. The YEAST specification language (described in detail in Section 9.3.1) lacked two features that were necessary to fulfill the role of the event-action component in PROVENCE.

First, the YEAST language did not provide constructs for capturing information about the context in which a matched event has occurred (such as the user identifier of the user who generated the event, or the machine on which the event was generated). Although this kind of information is not necessarily part of the event, it constitutes the context in which the event occurred. This information is needed by the Process Server to make the correct transitions in its enactment of the process model.

The second shortcoming was the inability to relate different event descriptors in the same event pattern by common variables or constraints. For example, one could not specify that the events that match various parts of the same event pattern must have been generated by the same user or on the same machine. This kind of constraint is often necessary for monitoring sequences of events in a multiuser distributed environment like PROVENCE, where similar events might be generated by different users and might occur on different machines.

We extended YEAST with the notion of *event context* and language constructs for accessing the information obtained in an event context and for constraining event matching based on this information. The elements of an event context include such things as the user responsible for the event, the time of the event, and the machine on which the event occurred. Capturing the context of a matched event and storing the values of its elements enables the monitoring system to make these values available both for matching and for the action part.

As explained in Section 9.2, YEAST distinguishes between polled events and announced events. While context is a generic concept, relevant to both polled events and announced events, it is impossible to capture the correct context of a polled event in YEAST. The reason is that a polled event is detected *after* it has occurred; thus, the context surrounding the occurrence of the event may be lost.

Unlike polled events, announced events occur within a context that can be captured at the time of the occurrence of the event. The reason is that the YEAST daemon is notified explicitly about the occurrence of these events immediately. In YEAST, a notification is generated explicitly by a user or a program to announce the value of a single attribute of a single YEAST object. In PROVENCE, all relevant events are announced either by users or by *n-DFS*. Thus, it is possible to capture the context of these events.

Several contextual elements are of interest to PROVENCE:

1. The name of the machine (*host*) from which the event was generated
2. The process identifier (*pid*) of the process that generated the event

3. The user identifier (*uid*) of the user who owns that process
4. The *value* assigned to the attribute involved in the event
5. The YEAST *object* on which the event occurred

Knowing the machine and the process identifier locates the source of the event, and knowing the user establishes ownership. The value element can be an aid in either matching additional events of the same pattern or in the action portion of the specification. The object contextual element enables the construction of event descriptors that match multiple announced events involving different objects. For example, the event pattern in the specification

```
addspec file /bin/% tested == true
do  notify file in /bin has been tested
```

contains a wildcard character (%); thus, it matches any announced event of the form

```
announce file /bin/<name> tested = true
```

where <*name*> is the name of any file in the directory /bin. By making the actual name of the object part of the context we capture, we can pass this name to the action part of the specification.

10.4.3.1   Naming Event Contexts

Once we capture and store the context of an announced event, we must be able to refer to it. We introduce naming of event descriptors as a mechanism for binding a name to the context of the event that matches the named descriptor. The syntax is

```
addspec N: <primitive event descriptor> ... do action
```

where *N* is an identifier and *primitive event descriptor* describes an announced-event descriptor. The name *N* is used as a placeholder for the context associated with the event that matches the event descriptor. In that sense, *N* can be thought of as a variable whose value is bound to the context of an announced event upon a successful matching.

Elements of the announced event's context that matched the event descriptor are accessed through the name using the syntax

```
N:<context_element>
```

where *<context_element>* is one of *pid*, *host*, *uid*, *object*, or *value*. The names of different event descriptors in the same specification must be different; otherwise, a syntax error results.

The information contained in the context of an announced event can be used in two places: in the action part of a specification, and in the matching constraints associated with other event descriptors in the same specification. We explain both uses in the next two sections.

10.4.4 Using Event Contexts in the Action

The information contained in the context of an announced event can be used in the action portion of the specification by referring to the name of the descriptor that matched the announced event and the announced event's contextual element within '%%' marks, as follows:

```
addspec N1: e1 and N2: e2 do .. %N1:uid% .. %N2:value% ..
```

where both *e1* and *e2* are primitive event descriptors that match announced events, and *N1* and *N2* are names that will be bound to the events that match *e1* and *e2*, respectively. Once an announced event matches either *e1* or *e2*, the values of the elements of the event's context are replaced in the string that represents the action part.

Consider the following improvement on the specification that monitors completion of testing of tools in the */bin* directory:

```
addspec N: file /bin/% tested == true
do notify Tool %N:object% tested by %N:uid% on %N:host%
```

When this specification matches an announced event, the notification program **notify** will have access to the actual name of the tool that was tested, the *uid* of the user who made the announcement, and the *host* of the machine on which the announcement was made. These three pieces of information can now be used in the notification program to send a more useful notification than the generic one we had before.

An anomaly can result in the case of an **or** combinator in the event pattern. Consider, for example, the following specifications:

```
addspec N1: e1 or N2: e2 do ... %N2:uid% ...

addspec N1: e1 or N2: e2 do notify .. %N1:uid% .. %N2:uid%
```

Say that an announced event that is matched by *e1* is received. Since the combinator used in the event pattern is **or**, matching *e1* is sufficient to trigger the action. In the case of both specifications, *e2* would not have been matched and, thus, YEAST would not be able to replace %N2:uid% with an actual value. There are three options: detecting such anomalies at the time the specification is added; aborting the action when an unbounded event name occurs in the action; or imposing an **and** semantics on the event pattern. The current implementation uses the second option. The use of event contexts to constrain matching in PROVENCE will be explained in a detailed example.

10.4.5   Visualization

Two kinds of visualization are possible in PROVENCE. The first is a high-level visualization of the process-related information (from the MARVEL database) by the *Enactor*. The second is a lower-level visualization of the YEAST specifications registered by the *Enactor*. We reuse *dotty* as the visualization component, and the manner in which both the high-level and low-level visualization is achieved is similar.

The low-level YEAST specifications can be visualized using the *fey* front end described in Section 9.6.2.2. There, YEAST opened a full duplex connection to a *dotty* process and sent notifications about changes in specification state resulting in an updated picture. The low-level visualization is likely to serve more as a debugging aid in PROVENCE.

For the high-level visualization, the *Enactor* initially translates the process-related information that MARVEL stores in its database into a *dot* specification and sends it to the *dotty* process. The display generated by *dotty* at this stage represents the process model, which shows all the possible transitions. Whenever a process transition occurs, the *Enactor* sends a message to *dotty* to update the visual representation of the process, showing the transition graphically. *dotty* might use color coding to indicate the initiation, progress, and completion of process steps.

```
PROJECT :: superclass ENTITY;
    business_plan: DOC;          # business planning document
    requirements: DOC;          # the requirements document
    release: MonitoredDir;       # the release area of the project
    arch_team: TEAM;            # the architecture team
    . . .
end

DOC :: superclass MonitoredFile;
    status: (Empty,Initial,Draft,Baselined) = Empty; # Default is Empty
    owner: user;                 # The user ID of the document's owner
    . . .
end
```

Figure 10.4   Data model of example in MARVEL.

Similarly, color coding and size of nodes may be used to indicate the completion status of a project component.

10.5   Revisiting the Example

To illustrate the realization of PROVENCE, we revisit the example discussed in Section 10.3.2, and present the details of how the various tools assist in carrying out the process. The example postulated a business planning team creating a business plan. When the plan becomes a draft, the requirements architects need to be notified about it so that they can proceed with their editing of the requirements document.

The first step is defining the information model described in Section 10.3.2. This includes the organization and structure of project data and the data that needs to be maintained about the process. Figure 10.4 shows the MARVEL classes that specify a subset of the information model. In this model, we need to represent two *real-world* objects: the business planning document and the requirements document. This is done by defining a class called DOC and making that a subclass of MonitoredFile, shown earlier in Section 10.4.1.

We also need to represent the *release area*, which is a directory that contains released documents. We can represent this as an instance of the

```
draft_bp [?proj: PROJECT]:
    (and (exists MonitoredDir ?rel suchthat (member[?proj.release ?rel]))
         (exists DOC ?bp suchthat (member [?proj.business_plan ?bp]))
         (exists TEAM ?arch suchthat (member[?proj.arch_team ?arch])))
    :
    # condition: If a document whose name is business_plan is
    # moved to the release area
    (and (?rel.inserted = true)
         (?rel.name = "business_plan"))

    {MAIL send_mail ?arch "draft of BP info available"}

    # effects:
    (?bp.status = Draft);        # business plan is in draft form
```

Figure 10.5   Process model rules in MARVEL.

class **MonitoredDir**, which is not shown but is similar to the definition of **MonitoredFile**.

Next, we define the process model of Section 10.3.2 in terms of the MARVEL rule shown in Fig. 10.5. The rule specifies that if a file named *business_plan* is inserted in the directory that represents the release area, then notify the architecture team (via e-mail) that a draft of the business plan exists. In addition, update the value of the attribute **status** of the object that represents the business plan document in the enactment model to *Draft*.

Given the rule and the data model, the *Enactor* generates several YEAST specifications to watch for the events that are relevant to the process. While many specifications are generated to monitor events on the requirements document and the business planning document, we discuss only one:

```
addspec repeat e1: file /proj/release/% syscall == created
do tell_enactor file_created %e1:host% %e1.pid%
                          %e1.uid% %e1.object%
```

The event descriptor in this specification is matched whenever a new file is created in the release area of the project. In the action part of the specification, the hostname, the process identifier, the user identifier, and the name of the created file are sent to the *Enactor*.

The *Enactor* maps this information to the rule **directory_modified**. The *Enactor* sends a message to MARVEL instructing it to fire the rule,

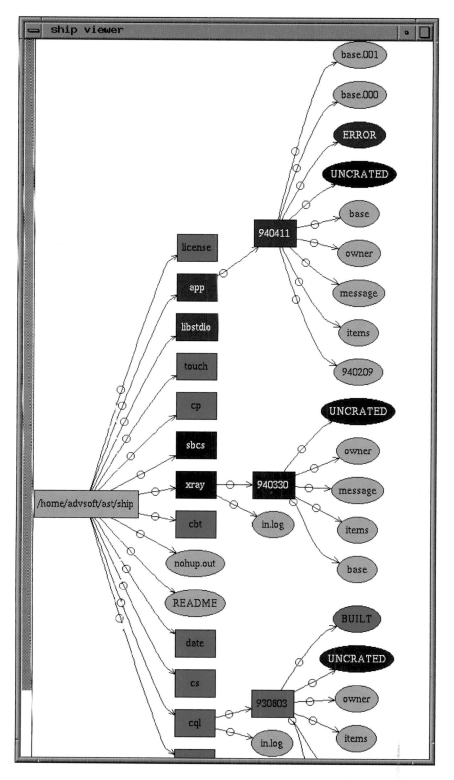

Color Plate 1 A snapshot of *shipview* in use.

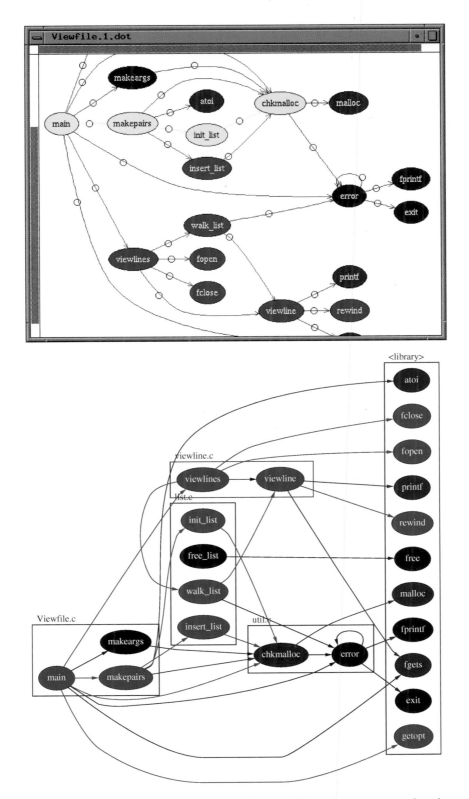

Color Plate 2 (Top) A sample of *Xray* snapshot. (Bottom) Using clusters to group function nodes.

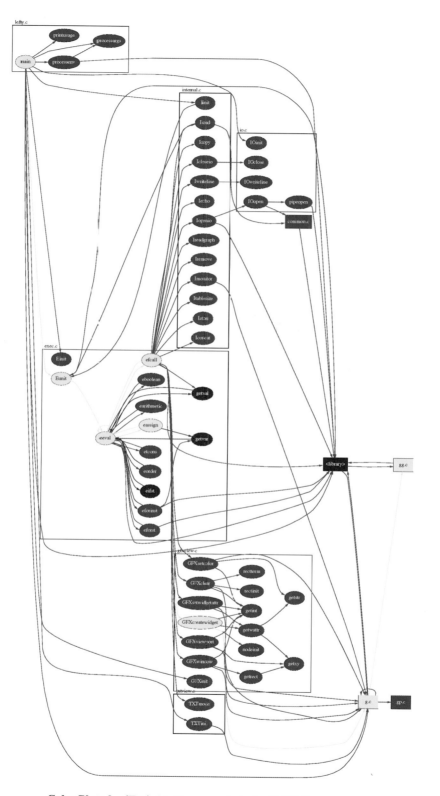

Color Plate 3 (Top) An *Xray* snapshot of a 12,000 line program.

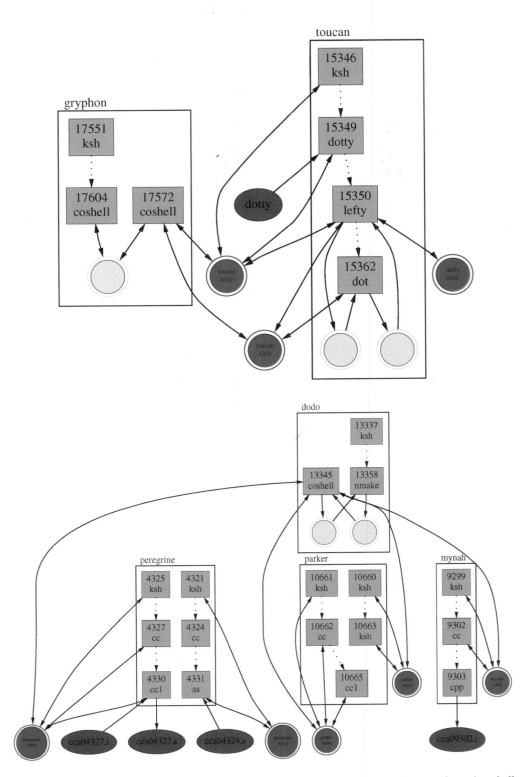

Color Plate 4 (Top) A sample VPM view. (Bottom) Distributed compilation using *nmake* and *coshell*.

and passes to it the object representing the release area and the name of the new file. Executing this rule causes a forward chain to fire the rule bp_draft just shown. The net effect will be that MARVEL will send a notification to the members of the architecture team and update information in its database, reflecting the process transitions that have taken place.

Note that the members of the business planning and architecture teams work without unnecessary intrusions by PROVENCE, since they do not have to inform PROVENCE manually about automatically detectable activities. Moreover, they can use any tools (editors, formatters, and so on) to perform their activities. The advantages of nonintrusiveness (through automatic data capture) and open environments are reflected in the foregoing simple example.

10.6   Reuse

10.6.1   Architectural Style

PROVENCE, a process-centered software development environment, consists of multiple components. The components range in architectural styles corresponding to their roles in PROVENCE. For example, YEAST supports the event-action style, MARVEL in the transaction processing style, and *n-DFS* in the filter style. PROVENCE provides an interesting test bed to contrast different styles being reused in a single "tool." There is a clear separation of components in PROVENCE, and their interaction is well defined. There is no direct link between YEAST and MARVEL, for example.

10.6.2   Architectural Services Used

dotty provides visualization service for PROVENCE. MARVEL has its own built-in visualization mechanism. *dotty* has been used to provide visualization for both the higher-level model and the lower-level event YEAST specifications.

As described in Section 9.6.2.1, fault tolerance service is provided to one of the components of PROVENCE: YEAST. Marvel has an external

daemon that starts up the server but, unlike *watchd*, the external daemon does not automatically restart the server if it were to die. The fault
tolerance (like visualization) is built into the MARVEL code.

10.6.3 Reuse of Libraries and Components

PROVENCE reuses four existing components: MARVEL (a tool built outside of AT&T), *n-DFS*, YEAST, and *dotty*; and it uses a new component
(*Enactor*). The internal components all use other libraries, as discussed
in their relevant chapters.

- Linking–libraries
- Configuration and assembling
- Component reuse in PROVENCE

10.6.3.1 Libraries

Several libraries used by the components were thus implicitly reused by
PROVENCE. The new code written (relatively insignificant compared to
the overall size of the project) was in the *Enactor*; the high-level model
was written in MARVEL's rule language, and the low-level specifications
were written in YEAST. *Enactor*, like YEAST, uses the connection stream
library (*libcs*) for communication as well.

10.6.4 Configuration and Assembling

MARVEL was an external tool that we used without modifications. Since
each of the components were developed independently, there was no over-
lap in building software. Assembling the components was straightforward,
since the interfaces to each of them were flexible enough to be combined at
the component level. Each component was assembled separately and then
connected. Component-level connection led to easier assembling once the
interconnection at the interface level was worked out.

10.6.5 Component Reuse in PROVENCE

PROVENCE is built by connecting existing components. We were able to
reuse all these components as described earlier. However, we were also

able to achieve significant reuse in the manner in which visualization support was added to FROVENCE. The code added to the MARVEL client to notify *dotty* about changes in internal state was similar to the manner in which the front end to YEAST, *fey,* (see Section 9.6.2.2) was created.

However, not all components were reused without modifications or extensions. Extensions to MARVEL did not require changing of the MARVEL language (see Section 10 4.1). We made an important addition to YEAST, matching semantics to take advantage of contextual (as described in Section 10.4.3) information in announced events. The changes were local to YEAST and did not affect any of the other components. The extension was generic enough to be usable in future YEAST applications.

10.7 Conclusions

We presented PROVENCE, a component-based architecture for modeling, enacting, and visualizing the software process. PROVENCE departs from recent work on process-centered environments in two main respects:

1. The main components of a process-centered environment have been identified and separated with clear interfaces, making them more easily replaceable. This contrasts with the monolithic architectures, where these components are tightly coupled and made to work only with each other.
2. The realization of PROVENCE we presented is based on existing tools that, together, can be used to provide the needed assistance in modeling and managing software processes. It is possible to replace any of the tools or to extend the set of tools. However, each of the tools must conform to the set of interface requirements for the component to which it is mapped to guarantee openness. For example, the operating system monitor component must provide information about file-related events and operating system process invocations in a format that is accepted by the event engine.

We believe that the open architecture of PROVENCE is more appropriate to the experimental nature of software process work. This is important because it is difficult to determine the forms of process-related assistance that are needed by development organizations. Thus, an architecture that can be easily extended or changed to incorporate different tools is more appropriate than one that fixes its components and functionality.

Currently, all the tools discussed in Section 10.4, as well as the interfaces between them, have been implemented. The pending portion of the implementation is the automatic generation of specifications for the *Enactor*. After implementing a prototype realization of PROVENCE, we shall conduct several experiments involving projects in development organizations. Our aim is to model the processes of these projects within our system, employ the system in a manner similar to what we have described in this paper, and measure the effects of employing the system on the software process. We hope that these experiments will help us achieve the following goals:

1. Identify the appropriate form(s) of process-centered assistance that development organizations need to increase their productivity. Expected forms of assistance include:

   - Monitoring of the process for the purpose of analyzing it both dynamically and statically
   - Automating parts of the process to relieve developers from menial chores
   - Measuring the actual duration of each step in a process for the purpose of planning future processes or the remaining parts of the process

2. Detect shortcomings and inefficiencies in existing processes.
3. Determine the effectiveness and feasibility of our approach.

From the reuse point of view, PROVENCE is proof of our ability to reuse at the component level.

11

Intertool Connections

Yih-Farn Chen, Glenn Fowler, David Korn, Eleftherios Koutsofios, Stephen North, David Rosenblum, and Kiem-Phong Vo

11.1   Introduction

This chapter presents a collection of interconnected tools built by the combining of tools described earlier in this book. The manner of connections vary, but a common theme linking the tools is vertical integration. The tools aid in visualization, testing, analysis, and animation of software.

A few principles that have served well in the integration process are:

- Instrumenting programs can pay rich dividends.
- Simple specification languages are an effective glue.
- Open interfaces and extensible architectures lead to rapid integration.

Section 11.2 discusses a graph editor that, owing to its malleability, has served as a vehicle for visualization of a significant number of tools, some of which are described here. *dotty* is built by combining *dot*, a graph layout mechanism, and *lefty*, a programmable graphics editor at a process level.

Section 11.3 describes a technique (and a tool called TESTTUBE) for selective regression testing by analyzing a software system. The static and dynamic analysis information available via CIA and APP are used to build TESTTUBE.

Section 11.4 describes a function call animator used to display the dynamic behavior of a program. *Xray* is built by combining APP, CIA, and *dotty*. APP helps generate a function trace log that is merged with the program database generated by CIA and fed to *dotty* to animate.

Section 11.5 describes VPM, a tool built by combining *n-DFS* and *dotty* to view real-time process execution on a network of machines. The process notification service of *n-DFS* is merged with the visualization ability of *dotty* to display system call invocations across multiple processes and machines.

11.2   *dotty*

11.2.1   Introduction

dotty [KN94] is a customizable graph editor. It can run as a standalone editor but, more importantly, it is also a programmable front end for other applications. Unlike most GUI systems, where the graphical elements are simple buttons, menus, and bitmaps, *dotty*'s main user interface objects are graph drawings and diagrams.

As discussed briefly in Section 2.4, graph drawings are one of the best ways to show relationships between objects. Data structures, database schemas, program call graphs, finite state machines, and source file dependencies are a few conventional examples of structures that can be made easier to understand when presented as graphs.

This section presents a set of tools for displaying and operating on graphs. From the user's point of view, the primary tool is *dotty*. Figures 11.1 and 11.2 show two snapshots of *dotty* in use. Figure 11.1 shows *dotty* running as a standalone editor. A graph depicting the historical relationships of our department's tool is being edited. Figure 11.2 shows *dotty* as a front end for VPM, a process management tool.

In its high-level architecture, *dotty* incorporates several fundamental trends in user-interface design:

1. It offers a convenient graphical user interface with operations controlled through a WYSIWYG (What You See Is What You Get) interface.

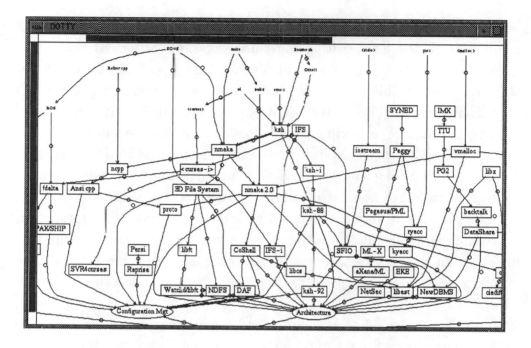

Figure 11.1 A snapshot of *dotty* as a standalone editor.

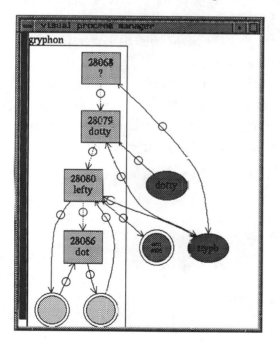

Figure 11.2 A snapshot of *dotty* as a graphical front end.

These include conventional menu-driven commands for viewing graphs in multiple windows, editing nodes and edges, updating attributes, and loading and saving graphs in the file language described in Section 2.4.

2. *dotty* is extensible. It was constructed by programming a generic 2-D graphics editor. This editor's control program is defined in a high-level scripting language. Scripts can be loaded to add or redefine functions controlling *dotty*'s behavior. For example, one could add a function that sets the color of every node as a function of its degree or distance from some other node. This allows reprogramming of the WYSIWYG interface. For example, one could rebind the left mouse button action to highlight all incident edges when a node is selected. This design, based on a high-level interpretive scripting language instead of a large class-based toolkit, reflects an important current trend in interactive systems.

3. *dotty* was designed to be a front end for other systems. Its language has primitives to start external processes and establish interprocess communication channels. In this context, graphs can represent state information maintained by a back-end process, and user actions can be bound to functions that translate graph operations to corresponding state change requests sent to the back end.

4. *dotty* works with external layout utilities and graph filters in a client-server relationship [BGST90]. It is not a monolith as are many other graph layout systems. Instead, *dotty* can work with differing layout programs and other language-based batch filters for graphs.

We have customized *dotty* for a number of applications including:

- Finite state machine animator

- C/C++ source code database browser

- Distributed process monitor

- Debugger with graphical data structure displays

- Program trace animator

- GUI for the YEAST event-action specification tool [KR91]

- GUI for the PROVENCE process modeling tool [KB93]

- GUI for the *ship* process

Internally, *dotty* is constructed from two cooperating processes, *dot* and *lefty*. *lefty* is a programmable graphics editor that displays graphs on the screen and allows the user to operate on them. *dotty*'s programming language is actually that of *lefty*. *lefty* executes *dot* as a separate process to make graph layouts. These programs communicate through pipes, a UNIX interprocess communication method. Figure 11.2 shows the two processes and the pipes that connect them (the bottom two nodes).

11.2.2 Design

We now describe the design of our tools and compare our design approach with that of some other graph editors: EDGE [PT90], GraphEd [Him89], daVinci (University of Bremen), the XmGraph toolkit (Douglas Young, University of Iowa), and the Graph Layout Toolkit [Tom] are some of the most widely known. Since *dotty* is built by combining other tools, we first present an overview of the pieces: the graph language and accompanying library, the layout tools, several graph filters, and the graphics editor *lefty*. Finally, we describe the design decisions embodied in *dotty* itself.

Graph language and library. All of our tools that read or write graphs use *libgraph*. Thus, there is no fixed set of attributes; any key-value pair can be specified in any file. While graph processing utilities may look up specific attributes, by default, any attributes that a tool ignores are passed through unchanged when the graph is written. This simplifies composing graph filters as pipelines; existing files and tools do not have to be changed when a new attribute is introduced. Almost all the other graph viewing programs do not provide enough language support for combining tools this way.

Graph layout tools. Our system has two main layout tools. *dot* makes hierarchical layouts of directed graphs [GKNV93] that are appropriate for software-related diagrams, where asymmetric relationships seem to be predominant. It was written as a successor to *dag* [GNV88], which incorporated results of Warfield, Carpano, and Sugiyama and others [War77, Car80, STT81]. *dot* usually makes good layouts and has an assortment of graphics and layout controls. *neato* is an undirected graph

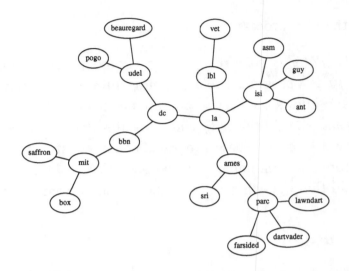

Figure 11.3 A sample layout from *neato*.

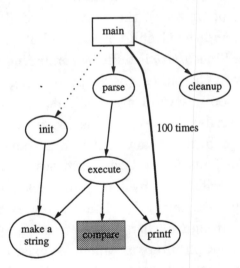

Figure 11.4 A sample layout from *dot*.

embedder based on the virtual physical models proposed by Kamada and Kawai [KK89]. Such layouts emphasize path distance and connectivity, and are more suitable for symmetric relationships (such as the computer network illustrated in Figure 11.3).

As both of these tools present the same interface (such as reading and writing graphs in our graph language), *dotty* can use either or both of them just by specifying a different pathname.

By default, *dot* draws directed graphs with edges aimed from top to bottom and drawn as solid lines; nodes are drawn as ellipses labeled by node names. These defaults may be overridden by setting certain attributes of the input graph. Tables 11.1 through 11.3 list the options. For example, *dot* can draw data structure graphs, displaying records as nested box lists, with node ports for connecting pointers. Figure 11.4 shows the *dot* layout for a sample graph. *dot* has the ability to emit graphs either in our graph language or in several graphical languages, such as PostScript and HPGL. In addition, *dot* incorporates an algorithm for drawing graphs with *clusters* or recursive node set partitions [Nor93]. A cluster is identified as any subgraph whose name has the seven-letter prefix `cluster`. Clusters at the same level are drawn in nonoverlapping rectangles. Cluster layout has applications in diagrams of hierarchical structures, such as dependencies of objects within nested source code modules.

neato has the same options as *dot* to control the drawing of individual nodes and edges (for example, to set sizes, shapes, colors, and fonts for nodes and edges). Its particular layout algorithm employs a *spring model*, so instead of using *dot*'s layout controls, the `weight` and `len` (ideal spring length) attributes of edges can be set to adjust node placement.

dotty benefits from having *dot* and *neato* to make layouts. Considerable effort was spent on developing their layout algorithms and creating robust and efficient implementations. They can make good quality layouts quickly and without extensive manual correction. This permits interactive graph layout (for most reasonably sized graphs) with acceptable response times. Robustness is also important because graphs from real applications often can have multiple edges, self-arcs, degenerate components, and so on. Some systems provide a wider variety of layout algorithms (GraphEd 3.0 had 18), but the implementations are often not robust or practical.

Being able to run *dot* as a standalone tool made debugging easier. It was debugged and profiled totally independent of other tools. *dot* was developed approximately a year before *dotty*. One drawback with using *dot* in the context of *dotty* is that *dot* always computes the complete layout of a graph. Whenever *dotty* needs a new layout, it sends the entire graph to *dot* and gets back positions and coordinates for all the nodes and edges. Such an exchange does not guarantee that making a small change to a graph will result in a layout that is close to previous layout.

Table 11.1 Node Attributes

Name	Default	Values
color	black	Node shape color
comment		Emitted by target code generator
fontcolor	black	Type face color
fontname	Times-Roman	PostScript font family
fontsize	14	Point size of label
height,width	.5,.75	Height and width in inches
label	Node name	Any string
layer		Selects active range in multi-page overlays
shape	ellipse	ellipse, box, circle, doublecircle, diamond, plaintext, record, polygon
style		graphics options, such as bold, dotted, filled

Table 11.2 Edge Attributes

Name	Default	Values
color	black	Edge stroke color
comment		Emitted by target code generator
decorate		If set, draws a line connecting labels with their edges
dir	forward	forward, back, both, or none
fontcolor	black	Type face color
fontname	Times-Roman	PostScript font family
fontsize	14	Point size of label
layer		Selects active range in multipage overlays
id		Optional value to distinguish multiple edges
label		Label, if not empty
minlen	1	Minimum rank distance between head and tail
style		Graphics options, such as bold, dotted, filled
weight	1	Integer reflecting importance of edge.

Table 11.3 Graph Attributes

Name	Default	Values
center		When true, center picture on page
clusterrank	local	May be global or none
color	black	Cluster box stroke color
comment		Emitted by target code generator
concentrate		Enables edge concentrators when TRUE
fontcolor	black	Type face color
fontname	Times-Roman	PostScript font family
fontsize	14	Point size of label
label		Any string
layer		Range in multipage overlays
margin	.5,.5	Margin included in page
mclimit	1.0	If set, adjusts mincross iterations by factor
nodesep	.25	Separation between nodes, in inches
nslimit		If set, factor bounds network simplex iterations
ordering		out (for ordered edges)
orientation	portrait	May be set to landscape
page		Unit of pagination, for example, 8.5,11
rank		same, min, or max
rankdir	TB	LR (left to right) or TB (top to bottom)
ranksep	.75	Separation between ranks, in inches
ratio		Approximate aspect ratio desired, or fill
size		Drawing bounding box, in inches

Sometimes, the graph layout changes significantly in response to a small change, and that is disconcerting to users.

We are currently designing incremental layout algorithms. Such algorithms will improve drawing stability and, perhaps, also improve throughput in movies of graphs.

dot is about 13,000 lines of C.

Graph filters. Layouts of large graphs are often complex and difficult to read. Though good layout algorithms help, sometimes a graph is simply too large or dense to understand visually. Effective techniques for filtering, partitioning, collapsing, and coloring can help to convey properties of interest. We have written utilities for these operations:

tred computes transitive reductions of directed graphs. When applied to dense graphs, it removes many edges but leaves reachability between nodes invariant.

unflatten adjusts lengths of leaf edges or wide fanout/fanin patterns. When applied to bushy graphs, this yields layouts having less extreme aspect ratios.

gpr (for *graph processor*) is a powerful, generic utility that applies a given predicate expression on nodes or edges to select a subgraph that is emitted. A command-line option enables path contraction on nonselected nodes and edges. One use is to remove long chains in control flow graphs by applying a node degree predicate and path contraction.

colorize allows setting *seed* colors on some nodes, then propagates these colors along edges to fill in the rest of the graph. This helps distinguish nodes that are logically related even when dispersed in the layout, taking advantage of the ability of the human eye to quickly locate similarly colored objects in a collection.

The graphical editor *lefty*. *lefty* [KD91] is a two-view graphics editor for technical pictures. This editor has no hard-wired procedures for specific picture layouts or editing operations. Rather, each picture is described by a program that contains functions to draw the picture and perform editing operations appropriate for the specific picture. Primitive user actions, such as mouse and keyboard events, are also bound to functions in this program. Programmability allows the editor to handle a variety of pictures, but is particularly useful for pictures in technical contexts, such as graphs and trees. Also, *lefty* can communicate with other processes. This feature allows it to run existing tools to compute layouts and similarly allows external processes to call the editor as a front end to display their data structures graphically.

The language implemented by *lefty* was inspired by the language in the EZ system [FH85]. It is at a higher level than C or C++, which is what programmers use to customize most other graph editors. This makes it more productive for building user interfaces (which is true for many other user-interface languages, such as *tcl* [Ous94]). Its main characteristic is the use of *tables*. A table is a list of key-value pairs, where the key is a scalar and the value is either a scalar or a subtable. Unlike C or C++ data structures, where the set of fields in a structure is fixed, any *lefty* table can contain any set of key-value pairs. *lefty* built-in functions that take tables as arguments look for specific fields in these tables. They do not, however, destroy or modify any fields they do not care about. This concept is similar to the graph attributes concept of our graph library. When *lefty* reads in a graph, the key-value pairs for the graph attributes become key-value entries in *lefty* tables.

lefty provides some convenient built-in functions. One important set contains functions for managing windows. *lefty* presents an abstracted view of the underlying window system. This view hides most of the details of the window system and provides extra features, such as mapping between world coordinates and pixel coordinates. This made it possible to port *lefty* fairly easily from UNIX/X Windows to Microsoft Windows. Only this library of windowing operations and the library for accessing some system services had to be changed. No changes were made to any *lefty* scripts (including those that implement *dotty*).

Another set of built-in functions allows *lefty* to open channels to other processes. Under UNIX, these channels can be pipes, sockets, or pseudo-tty connections. Under Microsoft Windows, we had to implement our own pipes. As these I/O functions were already separate, the changes were limited.

lefty provides a built-in function for reading graphs. This is not implemented by *libgraph*. Instead, *lefty* uses only the graph grammar description of *libgraph* (a *yacc* file). This was done because *lefty* needs to store graphs in its own tables. If we used *libgraph*, we would have to first load and store graphs in C data structures and then convert them to *lefty* tables, which would be inefficient. *lefty* is a 12,000 line C program.

The graph editor *dotty*. One drawback of *dag* and *dot* is that their pictures are static. Once generated, they can be printed out or viewed on a workstation using a PostScript viewer, but there is no way to interact with them structurally. We felt that having the ability to operate on graphs would significantly increase the usefulness of layouts. Many *dot* users were sending us similar comments. We felt that having a truly *graphical* user interface, involving drawings of graphs representing technical information, would provide a powerful user interface for many systems and applications. The graphs could represent the state of a system or some decision process, with its nodes and edges being objects that the user could select and perform operations and queries on.

Since we already had *dot* and *lefty*, we realized that creating an interactive system by combining them as two cooperating processes would be more practical than constructing a new system from scratch. Reuse at the process level has many advantages. Having several smaller tools, where each one performs a specific task well and has a cleanly defined interface, helps enforce a strict modular design. Individual modules can be tested and debugged independently. For example, *dot*'s layout algorithms can be debugged standalone; there is no need to involve *lefty*. Similarly, the *lefty* side can be driven through scripts and is thus easier to debug and profile. This is desirable because debugging user-interface programs by manually reproducing user actions is difficult.

This style of software reuse can be thought of as an extension to the UNIX/Shell concept of pipelines. The main difference is that in Shell-style programming, information usually flows one way (from one tool to another). The Shell itself, however, can be thought of as the text-based equivalent of *lefty*, a program that interacts with the user and can use several other programs to accomplish what the user wants. Process-level reuse is an obvious approach for constructing graphical user interfaces to preexisting text-based tools and systems.

One potential problem is that the final application may spend a significant fraction of its time merely in interprocess communication. This could result from having individual tools that do little processing in comparison to I/O. The design and selection of the process modules should therefore take this into account. For *dotty*, computing layouts does take longer than reading and writing the graphs (except for small graphs, where the total time is already negligible), so the balance is reasonable. By having separate layout processes, *dotty* achieves a form of parallel processing. The user can ask for a layout and, while *dot* is running in the background, switch to another graph and continue editing (or even ask for a layout of that graph as well, in which case, a second *dot* process is started in parallel).

Another problem is that some amount of duplicate code cannot be avoided. One example is interpreting node and edge labels. A label is a string containing control characters for indicating line breaks or field breaks (for record labels). *dot* needs to parse the labels so that it can allocate enough space for the nodes and edges in the layout computations. *dotty* also needs to parse the labels to extract the lines and fields, since these have to be drawn one at a time. Fortunately, for *dotty*, the duplicate code is a small fraction of the total system.

dotty is implemented as a *lefty* process, one or more *dot* processes and a program in the *lefty* language that customizes *lefty* so that it can handle graphs and their components. The program includes functions to insert and delete nodes and edges, as well as to draw these objects according to such attributes as color, shape, and style. There is also a function that computes the layout. This function sends the graph to a *dot* process running in the background. The *dot* process computes the layout and sends the graph (with layout information inserted as graph attributes) back to the *lefty* process. *lefty* then updates the node and edge coordinates and redraws the graph on the screen. Figure 11.2 shows how the two processes are connected.

The *lefty* program is organized in two layers. The lower layer (called the `dot` layer) implements the necessary data structure operations, such as insertion and deletion of nodes, edges, and subgraphs. This layer includes functions for reading and writing graphs from files, internet sockets, or UNIX pipes. The higher layer (called the *dotty* layer) implements the necessary graphical operations. For example, function `dotty.insertnode`

```
dot.insertnode =
        function (graph, name, attr) {
    ...
    graph.nodedict[name] = nid;
    graph.nodes[nid] = [
        'nid'   = nid;
        'name'  = name;
        'attr'  = copy (dot.nodeattr);
        'edges' = [];
    ];
    return graph.nodes[nid];
};
dotty.insertnode =
        function (gt, pos, name, attr) {
    ...
    if (~(node = dot.insertnode (gt.graph,
            name, attr)))
        return null;
    node.pos = pos;
    node.size = size;
    dotty.drawnode (gt.views, node);
    return node;
};
```

Figure 11.5   Functions for inserting a new node.

inserts a new node by calling function `dot.insertnode` and then drawing the node on the display using the node's color and shape attributes. Figure 11.5 shows the main parts of these two functions.

Overall, the *lefty* program implements the following operations:

- Create or destroy graphs

- Create or destroy views of graphs (a graph may have several views)

- Load or save graphs to files (or sockets and pipes)

- Insert or delete nodes, edges, and subgraphs

- Pan or zoom within a view

- Search for a node by name

- Geometrically move a node (and have all its edges follow)

- Edit attributes of an object

User actions can be bound to graph operations. For example, pressing the left mouse button can be bound to a function that inserts a new node at the position of the cursor. This can be done by writing a function called `leftdown` that calls the function `dotty.insertnode` with the appropriate arguments. By default, the left mouse button is bound to inserting or moving nodes, the middle button is bound to inserting edges between existing nodes, and the right button brings up a menu for selecting the rest of the operations mentioned in the foregoing list. There are also node- and edge-specific menus.

An important feature of *dotty* is that it can be easily customized, which amounts to modifying its *lefty* program. For example, the user interface functions (such as `leftdown`) can be redefined to perform different actions. Alternatively, the functions that operate on the graph data structures (such as `dot.insertnode`) could be modified to allow only operations that are appropriate for a specific type of graph. The most interesting class of customizations is the one where *dotty* is programmed to act as a front end for another process. In this context, a tool that generates and maintains information that can be expressed as a graph can use *dotty* to display this information graphically. *dotty* provides high-quality layouts and a simple way to implement a user interface. Graphs are first class citizens in such an interface; they are used not only to view information, but also as a way to operate on this information. An added advantage of this approach is that it requires little or no change to the original back-end tools.

The *lefty* program that implements *dotty* is 1,700 lines long. Most of this program is a library that is reused by the applications built on top of *dotty*.

11.2.3 *dotty* Applications

As mentioned at the outset, *dotty* has already been applied in creating graphical user interfaces for several applications. Many of these applications are described in other sections in this book.

Creating these applications has proved simple. It generally takes no more than a day or two to build a prototype. We can then make additions and changes depending on the features needed. Our largest applications are around 1,000 lines of *lefty* code.

The remainder of this section presents a short example. This application provides a graphical view of the *ship* area. Whenever a user receives a new tool or a new version of a tool through ADVSOFT, he or she uses *ship* scripts to unpack and build the tool. *ship* maintains a subdirectory per tool, where archives and other information is kept, including information about whether the tool was built. The owner of the software distribution process has such an area that contains all of our tools. As individual researchers send new versions of the various tools, they are installed and built in that area. As the number of packages grew, keeping track of the status of each version of each tool became hard. This led us to try a graphical approach.

Color Plate 1 shows a snapshot of *shipview*, the graphical user interface for *ship*. This is a trimmed-down version of our main *ship* area. Rectangular nodes represent directories, while ellipses represent files.

The first-level node (on the left) is the root of the *ship* directory. The second-level nodes represent tools. The third level shows specific versions of individual tools, such as the March 30, 1994 version of *Xray*. The fourth level shows the various files that each release contains. The nodes are colored to show the state of each tool. Red (such as node *app*) means that the build failed. In this case, the build of version 940411 failed. If there were several versions for that tool, the tool node would be colored according to the state of the latest version. Green (such as node *cql*) means that the tool was built successfully. Blue (such as node *Xray*) means that the tool was *uncrated* (the individual files were extracted from the archive), but no attempt was made to built it yet. Finally, gray (such as node *nohup.out*) is used when none of the foregoing criteria can be applied.

shipview initially displays the first two levels of nodes, colored white. Calculating the color for a node involves searching its subdirectories. Coloring all the level-two nodes (about 100 nodes) is time-consuming. Instead of requiring the user to wait while all the node colors are computed, *dotty* does this in the background; while there is no user input to service, *dotty* executes a function that picks a node from a list of white nodes and computes its color. Upon startup, *shipview* starts up a *ksh* process and establishes a two-way communication with it, using pipes. Whenever *shipview* needs to compute the color for a node, it sends the node name to the shell. The shell script that the shell is executing reads in the node name and searches its subdirectories to figure out the state of the node. The script uses *tw*, our tree walk program, to search the file system. When the state of the node is computed, the shell script sends the answer back to *shipview*, which uses the result to compute the appropriate color.

As this is happening in the background, the user can proceed to browse the graph and perform queries. If the user presses a mouse button over a directory node, it expands to show its contents (such as directory node *app*). If the directory is already expanded, it reverts to its closed state. Pressing a mouse button over a file brings up a text window showing its contents. The type of the file is checked to select the viewing method (for example, `vi`, `more`, `pax -v`).

Even though this is just the first version of this tool, it already seems useful. A quick look at the top-level picture is enough to inform the user which tools are built and which tools had problems. Checking to see what versions exist for a specific tool is also easy. Being able to browse around and inspect specific files helps detect the reason of any failures. An obvious improvement is to allow the user to ship packages to customers just by selecting the tools that must be sent.

This version of *shipview* took about one hour to build. This is because only 150 lines of *lefty* code and 80 lines of *ksh* code had to be written. *shipview* uses *dotty*, *ksh*, *pax*, *tw*, *file*, and a variety of standard system utilities. Such reuse encourages rapid prototyping and often leads to software that can be used on a regular basis.

11.2.3.1   Conclusions

We have described how new graphical applications have been created from smaller, general-purpose tools: a programmable graphics editor, graph layout tools, and text-based applications. The ease with which they were created suggests that small, well-focused, programmable tools can be a better starting point than large C or C++ libraries.

11.3   TESTTUBE

As software systems mature, maintenance activities become dominant. Studies have found that more than 50 percent of development effort in the life cycle of a software system is spent in maintenance; of that, a large percentage is due to testing [Mye79, LS80]. Except for the rare event of a major rewrite, in the maintenance phase, changes to a system are usually small and are made to correct problems or incrementally enhance functionality. Therefore, techniques for selective software retesting can help to reduce development time.

There is a clear analogy between retesting and recompilation of software. Good examples of tools for selective recompilation are *make* [Fel79] and *nmake* [Fow85]. These tools implement a simple strategy whereby recompilation is carried out only on source files that have changed and on files that depend on the changed files. Similarly, a test suite typically consists of many test units, each of which exercises or *covers* some subset of the entities of the system under test. A test unit must be rerun if, and only if, any of the program entities it covers has changed. However, unlike system recompilation, where the dependency between a program and its source files is specified in build scripts or *makefiles*, it is not easy to identify the dependency between a test unit and the program entities it covers. Computing such dependency information requires sophisticated analyses of both the source code and the execution behavior of the test units. Fortunately, the requisite technologies for performing such analyses are now available.

TESTTUBE is a system for selective retesting that identifies which subset of a test suite must be rerun to test a new version of a system. The basic idea behind TESTTUBE is illustrated in Figure 11.6. In the figure, the boxes represent subprograms and circles represent variables. The arrows represent static and dynamic dependency relationships (for example, variable references and function calls) among the entities in the system under test and the test units, with the entity at the tail of an arrow being dependent on the entity at the head. Suppose that the shaded entities were modified to create a new version of the system under test. Under a naive retest-all strategy, all three test units must be rerun in

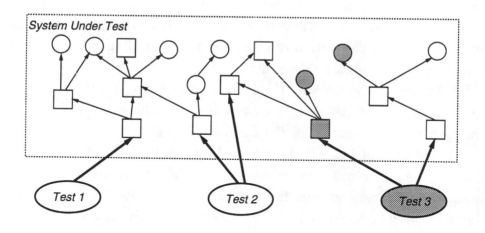

Figure 11.6 Selective retesting of a new version.

order to test the changes. However, by analyzing the relationships between the test units and the entities they cover, it is possible to eliminate test units 1 and 2 from the selective regression testing of the new version and rerun only test unit 3.

In a recent paper [CRV94], we described our initial results of applying TESTTUBE to some modestly large C programs, and we compared TESTTUBE to other approaches to regression testing that have been described in the literature. In this section, we focus on a description of the technology behind TESTTUBE and on the reusable components that we have used to implement a version of TESTTUBE for C.

11.3.1   The TESTTUBE Methodology

11.3.1.1   Basic Method and Terminology

The method underlying TESTTUBE is simple. First, we partition a software system into basic code entities. These entities are defined in such a way that they can be easily computed from the source code and monitored during execution. We then monitor the execution of each test unit, analyze its relationship with the system under test, and, in this way, determine which subset of the code entities it covers. When the system is changed, we identify the set of changed entities and then examine the previously computed set of covered entities for each test unit and check to see if any has changed. If none has changed, the test unit need not be rerun. If a test unit *is* rerun, its set of covered entities must be recomputed. Note that the notion of what constitutes a change in the system is programming-language dependent.

This approach works well if the code entities are defined so that the partitioning of a software system can be done efficiently while still allowing effective reduction in the number of test cases that are selected. At one extreme of testing, the retest-all approach is simply that of considering the entire software system as a single code entity. On the other hand, the data flow approaches mentioned in Section 11.3.4 treat each statement as a code entity and thus obtain extremely precise information about which code entities are covered by each test unit. But the large cost of data flow analysis may overwhelm the benefits of test reduction. To strike a balance, we consider a *software system S* as being made up of two sets of entities: *F, functions* and *V, nonfunctions.*

- *Functions*–These are the basic entities that execute program semantics by creating and storing values. We assume that every action of a program must be carried out in some functions. An advantage of using functions as a basic code entity is that there are readily available profiling tools that can monitor program execution and identify the set of covered functions.
- *Nonfunctions*–These are nonexecuting entities in a program, such as variables, types, and preprocessor macros. Variables define storage areas that functions manipulate. Among other things, types define the storage extent of variables. We assume that every storage location that is potentially manipulated by a function can be statically or dynamically associated with some variable. Typically, these entities cannot be directly monitored during execution without great cost. However, they can be deduced from the source code and function call trace.

Next, we define a program in the software system S as a composition of some subsets of F and V. A *test unit T* for the system S is defined as a program and some *fixed* input.* Fixing the input means that the set of functions covered by the test unit T can be determined by a single

---

*We view input as comprising both input data values and environment effects, such as signals.

execution. This set of functions is called T_f. The set of nonfunctional entities that are used by these functions is called T_v.

11.3.1.2   Safe Test Skipping

The working of TESTTUBE relies on a premise that all value creations and manipulations in a program can be inferred from static source code analysis of the relationships among the functional and nonfunctional entities. This premise is valid for languages without pointer arithmetic and type coercion. In that case, we can summarize TESTTUBE as follows:

Proposition *Let T be a test unit for a software system S. When changes are made to S, if no elements in T_f and T_v are changed, then T does not need to be rerun on the new version of S.*

However, with such languages as C and C++, it is not always simple to infer all value manipulations just from analyzing the variables and pointers used by functions. For example, the following C code uses type coercion to convert an integer value to an address value so that the creation of the value 0 in the memory store is not associated with any visible variable:

```
*((char*)0x1234) = 0;
```

Another problem with languages, such as C and C++, that allow arbitrary pointer arithmetic is that pointers may violate the memory extents of areas to which they point. This means that values may be manipulated in ways that are not amenable to source code analysis. In the following example, the pointer expression `*(xp+1)` points beyond the memory extent defined by the variable `x` (whose address has been stored in the variable `xp`). On many hardware/compiler architectures, it may, in fact, point to the same memory area defined by `y`, so the value of `y` is changed without ever referring to `y`.

```
int x, y;
int* xp = &x;
...
*(xp+1) = 0;
```

To account for such memory violations, we assume the following hypotheses:

Hypothesis 1 (Well-defined memory) *Each memory segment accessed by S is identifiable by a symbolically defined variable.*

Hypothesis 2 (Well-bounded pointer) *Each pointer variable or pointer expression must refer to some base variable and be bounded by the extent of the memory segment defined by that variable.*

For applications written in such languages as C and C++, the well-defined memory assumption is reasonable. This is because it is seldom the case that one needs esoteric constructs that would coerce a plain integer value to an address value, except for programs that require direct manipulation of hardware addresses, such as device drivers. However, in cases where they are required, the addresses represented by such integer values are usually well separated from the memory space occupied by normal variables. Thus, we do not need to worry about values of variables that are changed without ever mentioning the variable names. In addition, for maintainability, such values are often assigned symbolic names using macros, which *are* amenable to source code analysis.

On the other hand, the well-bounded pointer hypothesis sometimes fails in real C and C++ programs due to memory-overwrite and stray-pointer faults. These faults are among the hardest to detect, isolate, and remove. A number of research techniques and commercial tools are available to help detect these faults (for example, see Austin [ABS93], Purify [HJ92a], and others). Whenever such a fault is detected during testing, an attempt must be made to identify the entities that are affected by the fault; for example, memory overwrites are often confined to the functions that cause them. If the affected entities can be identified, then these entities must be added to the set of changed entities identified by TESTTUBE for the current round of testing. In extreme cases, where the effects of such faults are too difficult to determine, it must be assumed that all parts of memory are potentially damaged and, hence, all test units must be rerun in order to ensure thorough testing of any code that exercises the fault. The successful use of TESTTUBE depends on the quick removal of such faults so that they do not propagate from

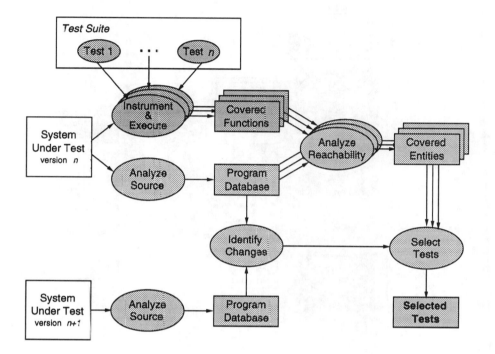

Figure 11.7 Application of the TESTTUBE methodology.

version to version. Once a software system has successfully grown into a maintenance phase, it is hoped that such faults will be few.

11.3.2 The TESTTUBE Architecture

We often use the name TESTTUBE to refer to the selective regression testing *system* that we have built for C programs. Yet, as was described in the previous section, TESTTUBE at its most general is a platform-independent, application-independent, and programming language-independent *method* for regression testing. This method imposes certain constraints on the functionality of the tools used to implement the method and on their order of invocation. Yet, by no means does the method require a particular architecture for its implementation. If there is such an architecture, it is a very open architecture of loosely coupled, highly independent components that may be easily interchanged with components of like functionality.

Figure 11.7 depicts the TESTTUBE methodology in terms of the com-

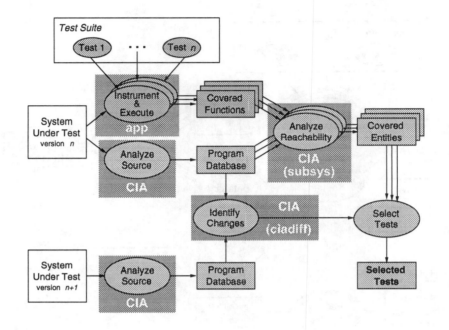

Figure 11.8   Implementation of the TESTTUBE methodology for C.

ponent technologies required for its application. The figure illustrates
testing of version $n + 1$ of some system under test, which was created by
making changes to version n. The figure shows how static and dynamic
analyses are applied to select test units for version $n + 1$ from an existing
test suite for the system. By necessity, the technology used to develop and
maintain the test suite will be highly application-dependent and heavily
influenced by the nature of the test cases and the means used to run them
on the system under test.

11.3.3   An Implementation of TESTTUBE for C Programs

Our version of TESTTUBE for C was designed and implemented around
a number of existing analysis tools. Figure 11.8 depicts our implementation of the TESTTUBE methodology for C, using the graphical diagram
of the method from Figure 11.7. The figure shows the existing analysis
components that we used for our implementation for C. In addition, we

built a number of new tools (all of whose names begin with the prefix `tt`) that basically serve to tie together these analysis components.

The collection of tools can be partitioned into three categories:

- *Instrumentation Tools*–The system source code is automatically instrumented by APP, the Annotation PreProcessor for C [Ros92]. The instrumentation causes each run of a test unit T to produce a *function trace list*, that is, the set T_f of all functions covered by T as defined in Section 11.3.1.

- *Program Database Tools*–For each version of the system under test, a C program database is built using the C information abstractor, *cia* (Chapter 6). This database contains information about the C entities that the system comprises and the dependency relationships among them. Then, for each test unit, the TESTTUBE tool `ttclosure` uses the program database to expand the function trace list T_f to an *entity trace list*, such as the set $T_f \cup T_v$ as defined in Section 11.3.1. When there are two versions of the source code, the TESTTUBE tool `ttdiff` uses the CIA tool *ciadiff* to analyze the two corresponding program databases and produces an *entity difference list*.

- *Test Selection Tools*–Three tools are provided to assist selective retesting: `ttselect`, `ttidentify`, and `ttcoverage`. The tool `ttselect` checks to see if there is an intersection between the entity difference list and the entity trace list of each test unit; test units with nonempty intersections must be rerun. To estimate retesting cost, the tool `ttidentify` computes the list of test units that need to be rerun if certain specified entities are changed. Finally, `ttcoverage` finds entities that are not covered by the existing test suite.

As was described in Chapter 6, C entities recognized by CIA are functions, variables (including pointers and their base variables), preprocessor macros, types, and files; however, only global entities that can be used across entity declaration and definition boundaries are recorded. A C entity is considered to be changed if any token in the sequence of tokens that constitute the entity has changed. Thus, the CIA database provides the right code-entity partition required by the TESTTUBE methodology.

We can illustrate the use of the TESTTUBE tools on the test suite of *incl* (Section 6.5.2), a program for detecting and removing unnecessary

`#include` directives from C programs [VC92]; such directives are used to incorporate interface or *header* files into C programs. There are eight test units for *incl*. We first instrumented version 1 of *incl* with APP and built a CIA database for it. We then generated the entity trace list for each test unit. Such lists are stored in files whose names end with `.clo`. Note that this initialization step is necessary only for the first version of *incl*. For later versions, only the entity trace lists of test units that are rerun need to be updated.

We then built a CIA program database for version 2 of *incl*. The following example shows that `ttdiff` was run to compare the two databases (contained in directories `v1` and `v2`, respectively) and to store the entity difference list in `tt.dfl`. Then, `tt.dfl` was printed out by *cat* to show that four program entities were changed from version 1 to version 2:

```
$ ttdiff -o v1 -n v2 > tt.dfl
$ cat tt.dfl
function;incl.c;dagprint
function;incl.c;dbeprint
function;incl.c;qexprint
macro;incl.h;N_LEVPRINT
```

We next ran `ttselect` to check for intersections between `tt.dfl` and the `.clo` files. The output of `ttselect` showed that four out of the eight existing test units for *incl* had to be rerun and that their `.clo` files had to be regenerated:

```
$ ttselect tt.dfl *.clo
rerun test t.3
rerun test t.5
rerun test t.6
rerun test t.8
```

While it is possible to use `ttselect` to predict the testing cost implied by a set of changes by manually constructing a hypothetical `tt.dfl` file, the tool `ttidentify` simplifies this process. Given a CIA entity pattern (which specifies an entity kind and a regular expression to match names of entities of that kind), `ttidentify` identifies which test units must be rerun if any matching program entities are changed. For example, the following query finds the list of all functions defined in `incl.c` whose names end with `print` and then lists the test units that cover them;

the output of the query shows that changes to different functions incur
different testing costs:

```
$ ttidentify 'function *print \
    file=incl.c' *.clo
incl.c dagprint:
        rerun test t.3
        rerun test t.6
incl.c dbeprint:
        rerun test t.8
incl.c dbvprint:
        rerun test t.8
incl.c exprint:
        rerun test t.1
incl.c levprint:
        rerun test t.2
incl.c qexprint:
        rerun test t.5
incl.c stprint:
        rerun test t.1
        rerun test t.2
        rerun test t.3
        rerun test t.6
incl.c subsysprint:
        rerun test t.3
        rerun test t.6
```

The entity trace lists provided by TESTTUBE can also be used as
an aid in evaluating the adequacy of a test suite. Given a CIA entity
pattern, ttcoverage finds entities matching the pattern that are not
present in any entity trace list. For example, the following command finds
all functions in *incl* that are not covered by any of the eight test units:*

```
$ ttcoverage 'function -' *.clo
NOT COVERED:
    incl.c subsys
    tree.c t_delete
    tree.c t_free
    util.c delNode
    util.c delSymbol
    util.c fatal
```

As seen in the following, the CIA tool *deadobj* finds that only t_delete
is truly not used by any *incl* code and, therefore, more test units should
be added to the test suite:

---

*The specifier "-" in a CIA entity pattern is a wild card that matches all entity names.

```
$ deadobj function
tree.c function t_delete
```

This completes our illustration of the TESTTUBE tools for C code. The tools do not require redesigning existing test suites or manually modifying code. They are driven by data readily obtainable from program analysis tools, such as APP and CIA. Furthermore, even the dependency on such program analysis tools can be removed. For example, if a project already uses a tracing tool that can provide function trace lists from program executions, then we do not need to instrument code with APP. With minimal textual transformation, the output from such a tool can be used by TESTTUBE. The same is true of CIA. Finally, outputs generated by TESTTUBE and the analysis tools find applications beyond selective retesting. In particular, CIA databases created for selective retesting can also be used to study program structure, eliminate dead program entities, and skip unnecessary header files during compilation.

11.3.4   Conclusion

We have described a system called TESTTUBE that implements a selective regression testing method through dynamic and static analysis of a software system and its test units. The choice of analysis methods used in any selective retesting strategy is governed by a spectrum of trade-offs between the desired detail and accuracy of the analysis and the time/space costs required to perform the analysis. For instance, data flow analysis can provide information about a system at the granularity of a source code statement, but its relatively poor time complexity may make it prohibitive for analysis of large systems. In comparison with previous selective retesting techniques, TESTTUBE employs relatively coarse-grained analysis of the system under test, producing a reasonable and practical trade-off between granularity of analysis and time/space complexity.

Each phase of TESTTUBE—instrumentation, program database construction, and test selection—contributes some amount of overhead to selective retesting. Instrumentation with APP for dynamic tracing typically increases object code size by about 19 percent, although compilation and linking with uninstrumented system libraries usually reduces this space cost to around 2 percent of the fully-linked executable. Furthermore, the

Table 11.4 Overhead of TESTTUBE for Selective Regression Testing

Phase	Space Overhead	Time Overhead
Instrumentation	19% of object code	≈ 0
Program DB	50 to 150% of source code	70% of compile time
Test Selection	$O(\text{TU})$	$O(\text{TU} \times \text{CE})$

runtime cost of generating the trace is insignificant, although this may not always be the case if low-bandwidth I/O devices are used to collect the trace (such as in an embedded real-time system). Construction of a CIA database typically requires about 50 to 100 percent disk space as the original source code (and about 150 percent in the worst case) and about 70 percent of the time needed to compile the source code. Note that projects that already use APP for assertion processing and CIA for source code analysis are already incurring these costs. The rest of the overhead of TESTTUBE comes from the test selection tools *ciadiff*, *subsys*, `ttselect`, `ttidentify`, and `ttcoverage`. *ciadiff* produces output that is linear in the size of the number of changed components. The test selection tools currently use naive algorithms for their computations; thus, we have not yet determined the minimum expected costs for these tools.

Table 11.4 presents a summary of the (current) overhead of using TESTTUBE for selective regression testing. TU is the number of test units, while CE is the number of changed entities. Note that while it is easy to bypass the tracing code at minimal runtime cost in a field-grade release of a system, projects that choose not to release instrumented code to customers must incur an additional complete recompilation.

11.4 *Xray*

11.4.1 **Introduction**

Xray is a program animation system that graphically animates the sequence of function calls that takes place during a program execution. The

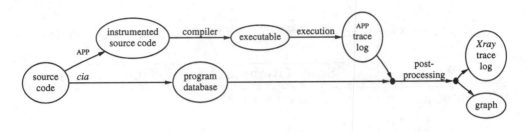

Figure 11.9   Processing steps for *Xray*.

pictures and animation information generated by *Xray* help the user analyze the performance of a program, visualize its dynamic behavior, and detect bugs or inefficiencies.

Xray was built by combining several tools. Figure 11.9 shows the processing steps of *Xray* and how a set of tools were invoked to create the static and dynamic information necessary for animation. APP is used to preprocess the user program to generate instrumented source code, which is then compiled to build an executable. A trace log of function calls is produced during each execution of that program against a test case. *cia* is used to analyze the program source to build a program database. The postprocessing step merges the static database information with the dynamic trace log to generate a merged program graph and a modified trace log with explicit call sequencing information. Finally, a front end based on *dotty* takes the final graph and trace log to animate the sequence of function calls both on the directed graph and on a stack.

The executable generated by APP is instrumented in such a way that it can be used both for TESTTUBE and *Xray* processing. The graph generated in the postprocessing step is basically the static call graph with possibly a few extra edges. These extra edges represent dynamic function calls through pointers that are not amenable to static analysis, but detectable by analyzing the trace log.

11.4.2   Program Animation with *Xray*

Color Plate 2 (top) shows an *Xray* snapshot. The graph shows the static and dynamic function-to-function references, represented as directed edges between function nodes. Colors of nodes and edges are changed dynamically when the animation is in progress. Different colors help distinguish between *hot* and *cold* spots, and to locate functions that are on or off the stack.

Active functions on the calling stack at a given point of execution and their associated chain of references are painted yellow in the graph. In the snapshot, the stack consists of `main`, `makepairs`, `init_list`, and `chkmalloc`. As the animation is played through, the yellow path extends and retracts through the graph, just as the stack drawn in a separate window grows and shrinks.

Unexercised functions and references during a particular execution are painted blue. For example, in the particular execution shown in the snapshot, `main` did not call `makeargs`. This is revealed in the picture by painting the node for `makeargs` and the edge between it and `main` blue. Most profiling tools (with the exception of *call path profiling* [Hal92]) concentrate only on statistics of individual functions, while *Xray* gathers and visualizes information on both functions and their calling paths. In general, a function might never be called if there was some flaw in the program logic or if the test suite does not provide adequate coverage. This can be detected visually by accumulating the results gathered from all trace logs during *Xray* animation.

Except for functions and references on the active stack, all others that are exercised at least once are painted green. For example, `viewline` was called in this test case, but only from `walk_list`, so that edge is painted green. On the other hand, function `viewlines` did not call `viewline`, so the edge between these two functions is painted blue.

A threshold n can be set so that all nodes or edges that are exercised more than n times in a trace are painted red to highlight *hot spots*, areas of focus for potential performance improvements.

The animation of function calls can be run either in continuous mode or single-step mode. The sequence can also be played in reverse. Playing the sequence continuously is useful for observing patterns in the execution of the program, while single-stepping is useful for detailed analysis of a section of a trace log. Breakpoints can also be set in the continuous mode so that the execution may run for a while and then stop at a selected node, possibly followed by detailed, single-stepped analysis of another program segment.

When running *Xray* on the previous test case in continuous mode, we see that the yellow path (representing the stack) first goes through the top section of the graph (above the **error** node), then moves to the bottom. By running *cia* source-retrieval queries on these functions to display their code, we find that the top portion of the graph corresponds to functions used for parsing the command line arguments, while the functions in the bottom portion execute the actions requested by those arguments.

To help highlight module-to-module dependencies, *Xray* can group all the functions defined in the same file into a single cluster, which is shown as a rectangle containing only the corresponding function nodes. Color Plate 2 (bottom) shows the cluster graph representation of the graph from Color Plate 2 (top). Note that all uninstrumented library functions are clustered inside the same rectangle labeled **<library>**.

11.4.3   Managing Complex Traces and Graphs

For large programs both the graphs and trace logs handled by *Xray* may become big and complex. A complex graph may not fit into a display window comfortably. Even with the *zoom out* and *scroll* features of *dotty*, either labels become illegible or edge crossings clutter up the picture, causing users to lose track of the animation. Moreover, large trace logs take a long time to generate and consume a lot of disk space when saved. *Xray* offers several ways to work around these problems:

- *Hiding uncovered code–Xray* allows a user to hide all uncovered code of a particular test case, such as all blue nodes and edges from the graph. The resulting graph tends to be much smaller, especially in large programs, since a single test case may exercise only a small portion of a program. However, hiding uncovered code also has the disadvantage of losing the visual coverage information of individual test cases.
- *Collapsing clusters to single nodes–Xray* can also collapse all the functions in a specific file to a single node. For example, in Color Plate 2 (bottom), the four functions in cluster **list.c** can be replaced with a single meta-node labeled **list.c**. Any edges from or to nodes outside the cluster will be replaced with edges to or from the meta-node. The trace log maintained by *Xray* is also adjusted accordingly. This option

can reduce the sizes of both the graph and the *Xray* trace log significantly. It is especially useful when the user is interested only in the details of a couple of modules (files); all other functions can be collapsed into their corresponding module nodes with only the interesting functions visible.

- *Selective deletion of nodes and edges*–Another alternative that *Xray* provides is to allow users to delete individual nodes and edges that they have understood or are not interested in. The user can remove a single edge, a single node, or all nodes belonging to a single module. The trace log is also adjusted to remove calls to the deleted objects. For example, every time the function `chkmalloc` in Color Plate 2 (bottom) is called, it in turn calls the library function `malloc()`. Once the user understands this, seeing the same calling sequence repetitively is not interesting. Also, if users are interested only in seeing how the functions they wrote interact with each other, they can first collapse all the library functions into a single node and then remove it. This will make the picture and the log much smaller and allow the user to focus on the user-developed functions in the program.

- *Pre-filtering of trace logs*–Users can also specify what functions to ignore during the generation of the trace log. This technique, as opposed to generating the full log and then removing functions from the graph, takes less time to generate the trace log and less space to save the log on the disk.

Color Plate 3 shows a snapshot from running *Xray* on a much larger program (12,000 lines of C). The graph shown here is about ten times smaller than the complete graph of the program. Several types of filters were applied: Prefiltering excluded several functions from appearing in the trace log, all dead nodes and edges were removed, and several groups of functions were collapsed into single nodes. Also, clustering was applied to show module dependencies.

11.4.4   Conclusion

Xray has benefited significantly from the components that it was built on. It inherits and takes advantage of their new features and performance improvements. For example, the new clustering operator in *dotty* was used effectively in *Xray* soon after it became available.

Using program animation provided by *Xray*, we have been able to identify some subtle bugs in certain projects that went unnoticed by their authors for a long period of time. Advances in *Xray*'s underlying technologies, including static analysis, dynamic analysis, graph drawing, and browsing tools, have made program animation a practical technique to help programmers understand, debug, and fine-tune their complex software systems.

11.5 Vpm

11.5.1 Introduction

Visual Process Manager (Vpm) is a tool that provides real-time views of processes executing on a network of UNIX machines. The processes, any system resources they use, and the computers they run on are shown as objects in a graph.

Color Plate 4 (top) shows a sample Vpm view. Outlined boxes, such as **toucan** and **gryphon**, represent computer systems. Filled boxes represent processes. Double circles shown within a computer box represent UNIX pipes, while double circles outside any boxes represent sockets. Finally, ellipses represent regular files. Processes and pipes are shown within a computer box to indicate that they can be accessed only from within that computer. Sockets and regular files are shown outside, since they can be accessed by other computers. There are two kinds of edges: edges between processes and edges between a process and a file (pipes and sockets are special kinds of files in UNIX). An edge between two processes indicates that these processes have a parent-to-child relationship. For example, process 17551 created (forked) process 17604. An edge between a process and a file indicates that the process has opened the file for input or output or both. For example, process 15349 has opened the file *dotty* for input (the arrow specifies that information is flowing from the file to the process that is, the file is opened for reading).

The picture shows a *coshell* server (process 17572) having started a *dotty* process on machine `toucan`. The user initiated this by running a *coshell* client (process 17604). The client sent the request to the server using the pipe shown in the **gryphon** box. The *coshell* server uses sockets (the two double circles outside the computer boxes) to collect any textual output that the processes on machine `toucan` may produce. Any such output is forwarded to the user's terminal.

Color Plate 4 (bottom) shows another VPM snapshot. *nmake* is being used together with *coshell* to run a distributed compilation of some tool.

VPM was built by combining several other tools and libraries. The trace log that VPM uses to generate its graphical views is generated by *n-DFS*. This functionality of *n-DFS* is implemented using *libcs*. The graphical views and user interface of VPM are implemented using *dotty*.

Previous work in the area of debugging and performance analysis for distributed programs has considered methods of collecting and examining trace logs. The most common software-only approach is to write trace logs via a debugging version of the standard programming library. Some systems also rely on special features of the operating system to monitor events, such as context switches, that would be transparent to a user process. Other systems require modifications to the operating system to allow them to collect tracing information.

PVM [BDGS93] has a library that implements its abstract parallel virtual machine. A debugging version of the library emits traces read by a monitoring process with an attached text log browser. ParaGraph [HE91] is a debugging system for a real-time multiprocessor without tasking, so only postmortem logs are available. HMON [Dod92] traces events using a combination of C library and kernel support to capture low-level trace information on a hexagonal mesh parallel computer. A language-based approach was proposed for concurrent Ada programs, but such issues as dynamic task creation were not considered. For UNIX system programming, the **proc** interface in Eighth Edition UNIX and Plan 9 provides a name space for distributed processes that aids debugging [PPTT90, Win94]. Plan 9 makes it easier to request state information on demand, but does not provide an event-monitoring scheme.

VPM differs from the systems mentioned here in several ways. Most of the other systems generate logs of events in some custom model of process interaction. To trace a distributed application, the application must be written or modified to obey that model. VPM traces the actual system calls so that any process and any distributed application can be traced. In fact, VPM is nonintrusive; there is no need to modify or recompile a program to trace it. *n-DFS* is implemented as a shared library that gets loaded at runtime and intercepts system calls as they are being executed. Also, VPM does not require any operating system modifications. This minimizes the effort required to integrate VPM into a user's environment. Finally, the modular design of VPM allows parts of it to be used independently. *n-DFS* traces can be generated and traced without the graphical front end. The graphical front end could be replaced by some other front end. A different trace log generator could be used to replace *n-DFS* and, as long as the trace is similar to *n-DFS* traces, the graphical front end could be used as is. This would be useful, for example, for animating traces generated by an embedded system.

11.5.2   Implementation

Trace generation is implemented using the ability in *n-DFS* to attach servers to specific parts of the file system and specific processes running under *n-DFS*. The tracing server is set up to apply to the entire file system and (by default) all the processes in an *n-DFS* user session. A per-process table is maintained, indicating which (if any) system calls to report and whether to use a verbose or terse format for each call. The following list of system calls can be selectively reported:

- *Process management system calls*, such as *fork*, *exec*, and *exit*–In Color Plate 4 (top), when *dotty* forks process 15350, this is shown by creating a node for the new process and linking it to the open file nodes of its parent (such as the socket 4269). When process 15350 execs a program called `lefty`, the label of node 15350 is updated correspondingly.
- *I/O channel management system calls*, such as *open*, *close*, *dup*, and *pipe*–Network connections are traced using *open* and *close* calls. For example, the two nodes at the bottom right of Color Plate 4 (top) are UNIX pipes created by the *lefty* process. `lefty` then spawned `dot`,

```
[ 15350 37506 ] fork ( ) = 15362
[ 15362 37506 ] fork ( ) = 15350
[ 15362 37506 ] exec ( "/home/ek/work/bin/lefty" ... ) = 0
[ 15362 37506 ] close ( 116842+2595 0x2ba8c3fb ) = 0
```

Figure 11.10 VPM trace sequence.

which also inherited the two pipes. Arrows in process-to-file edges show file access modes (read, write, or both).

- *I/O operations*, such as *read* and *write*.

The per-process table of system calls to report is inherited from process to process, but it can also be modified anytime during the lifetime of a process. This makes it possible to *focus* the visualization on a specific process by monitoring more system calls for that process only and by setting the monitoring mode to verbose.

Figure 11.10 shows an excerpt from the monitoring information generated by VPM. It corresponds to having process *dotty* in Color Plate 4 (top) spawn a process that eventually runs program *lefty*. When the *dotty* process performs a *fork*, two messages result: one from the parent and one from the child. The first number in brackets is the process id of the process performing the action. The second number identifies the host on which the process runs. The final *close* occurs because process *dotty* had the file descriptor for file *dotty* marked as close-on-exec.

The front end for VPM is implemented as a customized version of *dotty*. *dotty* reads the *n-DFS* message channel and translates its trace entries into graph operations. An *open* system call, for example, is translated to inserting a new node for the file (unless the file was already open by some process) and then inserting an edge between the process that performed the call and the file.

Tracing information for a process is generated by the process itself. This information is then sent to a single server process. The front end communicates with this server to receive the trace information. One problem with having each process generate its trace information is that if the process terminates abnormally, VPM never receives the final exit message from that process, so it does not know when to remove this process from the picture. To overcome this problem, we built a *pid* server. VPM starts up one *pid* server per machine. If VPM receives no message from a process for a while, it queries the *pid* server about this process. The *pid* server then replies, indicating whether the process is still around.

VPM can run either in real-time or in single-step playback mode. In real time, it reads the trace information as it is being generated and periodically updates the graphical view. Graph insertions are batched before a new layout is made (deletions and relabelings can be executed immediately). Layouts are not made online because *dot*'s algorithms are not incrementally stable and, even if improved algorithms are available, it probably will never be able to keep up with a burst of system calls. In single-step mode, VPM reads a previously written trace log and updates the graphical view after every step (or after a sequence of steps, depending on the user's selection). The real-time view is good for seeing things as they happen. The single-step mode provides a more detailed view and is better suited for debugging.

We are currently working on two features that would increase VPM's usefulness as a debugging tool. One feature is to allow the user to specify that one or more processes are to be suspended when they try to perform some specific task, such as opening a new file. When this occurs, the node representing the process changes color to red to show that it has been suspended. The user can then allow the process to continue by clicking on the node. Another debugging feature is that the user can click on a node representing a pipe and, from then on, any data flowing through this pipe are displayed in a text window.

12

Evaluation of Approach

David Belanger, Balachander Krishnamurthy, and Kiem-Phong Vo

12.1 Introduction

This book is a study of a collection of practical reusable software tools. Each of the individual tools or libraries was created to help some aspect of software development, for example: general purpose libraries, configuration management, application construction, security, software fault tolerance, reverse engineering, and software process. The process of building these tools helped to develop a variety of capabilities in both expertise and software modules. These capabilities have been used over many years to support hundreds of projects throughout the software development community within AT&T, and to create a highly synergetic environment in which to build new software. It is the latter that is the primary subject of this book. In this chapter, we discuss our experience to date in terms of what was done right, what could be improved, critical success factors, experience with technology transfer, and future directions.

12.2 What Went Right

At this time, many things have worked well. Notable among them are:

- *Impact*–Many of the tools and libraries described in this book are widely used in AT&T products as well as in the product development process.

From a corporation point of view, this has had significant positive impact in both development time and product quality.

- *Partnership*–Many of our members work closely with product organizations both in technology transfer and in learning problems that exist in these areas. This helps these organizations to quickly try and use new technologies. We freely share source code—this helps to increase trust in research software. Such collaborations help to mature technologies quickly and provide invaluable information on the detailed needs of software development.

- *Vertical integration*–Software tools, such as *ksh* and EASEL (Chapter 4), formalize powerful methods to build systems out of independent software components and are used widely to build products. Within our own work over the past few years, there have been many cases, such as VPM (see Section 11.5), in which we have been able to build sophisticated research prototypes quickly (for example, three weeks) by integrating many pieces of software across all of the levels described in Chapter 1. These applications would not have been attempted using standard processes.

- *Common view*–At face value, the structure of this work is technologically heterogeneous and appears to be a loosely coupled set of projects. They are bound by a common view of the needs of our customers, AT&T developers, and by an evolving view of the process of software creation. This common view has helped bring about a cohesive, supportive environment that values diversity in work directions. It has also supported a process of change in our work directions as the needs of product development have changed.

- *Teamwork*–Members with different types of expertise often collaborate on multiple aspects of software engineering research. Such teamwork is always driven by mutual interests in the problems to be solved. This helps us to solve problems quickly. It also helps to improve existing software, reduce code redundancy, and increase consistency across software tools. Over the years this mode of work has created a fertile environment both conducive to professional growth and helpful in orienting new members.

- *Continuous improvement*-In any multiyear, multiperson effort, there is ample room to make mistakes *and* to learn from them. We have made our share of mistakes and believe that learning from them has led to significant improvements in our software. For example, in Section 2.4, we discuss the lack of reusability of the data language of *dag* making it hard to create interactive browsers and other tools. This was rectified in *libgraph*, which defined a standard data language that aids in sharing at various levels, as a result of which graphs could be shared between programs.

12.3   What Could Be Improved

As with any process, there are areas for improvement. A few are listed in the following. Most of these are problems that have proven quite hard and, though there have been successes, we do not yet have a predictable process to ensure the successes.

- *Leverage*-Some of the technologies and tools described in this book have proven valuable in practice, but are still used at only a fraction of their potential value. There is considerable opportunity to increase practical value with appropriate, but limited, effort and expertise.
- *Distribution*-Some of the tools (such as *nmake*) have become de facto standards within large parts of AT&T. A few (for example *curses* and KornShell) have become standards outside; but often the technology has not been distributed widely or early enough to have effective impact on the software community at large.
- *Measuring benefits*-As with most of the software industry, we have not been able to quantify the benefits and costs of reusing most of these tools. In a few cases, we got estimates from production users but we do not yet have adequate measures.
- *Exit strategy*-It is difficult to gracefully reduce and end support of tools that are used by tens or hundreds of product developers, even when interest in them from a research perspective has been exhausted.

12.4   Success Factors

Several success factors for reuse have been discussed in the literature. We discuss a few aspects as outlined in [Dav93]: management, application development, asset development, and process and technology.

- *Management factors*–The colocation of the book's contributors in a stable environment for several years has clearly aided the development of reusable assets. This is a result of successful management. Another aspect of good technical management is establishing early connections between organizations with needs and appropriate research technologies. This leads to a more honest evaluation of the validity of the approaches and gives better, earlier feedback for improvements in the software.

- *Application development factors*–The contributors not only invent, design, and create the software, but often participate in evaluating ways it can be reused in the end products. This benefits both sides; we learn how to make our software more generic while the recipients discuss the software directly with the developers. In such cases as EASEL, *ksh*, and *nmake*, the high-level tools also act as the end products that reuse and drive improvements in other more basic components, such as *sfio* or *vmalloc*. Many of us also use environment tools, such as *ksh* or *n-DFS*, daily. We develop reusable software and use it in our own work. This close-knit interaction between development and use has proven to be tremendously valuable in compressing the evolutionary cycle of reusable assets and ensuring high quality in the resultant software.

- *Asset development factors*–A significant part of the software base, especially at the library level, is driven by our own needs during development of higher-level tools. Others are created as applications of certain theoretical considerations. In most cases, well-structured libraries with carefully thought-out interfaces are created first. This makes it possible to share new algorithms among a wide range of tools, developers, and projects. Then, concepts are developed at higher levels and implemented in specialized languages. Along with the code, there are documentation, regression test suites, and exemplary sample applications. In this way, reusable assets are created.

- *Process and technology factors*–Many of the higher-level tools and certain critical parts of the libraries are continually refined based on algorithm advances and new insights gained from usage of the tools. Direct and frequent communication among researchers helps to ensure that the tools fit well with each other. Conscious efforts are made to ensure that changes are either upward-compatible or documented clearly to help migration. By using *ship* (Section 3.1.4) as the software distribution mechanism, we make it easy to propagate changes to user sites. As all of us are engaged in full-time research, there has not been enough time spent on direct training and support except where direct partnerships are formed. However, all tools come with reference manuals and, in some cases, extensive user guides.

12.5   Technology Transfer Experience

Technology transfer is important to enabling wide-scale reuse in other organizations and plays a strong role in improving software quality and productivity. Three main ingredients in successful technology transfer are technology, application, and support. First, a set of reusable components is assembled. Then, a set of applications that can use these components needs to be identified. In cases where technologies were developed to meet known applications, this is easy. In other cases, where technologies are created without specific target applications, management must take a strong role in establishing connections with organizations that may have needs for such technologies. The third area of support deals with maintenance, documentation, training, process descriptions and ongoing monitoring of progress. We shall discuss more on support in the following.

In transferring a technology to different organizations, many barriers arise. Here are our approaches to reducing or removing such problems:

- *Not invented here*–Often, when a new piece of software is brought to an organization, a common hurdle is reluctance in accepting it due to either competing extant software or other ongoing work. By preparing for this *a priori* and introducing new software only in sites where there are clearly perceived benefits over locally available and commercial alternatives, we have been successful in getting over this hurdle.

- *Risk management*–Recipients of research software are often wary of using untested software that may upset their production environment. Over a long period of time, our record of successful transferring experiences and the quality of our software help to reduce this concern by recipients. In certain cases, where we feel that a closer relationship would increase trust and speed up the transfer process, we form a partnership with the target organization.

- *Radical changes in work/programming environment*–Nonintrusiveness of technology is vital; changes should be introduced gradually without requiring wholesale changes in the environment. We spend considerable effort to ensure this both in low-level libraries (such as *sfio* replacing *stdio*, as discussed in Section 2.2.1.9, and *n-DFS* ensuring unobtrusiveness, as discussed in Section 2.5.2) and in higher-level components (such as nonintrusive assistance in process automation; see Section 10.2).

- *Operability on application platform*–Portability is a large factor, especially in AT&T where a wide variety of platforms are used. This often requires that the tool creators do the necessary porting. Fortunately, our experience with portability is available in the form of consultation and documentation (see Section 3.2).

- *Continuing support*–A minimal requirement for successful technology transfer is adequate documentation (even for *self-explanatory* software) and training for recipients. But successful transfer of new technologies often requires continuing interactions between transferor and transferee for some period of time. In particular, ongoing effort must be applied to improve the technology transfer process. This is especially important in organizations, such as ours to reduce the workload for researchers. Our department has a group devoted to supporting technology transfer whose responsibility is to monitor the progress in improving transfer processes. The group assures interim support and creates a long term support program. This has helped assure users that their problems will be solved quickly.

12.6   Future Directions

This book has described ongoing work on the reuse of software at many levels. It cites some of the lessons we have learned from both organizational and technological viewpoints. Though the software described is extensive, it by no means covers all the needs. There are many aspects of software construction that we need to understand better. Among these are:

- *Software distribution*–The ADVSOFT process has gone a long way in providing a solution. Its configuration and distribution technology is advanced and will continue to be improved. But wide-area networks also are advancing; interactive speeds are possible even between continents. We must understand how software distribution should be done in such an environment.

- *Software testing*–This is an area that we have touched only peripherally. As larger and larger systems are built, more work must be done to ensure the quality of such products both in terms of defect discovery and online recovery from hidden defects. Research on testing and software fault tolerance will combine to achieve this goal. The combination of *n-DFS*, *nmake*, and TESTTUBE also offers a tantalizing hint at a software development process in which code and test development can be shared effectively among developers and testers. This integration can be made practical by minimization techniques in much the same way that *oldmake* and *nmake* made practical the reconstruction of large software systems during the development cycle.

- *Software architecture*–This area is growing quickly in the software engineering community. From a software reuse point of view, this should help in easing the construction of new software by matching architecture templates, and in choosing appropriate reusable components for implementations. Architecture deals with components and, more importantly, the linkages between the components. If we are able to identify a few templates that span many software applications, we can use the templates to classify new software. Once classified, we would be able to select reusable components as well as indicate the best manner in which the linkages can be made.

12.7   Summary

We have taken the view that break-through ideas can arise equally from theory or from observing and measuring the performance of software. This should be evident in reading about the projects described in this book. The collective experience has been presented from several angles in the hope that this will help other software researchers and developers.

In closing, note that the people involved in this work understand how *real* product software works, write code, and often work side by side with product developers. This has proved critical not only to create mutual trust between providers and users of software, but also to create a feedback process that generates better, more timely reusable assets. It is probably the most important factor in the success of this software reuse program.

Bibliography

[ABS93]   Todd M. Austin, Scott E. Breach, and Gurindar S. Sohi. Efficient Detection of All Pointer and Array Access Errors. Technical Report TR 1197, Computer Sciences Department, University of Wisconsin at Madison, December 1993.

[All86]   Eric Allman. An Introduction to the Source Code Control System. In *Unix Programmer's Manual Supplementary Documents Volume 1*. University of California at Berkeley, April 1986.

[ANS90]   American National Standard for Information Systems–Programming Language–C, 1990.

[Arn84]   K. C. R. C. Arnold. *Screen Updating and Cursor Movement Optimization: A Library Package, 4.2 BSD UNIX Programmer's Manual Supplementary Documents*. University of California at Berkeley, July 1984.

[AWK88]   Al Aho, Peter Weinberger, and Brian Kernighan. *The AWK Programming Language*. Addison-Wesley, 1988.

[BB91]   R. Bianchini and R. Buskens. An adaptive distributed system-level diagnosis algorithm and its implementation. In *Proceedings of the 21st International Symposium on Fault-Tolerant Computing*, pages 222–229. IEEE Computer Society Press, June 1991.

[BDGS93]   Adam Beguelin, Jack Dongarra, Al Geist, and Vaidy Sunderam. Visualization and debugging in a heterogeneous environment. *IEEE Computer*, 26(6):88–95, June 1993.

[Bel89]   Steven M. Bellovin. Security problems in the TCP/IP protocol suite. *Computer Communications Review*, 19(2):32–48, April 1989.

[Ber93]   L. Bernstein. Innovative Technologies for Preventing Net-
             work Outages. *AT&T Technical Journal*, 72(4):4–10, July
             1993.

[BGST90]   G. Di Battista, A. Giammarco, G. Santucci, and R. Tamas-
             sia. The architecture of diagram server. In *Proceedings of
             IEEE Workshop on Visual Languages (VL'90)*, pages 60–65,
             1990.

[BK89]   Morris Bolsky and David G. Korn. *The KornShell Command
             and Programming Language*. Prentice Hall Press, 1989.

[BK91]   Naser S. Barghouti and Gail E. Kaiser. Scaling Up Rule-
             Based Development Environments. In *Proceedings of the
             Third European Software Engineering Conference, ESEC
             '91*, pages 380–395, Milan, Italy, October 1991. Springer-
             Verlag. Published as *Lecture Notes in Computer Science*
             no. 550.

[BK95]   Morris Bolsky and David Korn. *The New KornShell Com-
             mand and Programming Language*. Prentice Hall Press, 1995.

[BP88]   Brian Bershad and Brian Pinkerton. Watchdogs: extending
             the UNIX file system. In *USENIX Association 1988 Winter
             Conference Proceedings*, pages 267–275, February 1988.

[BS92]   M. Baker and M. Sullivan. The Recovery Box: Using Fast
             Recovery to Provide High Availability in the UNIX environ-
             ment. In *USENIX 1992 Summer Conference Proceedings*,
             pages 31–43, June 1992.

[Car80]   M.J. Carpano. Automatic Display of Hierarchized Graphs for
             Computer Aided Decision Analysis. *IEEE Transactions on
             Systems, Man and Cybernetics*, SMC-10(11):705–715, 1980.

[CB94]   William R. Cheswick and Steven M. Bellovin. *Firewalls
             and Internet Security: Repelling the Wily Hacker*. Addison-
             Wesley, Reading, MA, 1994.

[Che76]   P. P. Chen. The Entity-Relationship Model–Toward a Uni-
             fied View of Data. *ACM Transactions on Database Systems*,
             1(1):9–36, March 1976.

[Che89]   Yih-Farn Chen. The C Program Database and Its Applica-
             tions. In *Proceedings of the Summer 1989 USENIX Confer-*

ence, pages 157–171, Baltimore, June 1989.

[Che94]   Yih-Farn Chen. Dagger: A Tool to Generate Program Graphs. In *Proceedings of the USENIX UNIX Applications Development Symposium*, pages 19–35, Toronto, Canada, April 1994.

[CI90]   Elliot H. Chikofsky and James H. Cross II. Reverse Engineering and Design Recovery: A Taxonomy. *IEEE Software*, 7(1), January 1990.

[Cic88]   S. Cichinski. Product administration through Sable and Nmake. *AT&T Technical Journal*, 67(4):59–70, July–August 1988.

[CL89]   Brent Callaghan and Tom Lyon. The automounter. In *Proceedings of 1989 Winter USENIX Technical Conf.*, pages 43–51, San Diego, California, 1989. USENIX Association.

[CL90]   Marshall P. Cline and Doug Lea. Using Annotated C++. In *Proceedings of C++ at Work*, September 1990.

[CNR90]   Yih-Farn Chen, Michael Nishimoto, and C. V. Ramamoorthy. The C Information Abstraction System. *IEEE Transactions on Software Engineering*, 16(3):325–334, March 1990.

[CRV94]   Yih-Farn Chen, David Rosenblum, and Kiem-Phong Vo. TestTube: A System for Selective Regression Testing. In *Proceedings of the 16th Internation Conference on Software Engineering*, pages 211–220, Sorrento, Italy, May 1994. IEEE Computer Society.

[Dav93]   Ted Davis. The Reuse Capability Model: A Basis for Improving an Organization's Reuse Capability. In *Proceedings of the Second International Workshop on Software Reusability*, pages 126–133. IEEE Computer Society, March 1993.

[DF93]   Mark Dowson and Christer Fernstrom. Towards Requirements for Enactment Mechanisms. In *Proceedings of the Third European Workshop on Software Process Technology*, pages 90–106, Grenoble, France, February 1993. Springer-Verlag.

[DoD85a]   DoD trusted computer system evaluation criteria, 1985. 5200.28-STD.

[DoD85b]   Technical rationale behind CSC-STD-003-83: Computer se-
           curity requirements, 1985. CSC-STD-004-85.

[Dod92]   PS Dodd. Monitoring and Debugging Distributed Real Time
           Programs. *Software—Practice and Experience*, 22(10):863–
           877, 1992.

[EP84]   B. Erickson and J. Pellegrin. Build—A Software Construc-
           tion Tool. *Bell System Technical Journal*, 63(6):1049–1059,
           July 1984.

[ER89]   M. W. Eichin and J. A. Rochlis. With Microscope and
           Tweezers: An Analysis of the Internet Virus of November
           1988. In *Proceedings of IEEE Symposium on Research in Se-
           curity and Privacy*, pages 326–345, Oakland, CA, May 1989.

[FCI92]   Federal criteria for information technology security, version
           1.0, December 1992. (Draft).

[Fel79]   Stuart I. Feldman. Make—A Program for Maintaining
           Computer Programs. *Software—Practice and Experience*,
           9(3):255–265, March 1979.

[Fer93]   Christer Fernström. State Models and Protocols in Process-
           Centered Environments. In *Proceedings of the 8th Inter-
           national Software Process Workshop*, pages 72–77, Schloss
           Dagstuhl, Germany, March 1993. IEEE Computer Society
           Press.

[FH85]   C. W. Fraser and D. R. Hanson. High-Level Language Fa-
           cilities for Low-Level Services. In *12th ACM Symposium on
           Principles of Programming Languages*, pages 217–224, 1985.

[FHKR93]   Glenn S. Fowler, Yennun Huang, David G. Korn, and Her-
           man C. Rao. A User-Level Replicated File System. In
           USENIX Cincinnati 1993 Summer Conference Proceedings,
           pages 279–290, June 1993.

[FHO92]   Glenn S. Fowler, J.E. Humelsine, and C. H. Olson. Tools
           and Techniques for Building and Testing Software Systems.
           AT&T Technical Journal, 71(6):46–61, Nov-Dec 1992.

[FKSV94]   Glenn S. Fowler, David G. Korn, J. J. Snyder, and Kiem-
           Phong Vo. Feature Based Portability. In *Proceedings of the
           USENIX Symposium on Very High Level Languages*, pages

197–207, October 1994.

[FKV89] Glenn S. Fowler, David G. Korn, and Kiem-Phong Vo. An Efficient File Hierarchy Walker. In *USENIX Summer 1989 Conference Proceedings*, pages 173–188, Baltimore, MD, 1989. USENIX Association, Berkeley, CA.

[Fow85] Glenn S. Fowler. The Fourth Generation Make. In *Proceedings of the USENIX 1985 Summer Conference*, pages 159–174, June 1985.

[Fow88] Glenn S. Fowler. *cpp*–The C language preprocessor, 1988. UNIX Man Page.

[Fow90] Glenn S. Fowler. A Case for *make*. *Software—Practice and Experience*, 20(S1):35–46, June 1990.

[Fow94] Glenn S. Fowler. *cql*–A Flat File Database Query Language. In *Proceedings of the USENIX Winter 1994 Conference*, pages 11–21, San Francisco, January 1994.

[Gau92] Philippe Gautron. An Assertion Mechanism Based on Exceptions. In *Proceedings of the Fourth C++ Technical Conference*, pages 245–262. USENIX Association, August 1992.

[GC90] Judith Grass and Yih-Farn Chen. The C++ Information Abstractor. In *Proceedings of the Second USENIX C++ Conference*, pages 265–277, San Francisco, April 1990.

[GHM+90] Richard Guy, John Heidemann, Wai Mak, Thomas Page, Gerald Popek, and Dieter Rothmeier. Implementation of the Ficus replicated file system. In *USENIX Conference Proceedings*, pages 63–71, June 1990.

[GI90] David Garlan and Ehsan Ilias. Low-cost, Adaptable Tool Integration Policies for Integrated Environments. In *SIGSOFT '90: Proceedings of the Fourth Symposium on Software Development Environments*, pages 1–10, Irvine, CA, December 1990. ACM SIGSOFT.

[GJSO91] David Gifford, Pierre Jouvelot, Mark Sheldon, and James OToole. Semantic File Systems. In *Proceedings of the Thirteenth ACM Symposium on Operating System Principles*, pages 16–25, October 1991.

[GKNV93] Emden R. Gansner, Eleftherios Koutsofios, Stephen C.

North, and Kiem-Phong Vo. A Technique for Drawing Directed Graphs. *IEEE Transactions on Software Engineering*, 19(3):214–230, March 1993.

[GLDW87] Robert A. Gingell, Meng Lee, Xuong T. Dang, and Mary S. Weeks. Shared libraries in SunOS. In *USENIX Conference Proceedings*, pages 131–145, Phoenix, AZ, Summer 1987. USENIX.

[GN91] David Garlan and David Notkin. Formalizing Design Spaces: Implicit Invocation Mechanisms. In *Proceedings of VDM'91: Formal Software Development Methods*. Springer-Verlag, October 1991. Published as *Lecture Notes in Computer Science* 551.

[GNV88] Emden R. Gansner, Stephen C. North, and Kiem-Phong Vo. DAG–A Program that Draws Directed Graphs. *Software— Practice and Experience*, 18(11):1047–1062, 1988.

[Gol84] A. Goldberg. *Smalltalk-80, The Interactive Programming Environment*. Addison-Wesley, 1984.

[GR93] Jim Gray and Andreas Reuter. *Transaction Processing: Concepts and Techniques*. Morgan Kaufmann Publishers, 1993.

[Gra92] Judith E. Grass. Cdiff: A Syntax Directed Differencer for C++ Programs. In *USENIX C++ Conference Proceedings*, pages 181–193, Portland, Oregon, August 1992.

[Gre94] Rick Greer. All About Daytona. AT&T Bell Laboratories Internal Memorandum, July 1994. Available from the author: rxga@research.att.com.

[GS91] J. Gray and D. P. Siewiorek. High-Availability Computer Systems. *IEEE Computer*, 24(9):39–48, September 1991.

[Hal92] Robert J. Hall. Call Path Profiling. In *The 14th Internation Conference on Software Engineering*, pages 296–306, 1992.

[HC88] Richard C. Holt and James R. Cordy. The Turing Programming Language. *Communications of the ACM*, 31(12):1410–1423, December 1988.

[HE91] M. Heath and J. Etheridge. Visualizing the Performance of Parallel Programs. *IEEE Software*, 8(5):29–39, September 1991.

[Him89]   M. Himsolt. GraphEd: An Interactive Graph Editor. In *Proceedings of STACS 89*, volume 349 of *Lecture Notes in Computer Science*, pages 532–533, Berlin, 1989. Springer-Verlag.

[HJ92a]   Reed Hastings and Bob Joyce. Purify: Fast Detection of Memory Leaks and Access Errors. In *Proceedings of the Winter 1992* USENIX *Conference*, pages 125–136. USENIX Association, January 1992.

[HJ92b]   Yennun Huang and Pankaj Jalote. Effect of Fault Tolerance on Response Time–Analysis of the Primary Site Approach. *IEEE Transactions on Computers*, 41(4):420–428, April 1992.

[HJK94]   Yennun Huang, Pankaj Jalote, and Chandra M. R. Kintala. Two Techniques for Transient Software Error Recovery. In M. Banâtre and P. A. Lee (Eds.), editors, *Hardware and Software Architectures for Fault Tolerance: Experience and Perspectives*, pages 159–170. Springer-Verlag (Lecture Notes in Computer Science No. 774), 1994.

[HK93]   Yennun Huang and Chandra M. R. Kintala. Software Implemented Fault Tolerance: Technologies and Experience. In *Proceedings of 23rd International Symposium on Fault-Tolerant Computing Systems*, pages 2–9, Toulouse, France, June 1993. IEEE.

[HKKF94]   Yennun Huang, Chandra M. R. Kintala, Nick Kolettis, and N. Dudley Fulton. Software Rejuvenation: Analysis, Module and Applications. Submitted for publication, October 1994. Available from: cmk@research.att.com.

[HKM⁺88]   John H. Howard, Michael L. Kazar, Sherri G. Menees, David A. Nichols, M. Satyanarayanan, Robert N. Sidebotham, and Michael J. West. Scale and performance in a distributed file system. *ACM Transactions on Computer Systems*, 6(1):51–81, February 1988.

[Hor82]   Mark Horton. The New Curses and Terminfo Package. In *USENIX Conference Proceedings*, pages 79–91, Boston, MA, Summer 1982. USENIX.

[IEE93]   IEEE Standard 1003.2-1992, ISO/IEC 9945-2, IEEE, 1993.

[ITS91]   Information technology security evaluation criteria (ITSEC),
           Provisional harmonised criteria, June 1991.

[Jal89]   P. Jalote. Fault Tolerant Processes. *Distributed Computing*,
           3:187–195, 1989.

[Joy80]   William Joy. An introduction to display editing with vi li-
           brary package, September 1980. Revised by Mark Horton.

[JV92]   Guy Jacobson and Kiem-Phong Vo.   Heaviest Increas-
           ing/Common Subsequence Problems. In *Combinatorial Pat-
           tern Matching: Proceedings of the Third Annual Symposium*,
           volume 644 of *Lecture Notes in Computer Science*, pages 52–
           65, 1992.

[Jya94]   Jyacc. Jam application development guide, 1994. Technical
           Publications Manager, 116 John St., New York, NY 10038.

[KB93]   Balachander Krishnamurthy and Naser S. Barghouti.
           Provence: A Process Visualization and Enactment Environ-
           ment. In *Proceedings of the Fourth European Conference on
           Software Engineering, ESEC '93*, pages 151–160, Garmisch-
           Partenkirchen, Germany, September 1993. Springer-Verlag.
           Published as *Lecture Notes in Computer Science* no. 717.

[KD91]   Eleftherios Koutsofios and David Dobkin. Lefty: A Two-
           View Editor for Technical Pictures. In *Proceedings of Graph-
           ics Interface '91*, pages 68–76, 1991.

[Ker84]   B. W. Kernighan. *PIC—A Graphical Language for Typeset-
           ting: Revised User Manual*. AT&T Bell Laboratories, 1984.

[Kil84]   T. J. Killian. Processes as files. In *Proceedings of the 1984
           USENIX Summer Conference*, Salt Lake City, UT, June
           1984.

[KK89]   T. Kamada and S. Kawai. An Algorithm for Drawing Gen-
           eral Undirected Graphs. *Information Processing and Letters*,
           31:7–15, 1989.

[KK90]   David G. Korn and Eduardo Krell. A New Dimension for
           the UNIX File System. *Software—Practice and Experience*,
           20(S1):19–34, June 1990.

[KK92]   Eduardo Krell and Balachander Krishnamurthy.   COLA:

Customized Overlaying. In *Proceedings of the USENIX Winter 1992 Conference*, pages 3–7, 1992.

[KN93]   Yousef Khalidi and Michael Nelson. Extensible File Systems in Spring. In *Proceedings of the Fourteenth ACM Symposium on Operating System Principles*, pages 1–14, December 1993.

[KN94]   Eleftherios Koutsofios and Stephen C. North. Applications of Graph Visualization. In *Proceedings of Graphics Interface 1994 Conference*, pages 235–245, Banff, Canada, May 1994.

[Knu73]   Donald E. Knuth. *The Art of Computer Programming, Volume 3: Sorting and Searching*. Addison-Wesley, 1973.

[Knu93]   Donald E. Knuth. *The Stanford Graphbase: A Platform for Combinatorial Computing*. Addison-Wesley, 1993.

[Koe88]   Andrew R. Koenig. Associative Arrays in C++. In *Proceedings of Summer 1988 USENIX Conference*, pages 173–186, 1988.

[KP84]   Brian W. Kernighan and Rob Pike. *The UNIX Programming Environment*. Prentice Hall Press, 1984.

[KR78]   B. W. Kernighan and D. M. Ritchie. *The C Programming Lanugage*. Prentice Hall Software Press, 1978.

[KR88]   Brian W. Kernighan and Dennis M. Ritchie. *The C Programming Language*. Prentice Hall Press, second edition, 1988.

[KR91]   Balachander Krishnamurthy and David S. Rosenblum. An Event-Action Model of Computer-Supported Cooperative Work: Design and Implementation. In K. Gorling and C. Sattler, editors, *International Workshop on Computer Supported Cooperative Work*, pages 132–145. IFIP TC 6/WG C.5, 1991.

[KS74]   Paul A. Karger and Roger R. Schell. Multics Security Evaluation: Vulnerability Analysis. Technical Report ESD-TR-74-193, HQ Electronic Systems Division, Hanscom AFB, MA 01731, June 1974.

[KV]   David Korn and Kiem-Phong Vo. Vdelta: An Efficient Delta Mechanism. Available from: kpv@research.att.com.

[KV85]   David G. Korn and Kiem-Phong Vo. In Search of a Better Malloc. In *USENIX 1985 Conference Proceedings*, pages 489–506, 1985.

[KV91]   David G. Korn and Kiem-Phong Vo.   SFIO: Safe/Fast
           String/File IO. In *Proceedings of Summer USENIX Con-
           ference*, pages 235–256. USENIX, 1991.

[LB85]   M. M. Lehman and L. A. Belady. *Program Evolution: Pro-
           cesses of Software Change*. Academic Press, 1985.

[LCM85]   David Leblang, Robert Chase Jr., and Gordon McLean Jr.
           The DOMAIN Software Engineering Environment for Large-
           Scale Software Development Efforts. In *Proceedings of the
           First International Conference on Computer Workstations*,
           pages 226–280, November 1985.

[LFA92]   J. Long, W. K. Fuchs, and J. A. Abraham. Compiler-Assisted
           Static Checkpoint Insertion. In *Proceedings of 22nd IEEE
           Symposium on Fault-Tolerant Computing Systems*, pages 58–
           65. IEEE, July 1992.

[LS80]   Bennet P. Lientz and E. Burton Swanson. *Software Mainte-
           nance Management*. Addison-Wesley, 1980.

[LST91]   David C. Luckham, Sriram Sankar, and Shuzo Taka-
           hashi. Two-Dimensional Pinpointing: Debugging with For-
           mal Methods. *IEEE Software*, 8(1):74–84, January 1991.

[Mey88]   Bertrand Meyer.   *Object-Oriented Software Construction*.
           Prentice Hall Press, 1988.

[MM93]   Steve Manes and Tom Murphy. C++ Development. *UNIX
           Review*, June 1993.

[Mor85]   Robert T. Morris. A weakness in the 4.2BSD UNIX TCP/IP
           software. Computing Science Technical Report 117, AT&T
           Bell Laboratories, Murray Hill, NJ, February 1985.

[Mye79]   Glenford J. Myers. *The Art of Software Testing*. Wiley-
           Interscience, 1979.

[NH93]   Michael N. Nelson and Graham Hamilton. High Performance
           Dynamic Linking Through Caching. In *Proceedings of Sum-
           mer USENIX*, pages 253–265, June 1993.

[NIT93]   The Canadian Trusted Computer Product Evaluation Crite-
           ria, January 1993. Version 3.0e.

[NNGS90]   John R. Nestor, Joseph M. Newcomer, Paola Giannini, and
           Donald L. Stone. *IDL–The Language and Its Implementa-*

tion. Prentice Hall Press, 1990.

[Nor93]   Stephen C. North. Drawing Ranked Digraphs with Recursive Clusters. *(submitted for publication)*, 1993. Abstract presented at Proceedings of ALCOM International Workshop on Graph Drawing and Topological Graph Algorithms, Paris, 1993.

[NV93]   Stephen C. North and Kiem-Phong Vo. Dictionary and Graph Libraries. In *Proceedings of Winter USENIX Conference*, pages 1–11. USENIX, 1993.

[Nye90]   Adrian Nye. *Xlib Programming Manual.* O'Reilly & Associates, Inc., 1990.

[Olc91]   Anatole Olczak. *The Korn Shell–User & Programming Manual.* Addison-Wesley, 1991.

[OTC86]   Mark Opperman, Jim Thompson, and Yih-Farn Chen. A Gremlin Tutorial for the SUN Workstation. Technical Report UCB/CSD 322, Computer Science Division, University of California at Berkeley, December 1986.

[Ous94]   John K. Ousterhout. *TCL.* Addison-Wesley, 1994.

[Par91]   Tim Parker. Pick a Pack of CASE. *Software Review*, 9(12), December 1991.

[PE85]   Dewayne E. Perry and W. Michael Evangelist. An Empirical Study of Software Interface Faults. In *Proceedings of the International Symposium on New Directions in Computing*, pages 32–38. IEEE Computer Society, August 1985.

[PE87]   Dewayne E. Perry and W. Michael Evangelist. An Empirical Study of Software Interface Faults—An Update. In *Proceedings of the 20th Annual Hawaii International Conference on System Sciences*, Volume II, pages 113–126, January 1987.

[Pet88]   Larry L. Peterson. The Profile Naming Service. *ACM Transactions on Computer Systems*, 6(4):341–364, November 1988.

[POS90]   POSIX–Part 1: System Application Program Interface [C Language], 1990. International Standard ISO/IEC 9945-1 IEEE Standard 1003.1-1990.

[PPTT90]   Rob Pike, Dave Presotto, Ken Thompson, and Howard Trickey. Plan 9 from Bell Labs. In *Proceedings of the United*

Kingdom UNIX Users Group, London, England, July 1990.

[Pri85]   Reuben M. Pritchard. Front End–A Multi-Interface Form System. *AT&T Technical Journal*, 64(9):2009–2223, November 1985.

[PT90]   F. Newbery Paulisch and W.F. Tichy. EDGE: An Extendible Graph Editor. *Software—Practice and Experience*, 20(S1):63–88, 1990.

[RC92]   G.-C. Roman and K. C. Cox. Program Visualization: The Art of Mapping Programs to Pictures. In *Proceedings of the 14th International Conference on Software Engineering*, pages 412–420, Melbourne, Australia, May 1992.

[RE89]   J. A. Rochlis and M. W. Eichin. With Microscope and Tweezers: The Worm from MIT's Perspective. *Communications of the ACM*, 32(6):689–703, June 1989.

[Rei90]   Steven P. Reiss. Connecting Tools Using Message Passing in the Field Environment. *IEEE Software*, 7(4):57–66, July 1990.

[Roc75]   Marc J. Rochkind. The Source Code Control System. *IEEE Transactions on Software Engineering (SE), Vol.SE-1*, 1(4):364–370, December 1975.

[Ros92]   David S. Rosenblum. Towards a Method of Programming with Assertions. In *Proceedings of the 14th International Conference on Software Engineering*, pages 92–104. Association for Computing Machinery, May 1992.

[Ros93]   Bill Rosenblatt. *Learning the Korn Shell*. O'Reilly & Associates, Inc., 1993.

[RP93]   Herman C. Rao and Larry L. Peterson. Accessing Files in an Internet: The Jade File System. *IEEE Transactions on Software Engineering*, pages 613–624, June 1993.

[Sch87]   Bruce Schneiderman. *Designing the User Interface*. Addison-Wesley, 1987.

[Sch93]   Christopher L. Schuba. Addressing Weaknesses in the Domain Name System Protocol. Master's thesis, Purdue University, 1993. Department of Computer Sciences.

[Sed78]   R. Sedgewick. *Algorithms, 2nd Edition*. Addison-Wesley,

1978.

[SGK⁺85] R. Sandberg, D. Goldberg, S. Kleiman, D. Walsh, and B. Lyon. Design and Implementation of the Sun Network Filesystem. In *Proceedings of the USENIX 1985 Summer Conference*, pages 119–130, June 1985.

[Spa89a] Eugene H. Spafford. An analysis of the Internet worm. In C. Ghezzi and J. A. McDermid, editors, *Proceedings of the European Software Engineering Conference*, pages 446–468, Warwick, England, September 1989. Springer-Verlag, Lecture Notes in Computer Science No. 387.

[Spa89b] Eugene H. Spafford. The Internet Worm Program: An Analysis. *Computer Communication Review*, 19(1):17–57, January 1989.

[SS92] D. P. Siewiorek and R. S. Swarz. *Reliable Computer Systems: Design and Implementation*, chapter 7. Digital Press, 1992.

[ST85] Daniel Sleator and Robert E. Tarjan. Self-Adjusting Binary Search Trees. *JACM*, 32(3):652–686, 1985.

[Str91] Bjarne Stroustrup. *The C++ Programming Language*. Addison-Wesley, second edition, 1991.

[STT81] K. Sugiyama, S. Tagawa, and M. Toda. Methods for Visual Understanding of Hierarchical Systems. *IEEE Transactions on Systems, Man and Cybernetics*, 11(2):109–125, 1981.

[Sum94] Steve Summit. Filesystem Daemons as a Unifying Mechanism for Network Information Access. In *Proceedings of Winter USENIX*, January 1994.

[Sun88] Sun Microsystems, Inc., Mountain View, Calif. *Shared Libraries*, May 1988.

[SVR90] AT&T. *UNIX System V Release 4 Programmer's Reference Manual*, 1990.

[Tho84] Ken Thompson. Reflections on Trusting Trust. *Communications of the ACM*, 27(8):761–763, August 1984.

[Tho91] Ian Thomas, editor. *Reprints of the Seventh International Software Process Workshop*, Yountville CA, October 1991.

[Tic84] Walter F. Tichy. The String-to-String Correction Problem with Block Moves. *ACM Transactions on Computer Sys-*

tems, 2(4):309–321, November 1984.

[Tic85]   Walter F. Tichy. RCS—A System for Version Control. *Software—Practice and Experience*, 15(7):637–654, 1985.

[Tom]   Tom Sawyer Software, 1824B Fourth Street, Berkeley, CA 94710. *Graph Layout Toolkit*, 1.08 edition.

[UNI86]   Computer Science Division, University of California at Berkeley. *UNIX Programmer's Manual, 4.3 Berkeley Software Distribution*, April 1986.

[VC92]   Kiem-Phong Vo and Yih-Farn Chen. Incl: A Tool to Analyze Include Files. In *Proceedings of the Summer 1992 USENIX Conference*, pages 199–208, San Antonio, Texas, June 1992.

[Vo]   Kiem-Phong Vo. Vmalloc: An Efficient Memory Allocator. Available from: kpv@research.att.com.

[Vo85]   Kiem-Phong Vo. screen(3X) - more <curses>: the <screen> library, 1985. UNIX Man Page.

[Vo90]   Kiem-Phong Vo. IFS: A Tool to Build Application Systems. *IEEE Software*, 7(4):29–36, July 1990.

[War77]   J. Warfield. Crossing Theory and Hierarchy Mapping. *IEEE Transactions on Systems, Man and Cybernetics*, SMC-7(7):502–523, 1977.

[Wei92]   Terry Weitzen. *C++ Standard Components Programmer's Guide*, chapter C++ Graph Classes: A Tutorial. UNIX System Laboratories, Inc., 1992.

[WHF93]   Y. Wang, Yennun Huang, and W.K. Fuchs. Progressive Retry for Software Error Recovery in Distributed Systems. In *Proceedings of FTCS23*, pages 138–144, Toulouse, France, June 1993. IEEE.

[Wil93]   Wilhelm Schäefer, editor. *Proceedings of the Eighth International Software Process Workshop*, Schloss Dagstuhl, Germany, March 1993.

[Win94]   Phil Winterbottom. ACID: A Debugger Built from a Language. In *USENIX San Francisco 1994 Winter Conference Proceedings*, pages 211–222, 1994.

[WO89]   Brent B. Welch and John K. Ousterhout. Pseudo-File-Systems. Technical Report UCB/CSD 89/499, University of California at Berkeley, 1989.

[Wol93]   Andrew D. Wolfe Jr. Three Touches of Class. *UNIXWorld*,
           July 1993.

[WS90]   Larry Wall and Randal Schwartz. *Perl*. O'Reilly & Asso-
           ciates, 1990.

[WWFT88]   Jack C. Wileden, Alexander L. Wolf, Charles D. Fisher, and
           Peri L. Tarr. PGRAPHITE: An Experiment in Persistent
           Typed Object Management. In *Proceedings of ACM SIG-
           SOFT '88: Third Symposium on Software Development Envi-
           ronments*, volume 13(5) of *SIGSOFT Notes*, pages 130–142,
           Nov 1988.

[Yan91]   Wuu Yang. Identifying Syntactic Differences Between Two
           Programs. *Software—Practice and Experience*, 21(7), 1991.

[You]   Douglas Young. Xmgraph. Contributed software to X11R5,
           Motif.

[ZL77]   J. Ziv and A. Lempel. A Universal Algorithm for Sequen-
           tial Data Compression. *IEEE Transactions on Information
           Theory*, 23(3):337–343, May 1977.

Index

Tools are listed first. General topics follow.

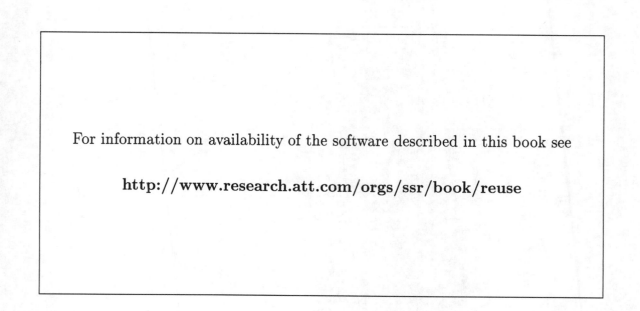

For information on availability of the software described in this book see

http://www.research.att.com/orgs/ssr/book/reuse